GW00359677

ABOUT THE AUTHOR

Gail Seekamp is personal finance editor at *The Sunday Business Post,* and has written about consumer finance topics for over seven years. She has worked as a journalist in Mexico City, London and Dublin for fifteen years and is a graduate of Sussex University.

PERSONAL FINANCE

1996/97

Gail Seekamp

Oak Tree Press

Oak Tree Press
Merrion Building
Lower Merrion Street
Dublin 2

© 1996 Gail Seekamp

A catalogue record of this book is
available from the British Library.

ISBN 1-86076-020-1

All rights reserved. No part of this publication may be reproduced or transmitted in any form or by any means, including photocopying and recording, without written permission of the publisher and the author. Such written permission must also be obtained before any part of this publication is stored in a retrieval system of any nature. Requests for permission should be directed to Oak Tree Press, Merrion Building, Lower Merrion Street, Dublin 2, Ireland.

The Personal Portfolio Planner (pp. 313–20) is adapted from *Personal Portfolio*, published by Cork Publishing Limited. Copies of *Personal Portfolio* are available from Cork Publishing Ltd., 19 Rutland Street, Cork, at a cost of £2.25 + 50p postage each.

Cover Design: Aileen Caffrey

Every effort has been made to ensure the accuracy of the contents of this book, including updated information from the 1996 Budget. However, changes in tax and Social Welfare may be introduced in the Finance and Social Welfare Bills later in the year. Neither the publisher nor the author can be held liable for any errors or omissions nor for any action taken as a result of information in this book. Readers are advised to take professional advice, where appropriate.

Printed in Ireland by Colour Books Ltd.

CONTENTS

Dedication

To the memory of John Murphy
who made an enormous contribution
to this book

ACKNOWLEDGEMENTS

Once again, this book took shape with the help of many people. Their professional input and support was much appreciated, especially in the weeks leading up to, and including, the Budget.

In Chapters 1 and 2, swift survey updates were provided by bank and building society staff, and members of other institutions. Douglas Farrell of National Deposit Brokers, Patricia O'Sullivan-Lacey of National Irish Bank, Paul Kenny of Irish Pensions Trust and staff at the Department of Social Welfare press office helped with two new case studies in Chapter 2. Staff in Davys gilts' department helped with another example.

Eilís O'Brien of Bank of Ireland updated the example in Chapter 4 and verified information in other chapters. John Farrell of the Mortgage Advice Shop gave information for Chapter 5, Buying a House.

My warm thanks to Eleanor Murphy and Barry Coleman of Finance Matters and Kathy Dillon of LifeWise, the insurance brokerage firm that specialises in financial planning for women. They provided new quotations for Chapters 6 and 8 in a very busy period prior to the 31 January pension deadline.

Jim Ryan, manager in Ernst & Young's personal tax division, and Brian Bohan, solicitor at the same firm, who specialises in inheritance planning, both gave vital and much appreciated help, particularly at Budget time.

Mark Carter, who deals with expatriate tax and personal financial planning at Craig Gardner, helped check Chapter 14.

Several organisations and individuals permitted useful information to be used in the book. My thanks to BZW and Phil Adams (for chart, Chapter 2); AIB Bank, for the use of their Budget Planner (Chapters 7 and 13); *The Irish Times*/Craig Gardner, who kindly agreed to the use of the Budget table (Appendix); and Davys Stockbrokers and *The Sunday Business Post* for the use of the equities table (Chapter 3).

Others deserve a mention and thanks. They include the staff in the Revenue and Departments of Finance and Social Welfare press offices, the Irish Insurance Federation, BDO Simpson Xavier and

Irish Life for their help. Apologies to anyone who has been omitted.

Finally, my thanks to Pierce for his moral support and the staff at Oak Tree Press for their sterling work. Emer Ryan, as production editor, made a huge and painstaking contribution; and David Givens, general manager of Oak Tree Press, was greatly encouraging and helped to steer the project forward.

All of the above contributed greatly. Any mistakes in the book remain my own responsibility, not theirs.

GAIL SEEKAMP
JANUARY 1996

1

STARTING TO PLAN

"Some people are masters of money, and some its slaves."

Russian Proverb

As 1996 opens, mortgage and other "borrowing rates" (overdraft, personal loan and credit card) are at their lowest in decades. Stock markets are booming. Inflation is under 3 per cent, and the economy is growing — fast.

The 1996 Budget has added a few pounds to most pockets but, as commentators pointed out, it was only a few pounds (see Appendix, p. 304). Ruairí Quinn gave with one hand and took away with another, as all Finance Ministers do. Instead of lowering the flat rates of income tax, still 27 and 48 per cent, he tinkered with "allowances" (which protect some of our income against tax) and made slight changes to the Pay Related Social Insurance régime (PRSI). Meanwhile, tax relief on mortgage interest repayments and VHI premiums was eroded further (see Chapter 11, Tackling Tax).

The impact of these changes depends on your own personal circumstances, but will be minimal for most. A married person, the sole income earner with a £15,000 salary and a middle-sized mortgage, gains just £2.50 per week, for example.

Arguably, the "macroeconomic" (large-scale) changes in 1995 will have more impact on most people's personal and family finances in the year to come. Low interest rates mean more cash left over after paying the mortgage each month. Indeed, Irish people are now saving a larger chunk of their disposable income — about 13 per cent in 1993. That was a sharp rise on the previous year.

So how can you invest and spend your hard-earned cash wisely? How can you plan your personal finances, and get the best value for money?

Personal Finance, in an updated second edition, will help you try to achieve this. It takes a needs-driven approach, which looks at key goals, like investing, buying a house or inheritance planning. Each chapter offers strategies for dealing with a particular "task", and points out the pitfalls and opportunities that you need to look out for.

Here's a checklist of the personal finance "tasks" covered by this book. Are any on your priority list for 1996?

CHECKLIST

Task	☑
• Budgeting (Chapter 13)	☐
• Buying a House (Chapter 5)	☐
• Inheritance Planning (Chapter 15)	☐
• Pension Planning (Chapter 10)	☐
• Protecting Your Family and Possessions (Chapter 6)	☐
• Savings and Investments (Chapters 2 and 3)	☐
• Tackling Tax (Chapter 11)	☐
• Travel, or Working Abroad (Chapter 14)	☐

Financial needs shift as you get older or your family circumstances change, so this book also looks at the broader issue of life-cycle planning. What should you do, for example, if you have a child? Or become self-employed? Or get married? Or lose your partner through separation, divorce or death?

The following are the different "life-cycle" and people-specific issues dealt with in this book.

- Marriage, Divorce and Separation (Chapter 7)
- Having a Child (Chapter 9)
- Self-employed People (Chapter 12)
- Widowhood (Chapter 15)
- Women (Chapter 8).

Alternatively, you can just dip into *Personal Finance* for information on a specific tax or financial product. For example, you may want to check the return on An Post's Savings Bonds, or compare the merits of annuity and endowment mortgages. You can access this data through the list of contents or index. There is a Glossary of key financial terms (p. 305), and the Appendix (p. 295) includes a list of addresses of places where you can get more advice or buy certain products.

This book is as relevant for high-income earners as it is for the self-employed, students, pensioners and single parents. The basic principles of money management apply to all of us, regardless of our income, age or marital status. Running a personal or family budget is a bit like managing a small business. You have an income, and expenditure. You need to maximise the return on your investments (without taking too many risks) and borrow as cheaply as possible. Like the businessperson, you also need to pay tax (unless your income is very low) and plan for long-term investments, such as your pension and your children's special educational needs. Finally, you need to get good advice and be well briefed. Otherwise, you could lose a lot of money through mismanagement, bad luck or even fraud.

STARTING TO PLAN

Let's start with the basics: your current account and how to get the best value from it. This is a convenient product for managing income. You can pay your bills, issue cheques, make payments (such as the mortgage) by standing order, and even save money, by setting up a direct debit into a separate deposit account.

In the past, people often opened a current account with a bank, got their chequebook and stayed put for life. Today's consumers are more demanding and less loyal. If they feel that their bank or building society is not delivering, they vote with their feet.

That's happening now. Bank charges are a hot issue, accounting for 6.17 per cent of complaints to the Ombudsman for the Credit Institutions in his 1995 report. The banks claim that they, like any other institution, are entitled to charge for services given, and that charges are low here, compared with Britain. Also, bank charges were static in 1995. Irish consumers, however, still think that bank charges are unfair and want to avoid them.

Can you?

That depends, as is often the case with financial planning, on your personal circumstances. Some people need a chequebook; others don't. Some run their account far more actively than others. The following is a list of product options and their strengths and limitations.

Associated Banks/Regular Current Account

There are four associated banks in Ireland — AIB Bank, Bank of Ireland (BoI), National Irish Bank and Ulster Bank. The vast majority of current account holders bank with one of these institutions.

A current account is a place where you can store money temporarily and make transactions, such as paying bills or cashing cheques. Most people have their salary or other income paid directly into their account, and then withdraw cash as they need it. You usually get a chequebook as part of the package (unless you are a student), plus a cheque guarantee card which allows you to cash cheques of up to £100. Current account holders also get a plastic card for withdrawing cash from the "hole in the wall" (the Automated Teller Machine — ATM). The associated banks have far more ATMs than the building societies — almost

800 in total — which gives you better access to your money. Furthermore, banks normally give overdraft facilities to clients who need to borrow money for a short while (see also Chapter 4). Building societies do not.

Convenience apart, bank-based current accounts have another big advantage. They can help you to build a commercial relationship with your bank manager, which may give you access to a cheaper mortgage in the future or gentler treatment if you get into financial difficulty (see also Chapter 16). But you have to run the account well, and not have a history of unauthorised overdrafts.

These accounts have drawbacks, too. It's hard to avoid bank charges, unless you keep a certain sum in the account each month (see "How Do They Compare?" table on pp. 10–11). Also, they rarely pay interest on credit balances, unless you pick a special account. Because of this, they are a bad place for parking large sums of cash.

Associated Banks/Interest-Bearing Current Accounts

All four banks, as well as giving you a cheque book, also offer current accounts which pay interest on credit balances, but the rewards are small, and the conditions strict. Here's a summary of both.

Institution	Product	Restrictions	Interest Paid	Other Benefits
AIB Bank	Credit Interest Account	No overdraft/ ATM Card. £300 min. opening balance.	0.25% on all balances.	Chequebook, cheque guarantee card and Eurocheque facility.
Bank of Ireland	Ascent	Under 25s only.	1.75%–2.25% depending on balance.	As per current account. Overdraft if needed. No transaction charges.
National Irish Bank	Freebank	No overdraft.	1.5% on all balances	No transaction charges etc.
Ulster Bank	Premium	£2,500 min. balance to earn premium interest. No overdraft.	1.50%–2.50% depending on balance.	Chequebook, own charge structure.

Source: Institutions listed.

Associated Banks/Deposit Account

This is a poor third choice. Some accounts allow you to withdraw funds with an ATM card, instead of via a "passbook" (deposit book). Ordinary bank deposit accounts pay very little interest on your balance, and the yield is further reduced by Deposit Interest Retention Tax (DIRT). This is still 27 per cent.

You can pay bills, for a fee, but get no chequebook on these accounts.

> **Note:** The main banks also offer special budget accounts, which can help to balance your income and expenditure during the year. See Chapter 13 on Budgeting, for details. You should also decide whether you want a joint or single account.

Building Societies/Deposit Accounts

Building societies do not offer current accounts as such. The alternative is a deposit account with access to cash via an ATM machine.

These accounts do not offer a chequebook or overdraft facility. Moreover, it can take much longer (up to two weeks) to clear a cheque deposited into a building society account. This can cause cash-flow problems. They have fewer ATMs, about 70 in their shared "Cashere" network, though most have also linked up with a retail bank to increase access. On the other hand, building society accounts pay slightly higher interest rates than bank-based accounts. Also, they offer a bill-paying facility and may offer other services, such as bureau de change. Last but not least, they don't charge transaction fees (for ATM withdrawals, etc).

This may make them an attractive alternative to a regular bank current account. Building societies, like banks, will sometimes give you a cheaper mortgage rate if you have an account with them.

Other Options

ACCBANK/Current Account

This is an ordinary current account, which comes complete with chequebook and cheque guarantee card. It even pays interest (albeit low) on balances, and has ATM access (12 ACCBANK; 315 BoI). Customers who do not need a cheque guarantee card or an overdraft may obtain an economy version called Cheque Save which has no quarterly charge

Credit Union/Share (Deposit) Account

This will probably supplement, not replace, an ordinary current or deposit account. However, it may be possible to have a full current account with a credit union in the near future.

Credit unions are run on a co-operative basis. They are based in the community, and are open to people who live in a certain geographic area or are united by another common bond, such as membership of a trade union or company. Credit unions offer a very valuable service, but they do not yet offer full banking services, including current accounts. This situation may change with new legislation. In the meantime, they give their members access to cheap loans (see Chapter 4). Some also have bill-paying facilities, provide cut-price home insurance and VHI premiums, and a tiny few allow ATM access. Your cash deposit is used to lend money to other members in the credit union, and is always held intact even when you borrow yourself.

Irish Permanent/Current Account

Launched in late 1994 as a fully-fledged bank, the Irish Permanent offers a suite of four current accounts. Each offers a slightly different package, in terms of services, fees and interest yield. Irish Permanent shares its ATM network with Bank of Ireland. Customers can access over 300 machines nationwide.

Merchant, Investment and Private Banks/Current Account

Since Spring 1995, AIB Bank, Bank of Ireland and Guinness & Mahon have offered a full banking service for wealthy individuals. This is called "private banking", and includes extra facilities, investment advice, etc. Other merchant/investment banks like ABN Amro do not have current accounts but offer deposit-taking and advice services.

Post Office/Savings Account

You can open a regular account at the Post Office Savings Bank. The amount of interest that you earn depends on the credit balance in the account — it starts at 0.5 per cent (deposits up to

£999) and rises to 2 per cent (£5,000 plus) before DIRT is deducted.

You can pay a range of bills, including the TV licence, local authority bills, gas bill, and telephone bill, through Bill Pay. People who are living on social welfare payments can also pay bills directly through the Household Budget scheme (see also Chapter 13, Budgeting). The Post Office has long opening hours — 9.00 a.m. to 5.30 p.m. at most main branches — but no ATM network.

TSB/Current Account

TSB Bank offers a wide range of services, including mortgages, personal loans, a chequebook facility and access to ATMs. The TSB also has longer opening hours than the main associated banks, and its transaction charges are lower. TSB Bank shares its ATM network with AIB Bank. Customers can access nearly 400 machines in total.

WHICH ONE TO CHOOSE?

That depends on your needs. If you already have a current account, look at your bank statement and check what bank services you are now using — such as a standing order or direct debit, for example. Are you paying charges? If so, how much?

The section below deals with bank charges and how to avoid them. Meanwhile, here's a summary of your options:

BANK

Product	Pros	Cons
Current Account	Big ATM network. Full range of banking services.	Hard to avoid charges. Short opening hours.
Deposit Account	Pays interest on balance. ATM access on some accounts. No transaction charges, except on ATMs, bill-paying, etc.	Deposit interest is very low. No chequebook/overdraft. Short opening hours.
Interest-Bearing Account	Pays interest. Chequebook/overdraft facilities etc.	Deposit interest is low. Strict conditions. Short opening hours. ATM access may be limited.

BUILDING SOCIETY

Product	Pros	Cons
Deposit Account	Pays interest. No charges. Bill-paying facilities. Long opening hours.	No chequebook/ overdraft. Fewer ATMs, branches.

OTHER OPTIONS

Product	Pros	Cons
ACC BANK: Current Account	Pays interest, low charges. Chequebook/overdraft. Long opening hours.	Fewer ATMs.
Credit Union: Share (Deposit) Account	Pays interest. Loans and insurance available. Bill-paying facilities. Open evenings and Saturdays.	No chequebook/ overdraft facility yet. Very restricted opening. Very few ATMs.
Irish Permanent: Merit Account	Pays interest. Full banking facilities. No transaction charges. Long opening hours.	High annual fee (£40). Fewer ATMs than associated banks' shared network.
Merchant/Private Bank: Current Account (BoI, AIB and Guinness & Mahon)	Pays interest. Full banking facilities. Prestigious. May have ATM access.	Wealthy customers only.
Deposit Account	High interest. Prestige. BoI/AIB clients have access to ATMs, Merchant bank clients may not.	Wealthy customers only. No chequebook/ overdraft. Short opening hours.

OTHER OPTIONS (CONTINUED)

Product	Pros	Cons
Post Office	Pays interest, no charges. Long opening hours. Bill-paying facilities.	No chequebook/ overdraft. No ATMs.
TSB Bank	Chequebook/overdraft. Long opening hours. Full banking facilities. Low charges.	Fewer ATMs

Source: Institutions listed.

BANK CHARGES

Because of the convenience factor, most people end up choosing a bank-based current account. Here's a list of the charges that applied in January 1996:

HOW DO THEY COMPARE?

Transaction	AIB	BoI	NIB	Ulster	ACC	IP	TSB
ATM Withdrawal/ Deposit*	17p	19p	15p	18p	20p	Nil	10p†
Cheque Card	£3	£3.15	£5‡	£3‡	£2.50	Nil	£2.50
Direct Debit (set up)	Nil	£2.70	£2.50	£2.50	£2	Nil	£2.50
Direct Debit (transaction fee)	17p	19p	15p	18p	15p	Nil	15p
Paper Withdrawal/ Deposit	24p	26p/22p	24p	25p/24p	22p	Nil	23p
Standing Order (set up)	£3	£2.70	£3	£3	£2	Nil	£2.50

* Not all banks have a deposit facility on their ATMs.
† From TSB Bank's own ATMs. 20p charge for transactions on AIB Bank ATMs.
‡ Fee charged every two years.

HOW DO THEY COMPARE? (CONTINUED)

Transaction	AIB	BoI	NIB	Ulster	ACC	IP	TSB
Standing Order (transaction fee)	29p	31p	27p	37p	30p	Nil	30p
Statement	Nil	Nil	Nil	Nil	Nil	Nil	Nil
Quarterly Fee	£3.75**	£4.15††	£3.75	£3.90	£3	£10‡‡	£3

** If you also want an overdraft facility with a chequebook, AIB charges an extra £20 annual fee, on top of the transaction charges listed above. If you want an overdraft facility but no chequebook (called an "on line" overdraft) there is a fixed £12 quarterly fee, but no transaction charges.

†† BoI also charges an annual £20 fee, on top of the quarterly and transaction fees, for standard customers who want an overdraft.

‡‡ All details are for IP's Merit Account. It also pays interest at 0.90% gross (£1–£999), or 1.40% (£1,000+).

Key: ACC = ACCBANK; AIB = AIB Bank; BoI = Bank of Ireland; IP = Irish Permanent; NIB = National Irish Bank; TSB = TSB Bank; Ulster = Ulster Bank.

Source: Institutions listed. Note that the comparisons are based on current accounts only. Credit union and building society accounts are not included for that reason. Merchant/investment/private bank deposits are not included because of the requirement for a high minimum balance.

Free Banking

If you meet certain conditions, your bank will waive the quarterly fee and most transaction charges. This is called "free banking". It's a bit of a misnomer, as you still have to pay some charges, such as the cheque-card fee, standing-order set-up charge and yearly government stamp duty on ATM card, which was increased to £5 in the January 1996 Budget. The conditions for "Free Banking" are listed in the table on p. 12.

Avoiding Bank Charges

It isn't easy. Few people can discipline themselves into keeping a £100 balance in their account all the time. The best way to deal with bank charges is to check your statement and find what you are paying. Do you need a chequebook or overdraft facility? If not, you could move to a deposit account which allows you to access your cash through an ATM.

THE CONDITIONS FOR "FREE BANKING"

Bank	Conditions
AIB	Customers who keep a minimum £100 balance in the account during the quarter. Also, customers who have their salaries paid directly into the account via the "PayPath" scheme (charges waived for the first 18 months only); full-time students in credit, "One to One" customers (60+, widowed, visually impaired) and some others. Ask at the bank.
BoI	Minimum balance of £100 in the account during the quarter. Also, customers who have their salaries paid directly into the account via "PayPath" for the first 18 months, students and "Golden Years" (elderly) customers.
NIB	Customers who remain in credit for the charging quarter. Freebank customers, and those with salaries paid direct via "Safepay".
Ulster	Customers who remain in credit for the charging quarter.
ACC	Does not offer "free banking". However, it pays interest on daily credit balances over £200.
IP	Only the over 60s and "Prestige" account customers qualify for "free banking". The latter need a £5,000 minimum balance.
TSB	Customers who keep a minimum cleared £100 balance or, if the balance dips below that, an average cleared daily balance of £300 throughout the quarter. Also, PayPath customers whose salaries are paid in directly (first 18 months only), students and the over 60s.

The next time you are in your bank, ask for a leaflet about bank charges and ask a staff member what alternative products the bank offers with lower charges.

Or, pick a bank which only charges you when you slip into the red. Don't ask for an overdraft facility or, if you do, try to clear it within three months.

Here's what a typical customer pays.

Joan has an account at a leading bank. She writes about five cheques a month, and uses the ATM machine three times a week, on average. She has two direct debits on her account for the mortgage payment and mortgage protection policy, and a standing order for a life assurance payment. Joan's account balance usually drops to a few pounds at the end of each month, so she doesn't qualify for free banking at her bank. This is what her bill looks like after one year:

	Service	Annual Fee
60	cheques	£14.40
156	ATM transactions	£26.52
24	direct debits	£4.08
12	standing orders	£3.48*
4	quarterly fees	£15.00
Total		£63.48

* This includes the bank's own charge of £2.04 (17p x 12), plus a £1.44 fee (12p x 12p) which would be levied regardless of whether or not Joan qualified for "free banking".

Joan might feel that £63.48 is a small sum to pay for a full banking service. But she could get the same service elsewhere for just £1.44 (the standing order fee) if she switched to a bank that offered "free banking". If she asks for an overdraft, the cost will rise by another £20 per year.

CHECKING YOUR ACCOUNT

It pays to examine your bank statement very closely. Bank clerks make errors, just like every other human being. Machines can make them, too. You may be charged too much interest on a loan as a result. Several companies offer statement checking services which can spot overcharging (see Appendix). If you have any problem with your bank or building society over a current or deposit account, discuss the problem with that institution's customer services department. If that fails, contact the Ombudsman for the Credit Institutions, 8 Adelaide Court, Dublin 2 (tel: (01) 478 3755).

CONCLUSION

Taking a critical look at your current account is a good way to start getting your personal finances on track. It should focus your mind on a few key issues: namely, your budget (or lack of one), the cost of running your account and whether you are using the right product.

If you have a current account, your bank statement should give you a breakdown of any fees charged. Ask yourself whether you can avoid these charges and still get the level of service you need elsewhere. Are you getting value for money? If the answer is no, you might consider the alternatives.

Don't forget the bigger picture either, and the reason why you bought this book!

- Personal financial planning can be viewed as a series of "tasks". You can solve a problem or achieve a certain goal by tackling a "task".
- You should be aware of your needs, and then match these with a financial product — not vice versa.
- Remember that your needs may change, so keep your plans flexible.

2

SAVINGS

"Men do not realise how great a revenue thrift is."

Cicero (106–43 BC), Roman Consul

Regular saving is a key element of financial "health". It can finance a holiday, build a pension or an emergency fund. A nest egg can prevent a short-term problem — being out of work for three months through sickness or redundancy, for example — from spiralling into a major crisis.

However, deciding where and how to save is tough. Because of volatile stock markets and commission-hungry life-assurance reps, many consumers no longer trust insurance-based funds, though these can pay handsomely over a 15- or 20-year period. Returns on ordinary savings accounts were pitiful in 1995: some paid just 0.25 per cent on £10,000 or more.

Choices will be even tougher in 1996. Even people with a few pounds to spare face a bewildering range of savings products, with very different rewards and conditions. Wealthier investors may also agonise. Has the "bull run" finished on Irish and overseas equities? Can a Special Portfolio Investment Account (SPIA) pay off? Is property a good bet?

We can't predict what the future will bring, but *Personal Finance* will help you to work out a savings plan and make informed investment choices.

USING THIS CHAPTER

This chapter looks at short- and mid-term savings products which do *not* put your capital at risk. If you want to find out about a specific product, go to the alphabetised section which starts on p. 22. If you want to plan your savings/investment portfolio, read the "Defining Needs" section below. Best options for short- and mid-term savings are shown on p. 31 and p. 32.

Chapter 3 covers more aggressive investments for long-term savers and high-income earners, including life assurance-based schemes (unit-linked and "with profits" plans), equities and property, etc. Remember that choosing these products *may* put your capital at risk.

DEFINING NEEDS

Now, ask yourself a key question: "Why do I want to save?" Remember that being clear about your goals makes it easier to pick a suitable product.

Here's a list of typical savings targets:

Short Term (0–3 Years)	**Mid-Term (3–10 Years)**	**Long Term (Over 10 Years)**
Holiday	Emergency Fund	Pension
Christmas	Car	Children's Special Educational Needs
Washing Machine, or another large household item	Marriage	
College Course	New Kitchen	
Decorating Job	House Deposit	
	Big Trip	

They fall into three broad time frames — short, medium and long. Income permitting, most people can save for Christmas or a holiday in under a year, but short term can mean up to three years in the investment world. Saving £5,000 for a car, a new kitchen or a round-the-world trip can take five years or more, although many people would prefer to finance projects like these through borrowings. Building a cash fund for a pension, in particular, is a long-term venture and can take over 20 years.

As a general rule, the more distant your savings horizon, the more you can afford to risk some capital. It would be rash to invest £250 in speculative shares to "save" for Christmas. Your money would be safer earning a small return in the bank, building society or Post Office. Over the long term, however, the average *yield* (profit) on shares outperforms the average interest paid on deposit accounts. It's not wise to bury your money in a building society for 20 years where it will earn very low interest (see "Risk/Reward" below).

Ideally, try to match the chosen savings term with an appropriate product. It's not always possible to define *why* you want to save, or for how long. You may simply have £50 a month or a £5,000 lump sum that you want to invest. Or, you may have several savings goals — a holiday, home improvement plans and pension — and very little income to spare.

A flexible portfolio should contain a mix of assets geared at short-, medium-, and long-term returns. The golden rule is to *spread* your investments. A balanced portfolio should safeguard a large percentage of your capital from any loss, and give you access to cash in an emergency, but it may need to contain longer-term (and more risky) investments as well.

Finally, defining needs is not just a matter of working out what you want to save money for. Do any of the following issues concern you?

CHECKLIST

Issue	☑	See Page
• Access to Your Cash	☐	18
• Confidentiality	☐	18
• Income	☐	19
• Inflation	☐	19
• Risk/Reward	☐	20
• Strategy	☐	21
• Tax	☐	21

Access to Cash

When planning an investment, ask: "Will I be able to get hold of my cash, without penalty, in the event of an emergency?"

Breaking an investment contract can be costly. You may lose interest income if you cancel a short-term deposit account. Encashing a unit-linked investment is even more costly. Typically, insurance companies deduct all the first year's premiums to pay commission to the broker and cover administration costs. You may not get all your money back if you cancel within seven years, let alone get any return on the investment. Ideally, aim to hold a unit-linked investment for at least 10–15 years.

Try to plan a portfolio that will give you immediate access to emergency cash, but also offer mid- and long-term gains. This will be discussed below when dealing with investing over particular time periods. As a general rule, insurance-based products (such as unit-linked funds, tracker bonds and investment bonds — see Product list later in this chapter) are liable to severe early encashment penalties. An Post, bank and building society products are not.

Confidentiality

If you are a high-income earner or have brought cash back to Ireland on which you have never paid tax, this may concern you.

A product is "confidential" if the Revenue Commissioners (tax authorities) are not informed about your investment. All of An Post's savings products are confidential, as are life assurance-based investment plans (unit-linked funds, etc). New legislation, aimed at curbing money laundering and other fraud, now requires banks and building societies to question clients who suddenly deposit large cash sums.

Some products, especially those offering generous tax breaks, are not very confidential. They include Special Savings Accounts (SSAs), which still pay Deposit Interest Retention Tax (DIRT) at 15 per cent, instead of the usual 27 per cent rate. SSA investors must complete a form at the bank or building society, which can be checked by the Revenue Commissioners. Business Expansion Schemes (BES), which give tax breaks for people who invest in authorised companies, involve detailed paperwork which must also be vetted.

Income

Some financial products pay all or part of the interest in the form of an income, instead of a lump sum when the investment matures. Income may be paid monthly, every three months (quarterly), half-yearly or annually. This option may suit pensioners and people who have no other income source.

Be careful of products that seem to guarantee a very high income. Ask if taking this income will eat into your capital, or if returns may fluctuate from year to year (see also Chapter 3, Investments). Also, ask if there are any charges and find out how much they will eat into your income (see also Chapter 3, p. 60).

Inflation

This erodes the buying power of your pound over time. If inflation averages 10 per cent per annum, your £10 will buy only £9 worth of goods after 12 months. Its nominal value will be the same, but its *real* value will have decreased. The table "Real Value of Your Money" shows how inflation could eat into the Irish pound over the next 30 years.

The idea — albeit unlikely — that your £1,000 may be worth just £57 in 2025 is shocking. Clearly, any mid- or long-term investment product you choose will at least have to keep pace with inflation to protect the real value of your nest egg.

Bank and building society deposits often fail to do this, so you need to pick a more risky investment, like equities, which *may* grow faster than inflation over the long term.

REAL VALUE OF YOUR MONEY

Year	3% inflation	5% inflation	10% inflation
1995	£1,000	£1,000	£1,000
2000	£863	£784	£621
2005	£744	£614	£386
2010	£642	£481	£239
2015	£554	£377	£149
2020	£478	£295	£92
2025	£412	£231	£57

Source: Central Bank.

Risk/Reward

As a general rule, the return on an investment is inversely related to risk. Money which sits safely in a deposit account earns a low rate of interest. You can get double-digit returns on unit-linked funds, but may lose some capital if the stock market plunges. Some people — like those approaching retirement age or on tight budgets — can ill afford to take risks. More affluent people, and those who are saving over a longer term, can.

Time is an important factor in risk-related investments because it smooths out the effect of short-term gains and losses.

The following chart shows the average *return on equities, gilts and cash over the past 20 years. It assumes that a person invested stg£1,000 on 31 December 1975.*

THE GROSS (PRE-TAX) VALUE OF STG£1,000
INVESTED ON 31 DECEMBER 1975

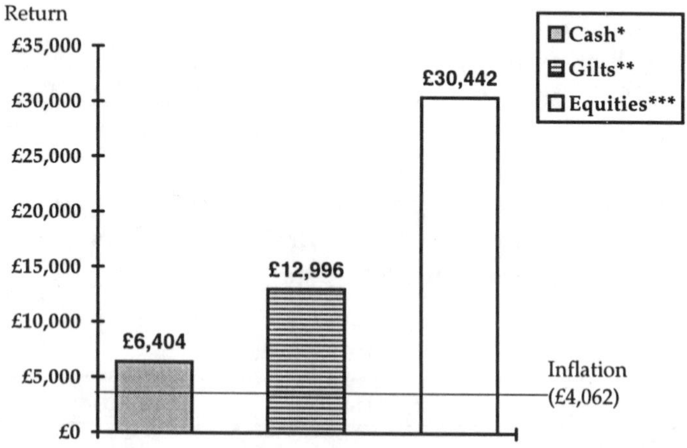

Notes: * Estimate of average building society yields. Assumes a 3.9% (gross) return in 1995.

** Based on index of long-dated gilts which are held to maturity. Figure is gross of taxes and charges, and assumes gilt income is reinvested in more gilts, instead of being paid annually.

*** Based on growth in the FT All Share Index, which now reflects the value of roughly 800 shares.

Source: BZW, London.

> **Note:** Never take risks with capital you cannot afford to lose. Also, beware of investment advisers or financial institutions that offer spectacular gains. Your savings may not be safe. Insist on a capital guarantee if you do not want to lose any money, and make sure that you deal with reputable brokers and institutions.

Strategy

Think strategically when you save.

For example, if you are saving a deposit for a house, why not choose a bank or building society that offers a reduced rate for its own savers? Or one that has an attractive mortgage package? Your £2,500 deposit will not earn a lot of interest, but a competitive mortgage rate could save you a lot of money over a 20-year term.

Credit unions pay their members about 6 per cent interest on savings, and give them access to competitively priced loans. Opening a credit union account will also discipline you into regular saving.

Tax

Investment products are taxed in different ways, and some not at all. So, tax is a key issue for savers and investors, especially if your PAYE earnings are taxed at 48 per cent.

Briefly, most bank and building-society deposit accounts and life assurance-based investments (unit-linked funds and "with profits" funds — see Chapter 3), deduct 27 per cent tax from your profits. This means that they pay the return *net* of tax. The tax rate on SSAs was increased from 10 per cent to 15 per cent in the 1995 Budget, but is still low. Many Post Office products are totally tax-free.

Other products pay returns *gross* of tax. This means that you have to declare to the Revenue Commissioners any profit which is paid either as a regular *income* or final *gain*. Make sure that you look at net (post-tax) returns when comparing products.

Top-rate taxpayers usually pay tax at 48 per cent on investment incomes, such as interest from a foreign bank account. Profits which are taken when the investment is *encashed*, or has *matured* — for example, equities (see Chapter 3) — are usually liable for Capital Gains Tax (CGT). This tax, usually 40 per cent, is charged on the "profit" made on the difference between the purchase and sale price of the investment. You can make a yearly gain of £1,000 (£2,000 for married people) before paying CGT. There is a special 27 per cent CGT rate on some shares (see "Equities", Chapter 3). People who invest in equities through a Special Investment Account (also called Special Portfolio Investment Account) pay a special low tax rate of 10 per cent on all profits.

All investors, large and small, should maximise gains on their savings by putting at least some cash in a tax-free or low-tax deposit product. Ironically, these products already pay high returns because of competition for new customers. But investors can use tax perks, like the CGT allowance and investment-related tax benefits, to cut the tax bill on riskier (and potentially more rewarding) products.

Note: People aged over 65 or permanently disabled do not have to pay DIRT on their savings. They can claim a refund by filling out a form at the bank or building society and sending it to the Revenue Commissioners.

WHAT'S AVAILABLE?

Here are the different product options. They are listed alphabetically under five main groups:

- An Post
- Bank/Building Society
- Credit Union
- Government
- Insurance Company.

If you want to check the "best" options for different savings periods first, see tables on p. 31 and p. 32.

An Post

Deposit Accounts

Like banks and building societies, An Post offers an ordinary deposit account which pays low interest. There is also an SSA option. The rate on its SSA account is currently very competitive. Three other products offer an excellent choice for the short-term and mid-term saver. Returns are paid tax-free, and the investment is fully confidential.

National Instalment Savings

NIS pay 50 per cent interest after six years. Unlike Savings Certificates and Bonds, they do not require a lump-sum investment. Instead, you save an agreed amount (between £10 and £200) each month for a year, and then leave the money untouched for another five years.

If you miss one payment, the maturity date is put back a month. If you miss two, the agreement is cancelled. Like Savings Bonds, these can be encashed after each full calendar year. They are also inflation proof and confidential. Here's how £1,000 (roughly £84 per month) grows each year:

One Year	£1,080
Two Years	£1,170
Three Years	£1,280
Four Years	£1,390
Five Years	£1,500

NIS will only guarantee a rate for up to five years. However, you can lock up your cash again at another guaranteed rate, or switch it into another An Post product, like Savings Bonds. This may suit parents who have less than 10 years to save for their child's special educational needs, and cannot risk losing their capital in a unit-linked fund. See also Chapter 9, Children.

Savings Bonds

They pay 20.4 per cent interest over three years. You can cash them in early and get your capital back, plus interest, but must leave your money in for a full calendar year. They are bought in £50 units. Here's how a £1,000 investment grows after three years:

One Year	£1,055
Two Years	£1,113
Three Years	£1,204

The Compound Annual Return (CAR) on Savings Bonds is 6.39 per cent although part of the interest is paid as a "bonus" in year three. If you withdraw your money between anniversary dates, you will be paid interest to the last anniversary date, plus the gross Post Office Savings Bank rate on interest due since then. You will get no interest if you cash in your bonds within the first 12 months. Savings Bonds are index-linked. If inflation is higher than the guaranteed minimum, you will be paid the higher sum. As with Savings Certificates, the maximum investment is now £60,000 per person.

Savings Certificates

These can be held for up to five years and nine months, and pay 40 per cent interest on maturity. But interest is added at six-monthly intervals, which makes them a more flexible product than savings bonds. They are an excellent choice for lump-sum investors who want a tax-free, confidential return, and a married couple can invest up to £120,000 jointly. You can also generate an income from Savings Certificates (see p. 61).

Prize Bonds

These pay no interest on your savings. Instead, your capital is guaranteed and you are entered for regular draws for cash prizes. They are a good place to stash away a lump for a year but remember that inflation will soon eat into your capital.

Bank and Building Society Accounts

Demand Accounts

They give instant access to your cash, but pay very low yields — as little as 0.25 per cent in 1995 — and are usually taxed at 27 per cent. They are offered by both banks and building societies and are also called "instant access" or "ordinary" deposit accounts. You should only use them as a temporary home for money. Other deposit products pay far higher rates.

Fixed-Term Accounts

These commit your money for a specific term, typically between one month and several years. They pay a pre-agreed interest rate. People who invest in fixed-term accounts are taking a bet on interest rates, just like those who opt for fixed-rate mortgages. Say you invest £2,000 in a two-year fixed-term account that pays an annual return of 6 per cent gross. This yield will remain constant, even if interest rates rise, for the two years. They are a good bet for "lump-sum" investors, who want to lock up their cash for a short period.

Guaranteed Interest Accounts

These are fixed-term accounts by another name. Rates are usually quoted for the full investment term — for example, 20 per cent over three years. This makes it easier to compare returns with An Post's popular short-term savings options, but remember to compare *net* yields. An Post's savings certificates and other products pay a tax-free profit; bank and building society accounts are liable to DIRT (either at the SSA or ordinary tax rate).

Notice Accounts

These pay slightly higher returns than demand accounts, but you have to give prior warning — typically one month — before taking out your savings. The bank or building society may return your cash without applying the notice period in a real emergency, but you will lose interest income.

Regular Savings Accounts

These are available at both banks and building societies. You have to save a specific amount, usually each month, for an agreed period. In return, the bank or building society may offer special incentives, such as a higher interest rate or prizes.

Special Savings Accounts (SSAs)

SSAs were first launched in January 1993, and accounted for an estimated £3.7 billion in savers' funds by late 1995. They can be opened at banks, building societies and An Post. SSA customers pay 15 per cent tax on their interest. This went up from 10 per cent in the 1995 Budget but is still low compared to the regular DIRT rate of 27 per cent. Even better for the consumer, gross (pre-tax) rates on SSAs are very good, thanks to fierce competition for business.

SSAs are subject to strict conditions:

- You must be 18 or over to open one.
- You can only have one SSA account, although married couples can open two single or two joint accounts.
- You can invest a maximum of £50,000 (£100,000 for married couples).
- The account must be designated as an SSA by the bank or building society. The Revenue Commissioners can check details of your account.
- You and/or your spouse must be the beneficial owner of the SSA. In other words, the account must belong to you and not be opened on someone else's behalf.
- You cannot withdraw money within three months of opening the account. After the first 90 days, you must give 30 days' "notice" of any withdrawals.
- Bank and building societies also offer fixed-rate SSAs, as well as a floating-rate option where the interest paid can fluctuate from month to month. However, you can only "fix" an interest rate for a maximum of two years.

Note that a lot of the products described earlier — notice and fixed-term accounts — are often available as SSAs. You pay less tax as a result.

Tracker Bonds

These were very popular in 1995, when stock markets boomed. They suit people who want to dabble in equity-based investments, without risking their capital. They are launched by banks, building societies and insurance companies. Their tax treatment can differ, however.

They "track" the performance of one or more stock markets during the investment period, typically 3–5 years. If the stock market index rises during that time, you make a profit. If it falls, you just get your money back unless the institution has agreed to "lock in" any gains achieved early in the investment term, or pay a minimum "guaranteed" return. Some institutions also average out losses and gains in the last 12 or 6 months. So, if the stock market crashes the day before, you may still make some profit.

Here's an imaginary example:

The "Double" tracker bond is launched by a building society in March 1996. It is a four-year bond, and the minimum investment is £5,000. It will track two stock-market indices: the FTSE 100 (which reflects the performance of Britain's top 100 companies) and Japan's Nikkei Index. You are promised 100 per cent of the "combined" growth in these markets.

The bond matures four years later, in March 2000. The FTSE has fallen by 12 per cent, but the Nikkei has climbed by 40 per cent. So you make 50 per cent of the Nikkei's rise — a gain of 20 per cent. Your £1,000 profit is taxed at 27 per cent, reducing it to £730.

Some tracker bonds promise a tax-paid return; others deduct tax from any guaranteed return. They have some draw-backs; your money is usually locked up for the full investment term and the minimum lump sum is high — around £3,000–£5,000.

Credit Union

Credit union accounts are an excellent choice for single people, young families and older savers who plan to take out low-cost loans. They are not savings accounts, as such, because you cannot really withdraw your cash unless you close the account.

To borrow from the credit union, you must build a relationship based on your savings and loan repayment record. When you first open the account, you must save regularly, even if it is only a small amount. Your savings are called "shares", and entitle you to credit union membership. After about 12 weeks, or less, you can apply to take out your first loan (see also Chapter 4, Borrowing).

Credit unions pay about 6 per cent interest, which is very high compared to ordinary bank/building-society deposits. Interest (called dividends) is paid once a year on savings. DIRT is not deducted, and profits should be reported to the Revenue Commissioners in your annual income tax return.

Government

Gilts

Gilts are IOUs which are sold by the government when it needs to raise money. They used to be issued on paper which was edged with gold — hence the name "gilt-edged securities". Today they are more commonly called government gilts, government stocks, or government bonds.

They are sold in £100 units as part of a gilt "issue". Gilts are usually snapped up by large institutions, like banks and insurance companies, which buy a large chunk of each issue. Because of this, they can be difficult to buy (or sell) in small quantities (even under £20,000). A recent survey found that only 2 per cent of Irish households had invested directly in gilts. Despite this, and the fact that they can be hard to buy if you're a small investor, gilts deserve a place in some portfolios.

They pay an income, usually twice-yearly, which is invariably fixed until the gilt reaches *redemption* date. This income is paid gross of tax, which gives you the use of it until you have to settle the tax bill. Also, it means that people who do not have a taxable income, like students, can avoid tax totally. They cannot do this with deposit accounts because DIRT is deducted automatically. Gilts are "safe" investments, which guarantee your capital if you hold them to maturity. These factors can make them a good place to park a large sum of cash. They can also pay a tax-free capital gain when they mature, depending on the price at which they were purchased. Thus, a 48 per cent taxpayer may be better off buying a gilt that pays low interest, but offers a fat, tax-free, capital gain.

Let's look at one stock, 6¼ per cent Treasury 1999, to see how gilts work:

This stock will pay 6.25 per cent interest per year, in two six-monthly instalments, until 1 April 1999 when it reaches the redemption date. This annual yield is also called the coupon.

On 8 January 1996, this gilt was being traded on the market at £99.15 per £100 worth of stock, but you will get £100 back by holding the gilt to maturity. This means that you would make a tax-free capital gain of £0.85 for each £100 worth of stock bought, in addition to earning the 6.25 per cent interest each year. This brings your total "yield to redemption" to 6.44 per cent.

Gilts have other names like "Capital" and "Exchequer". These titles are irrelevant. The interest rate that they pay and their total *yield to redemption* are far more important. The latter, which is usually expressed as a percentage, takes into account both the gilt's coupon yield and its projected capital gain. You can only be sure of making a capital gain if you buy a stock that is sold *below par* and hold it to maturity. This means that you are buying a stock at a price below its promised redemption value.

The 6¼ per cent Treasury 1999 gilt is one example of a *below par* stock. Gilts that promise a high fixed-interest rate are sometimes sold *above par*. Thus the 8 per cent Treasury bond 2006 traded in early January at £103.775 per £100 worth of stock. You would make a *capital loss* by holding the gilt to maturity, but get a high coupon by way of compensation. The "yield to redemption" is 7.33 per cent.

Not everyone holds gilts to redemption date. Gilts are traded on the stock market by banks, building societies and other large "institutional investors". Their sale price fluctuates in line with interest rates. Thus, if interest rates rise, the price of the gilt falls, and vice versa. These movements are not usually relevant to small investors who want to earn an interest income on their gilt until it matures.

Not all gilts offer a fixed-interest return. A small number pay a floating interest rate. Some offer an index-linked return, which links the yield to interest rates. Finally, gilts fall into three main age categories. Short-dated gilts mature in five years, medium-dated gilts run from 5 to 15 and long-dated gilts mature later, after 15 years. Long-dated gilts are a more risky prospect, because their buy/sell price fluctuates more in response to interest rates, and investors may not be able to hold them to maturity.

Buying Gilts

This is usually done through a stockbroking firm. Large firms usually set a high minimum investment, perhaps £20,000, so it's best to buy through a smaller firm. You will pay a commission charge ranging from £25 to £40, depending on the amount of stock you buy. As stated before, gilts can be difficult to buy in small quantities. However, financial institutions have traded more actively in gilts since 1995 when they were permitted to become *market makers*.

> **Note:** You can invest in gilts through a unit-linked fund marketed by a life-assurance company, too. These funds spread your investment across a number of gilts, and you can also invest in a fund that holds European or other foreign bonds, as they are normally called outside Ireland and the UK. The minimum investment is smaller, typically £1,000 or more, and yields are paid tax-free. But you can lose part of your capital in a gilt fund as fund managers "trade in" their collection of gilts.

Insurance Companies

Guaranteed Bonds

These are similar to the fixed-term deposit accounts available at banks and building societies. They pay a pre-agreed interest rate over a set term, typically two years or more. There is a crucial difference. An insurance company may refuse to repay your cash early, or charge a large penalty. However, returns are paid tax-free.

Bonds can be tricky investments. Ask these questions if you are thinking of buying one:

- Is my capital fully guaranteed?
- Will tax be deducted?
- What will I get back for my lump sum when the bond matures?
- Can I get an income?
- What are the penalties for early encashment?

Tracker Bonds

Also marketed by insurance companies, these pay returns net of 27 per cent tax, like bank and building-society tracker bonds.

Some trackers invest in exotic places like Japan. They suit people who don't want to risk their capital but fancy the prospect of a higher return. Note that trackers lock up your cash for the full term. You cannot encash them early.

SUMMARY POINTS

Reviewing the Options

Picking the right savings or investment product is tricky, given the range of issues to consider and the sheer number of products. It can be quite confusing.

Try to prioritise. If you are a short-term saver, you probably want to keep your capital safe, readily available and paying a good return. You may also want a home for "rainy-day" cash, if an emergency strikes. You won't be too worried about inflation, however. Mid-term savers also need access to their cash, in an emergency, but they might be concerned about inflation. Their goal is usually to maximise return and minimise tax. An Post offers options for these savers. The investment that you pick will also depend on whether you want to invest a lump sum or smaller amount — £10 upwards — on a regular basis.

Here's a summary of the best choices for short- and medium-term savers. Long-term savers are covered in the next chapter.

WHICH IS BEST?
SHORT TERM (0–3 YEARS)

✓ Good Option	? Be Wary	✗ Avoid
Credit Union*	Gilts	Demand Accounts
Notice Accounts	Guaranteed Bonds (Insurance companies)	Equities
Prize Bonds		Property
Regular Savings Account		Unit-linked Funds
Savings Bonds*		Tracker Bonds
SSAs*		"With Profits" investments

* Recommended.

MID-TERM (3–10 YEARS)

✓ Good Option	? Be Wary	✗ Avoid
Credit Union	Equities	Demand Account
Guaranteed Interest Account	High-yielding Bonds	Offshore Insurance Funds
National Instalment Savings*	Gilts	
Savings Certificates*	Unit-linked Funds	
Tracker Bond*	"With Profits" investments	

* Recommended.

CREATING A PORTFOLIO

This is largely a matter of analysing your needs, and spreading your available cash over a range of savings options. Here are a few examples. These are imaginary people, but their dilemmas are quite real:

Case Study 1: Married man, gets windfall which he wants to invest wisely.

Michael (36) earns £20,000. He has three children, aged 18, 15 and 12. His wife does not work outside the home. They have a £50,000 mortgage, now seven years into a 20-year term, and still owe £40,000. Michael gets an £8,000 inheritance from his uncle. Should he invest the money or pay off his mortgage?

Michael should probably do both. If he paid a lump sum of £5,000 off his mortgage (in year 8), he could cut his total interest bill by £6,660 and repay his mortgage two and a half years early. That would leave £3,000 for repaying other high-interest debts (such as a credit card bill, overdraft or car loan). He could also "park" £1,000 in the credit union, which would give him access to cheap loans in the future and, if he has no debts, invest the balance in An Post Savings Bonds or Savings Certificates.

Taking out a life assurance-based "single premium" policy is probably not a good idea. He may have to lock up his cash for at least 10 years to get a decent return, and he may face college-related costs a lot earlier than that. If he can't decide what to do, he could put all his money in a Special Savings Account until he thinks out his priorities.

This would lock up his cash for a minimum of just three months. Based on rates in January 1996, an SSA would earn interest at 6 per cent (or more), and his "profits" would be taxed at just 15 per cent. He can store his money in an SSA for up to two years (at a fixed rate) and then decide what to do.

Case Study 2: Single woman, made redundant and gets lump sum. How should she invest it?

Anne (53) is made redundant by her employer and gets a £60,000 lump sum (after tax). She has a very small mortgage — her repayments are now less than £100 per month — and has just a few years before the loan is totally repaid. She has no other debts. Anne has been offered a reduced pension, in addition to her lump sum, but can also wait until 65 to take out a "full" pension.

As Anne's mortgage is low, it may be a good idea to keep it as she will get some mortgage interest relief on repayments if she starts working again. That leaves her £60,000 lump sum intact for investment purposes. Anne can opt for an early pension, and then supplement this with her lump sum, but this may be a poor choice. Her pension income will be small, and her capital may erode quickly. As she has a company pension scheme, she may opt, instead, for making a last-minute Additional Voluntary Contribution into the scheme before she leaves the company (see Chapter 10, Your Pension). A £5,000 contribution would cost just half that, after tax relief, because Anne is a 48 per cent taxpayer. Also, her investment will roll-up tax-free, until she reaches 65, boosting her final pension in retirement.

Anne will probably be entitled to Unemployment Benefit for the first 15 months after she leaves work. This is based on her PRSI contributions, so her lump sum should not affect this entitlement significantly, but it is taxable. She could invest £50,000 of her funds in a two-year Creative Quality account, earning 6 per cent gross. This would be taxed at 15 per cent and could generate an income. She could put the balance in An Post's Savings Bonds or Savings Certificates for longer-term growth.

Anne's income will be assessed for Social Welfare purposes when the benefit period ends, and she may not qualify for a full unemployment allowance. She might have to live solely off her capital and income, but should continue to sign for Social Welfare credits (towards her State

Contributory pension). Anne can generate an income by investing in An Post's Saving Certificates (see Chapter 3, Investments), or opting for a series of income-generating SSAs. National Deposit Brokers, based in Dublin, could advise her on this. Anne should also be wary of insurance-based investment, because she is close to retirement. But she might want to lock up some cash in a guaranteed bond, which will pay an agreed sum after three, four or five years, or she could pick a tracker bond, investing just £3,000 or £5,000 at most.

To summarise. Planning a portfolio is very, very tricky. It's vital to get good independent advice to make sure that your choices are well-informed and based on *your* needs.

CONCLUSION

Deciding how to save money is about personal choices. A product that suits a teenager may not suit a pensioner, a single woman or a married 49-year-old man. Ideally, you should sit down, analyse your needs and capacity to save. Then, when your ideas are clearer, look for professional advice. Remember that a financial adviser may "push" a certain product. You must specify what you want.

Make sure that any insurance broker with whom you deal is a member of the Irish Brokers' Association (which represents independent brokers) and has a professional qualification in accountancy or investment services.

Prepare your own questions before going for advice or a sales pitch. You should also keep a record of the conversation and of all future correspondence. Be sure to keep these in a safe place.

When you take out an investment, keep track of its performance. Make sure that you get a regular statement, which shows how your deposit/fund is performing. Review your investment strategy regularly to take into account changes in your personal circumstances or interest rates.

A final point. Millions of pounds are stashed in "dormant accounts", because the account-holders have either forgotten their existence or died. Similarly, thousands of Prize Bonds winnings have never been collected — details of these are kept by the Prize Bonds office, c/o Fexco, Killorglin, Co. Kerry (tel: (066) 61258). Keep a record of your investments, and leave a copy with your family solicitor.

3

INVESTMENTS

"Buy cheap, sell dear."

Thomas Lodge (1558–1625), English poet

This chapter is about more aggressive investments. Unlike those covered in Chapter 2, they involve a degree of risk. In other words, you may lose money instead of making a profit.

Some people tolerate risk because they want a long-term investment that *may* beat inflation. Some thrive on it. Others — like pensioners, families on modest incomes, or anybody who wants to protect their nest egg — should be very wary of it. This chapter deals with various options for risk-based investments. It explains how to invest in them, the pitfalls and how they are taxed. Finally, it looks at earning an income from your investment.

The options are:

Stock-Market-Related

Other Investments

EQUITIES/SHARES

What are They?

Companies issue shares on the stock market to raise capital. When you become a shareholder, you buy a piece of a company and invest in its future. In return, you get certain rights and the chance to make a profit on your investment.

You can make a profit in several ways. Companies usually divide up some of their profit and distribute it amongst their shareholders. This is called a *dividend*. It is usually paid twice a year, and the amount each investor gets is in direct proportion to the size of their shareholding.

Here's an example:

Jack buys 1,000 shares in Ace Manufacturing. They cost him £1.50 apiece. The company makes a good profit in the financial year ending 31 December 1995, so the board decides to pay a dividend of 5p per share. Jack has 1,000 shares, so his gross (pre-tax) dividend is £50.

Ace Manufacturing deducts tax at 27 per cent from Jack's dividend cheque, leaving him with £36.50. He's a 48 per cent taxpayer, so he will have to pay more tax on this "income" and must declare this income to the Revenue Commissioners in his annual tax return.

You can also make a profit if the share price rises. Shares are traded daily, from Monday to Friday, on the Irish Stock Exchange. The closing prices after each day's trading, plus the highest and lowest price recorded for each share in the current year, are published in the financial pages of the daily papers.

EQUITIES TABLES

	A	B	C	D	E	F
Company	Price	Change %		NAV	No. (M)	Mkt Cap
	(p)	Wk	YTD	(p)	Shares	£m
AIB	354.0	4.4	4.4	174	673	2381
Bank of Ireland	466.0	2.4	2.4	185	480	2234
CRH	473.0	0.6	0.6	167	352	1665
Smurfit Group	158.0	6.8	6.8	114	1052	1662
Élan Corporation	3060.6	1.3	1.3	510	36	1099
Kerry Group	495.0	1.0	1.0	143	164	811
Irish Life	250.0	5.0	5.0	320	307	767

Key: A = The current price of each share in pence
B = Increase/decrease in the share price in last seven days
C = Increase/decrease in the past 12 months
D = Net Asset Value (value of company's assets)
E = The number of shares issued (in millions)
F = The company's current market value, i.e. A multiplied by E.

Source: Davy Stockbrokers and *The Sunday Business Post*, 7 January 1996.

Usually, when a company performs well and looks like a promising investment, demand for its shares increases and the price goes up. This is because the "market" — institutional investors and stockbrokers — view it as a good buy.

Risk

Last year was a boom year in the Irish stockmarket. The ISEQ Index, which tracks the performance of the top shares, surged by about 25 per cent. But share prices can be very volatile, reflecting not only a company's performance and strength but also market mood and perception. Rising inflation or unemployment figures, an outbreak of war or a plunging dollar can trigger a mass exodus from equities, as big investors sell their holdings and retreat to cash and safer investments. Millions of pounds can be "wiped off" the value of the stock market overnight.

When this happens, share prices fall and the market is said to be "bearish". When investors are positive and buy large volumes of shares in the hope of making profits, share prices rise and commentators describe the market as "bullish". These fluctuations create paper losses and gains for most shareholders. You are not really affected until you sell your shares, so it's best not to panic and ditch your holding when the markets fall, unless the shares are becoming worthless. Try to take a long-term view instead. Too many small investors buy into the market when shares are high, and sell when they plunge.

Shareholders don't always make a profit. The company may report losses, run up debts and be unable to pay a dividend. The share price may fall, or even collapse. That's why equity investment is a high-risk business. In the long term, average returns on shares are better than yields on bank or building-society deposits, which barely protect your money against inflation. But the average return hides the fact that some investors lose their shirts, and others make a killing. Some shares are a lot riskier than others.

As an ordinary shareholder, you can attend the company's Annual General Meeting (AGM) and vote on matters affecting your interests, such as poor commercial performance, takeover bids and appointments to the board. Institutional investors often hold most of the shares, so your voting power will be limited.

You may also make a profit if your company is taken over by another firm. That's because, in order to encourage the shareholders to sell, the company making the acquisition will offer them a bid price that represents a profit on their shares.

Shares

Unitised v. *Direct Purchase*

You can invest in shares via two main routes: unitised (unit-linked fund or unit trust) investment or direct purchase. What are the pros and cons of each?

Unit-linked funds and unit trusts are "pooled investments". Your money is spread across a range of shares and/or other assets. The percentage invested in a particular class of asset — such as cash, property or shares — will depend on the category of fund that you pick. See also "Life Assurance-based Funds", p. 41.

Equity funds invest your money exclusively in shares. The fund manager trades in these holdings, adding dividends and other profits to the fund. This has the advantage of smoothing out losses and gains, because you are investing in a "basket" of shares, not just one or two. It's also easy to invest outside Ireland's tiny stock market through a European, Far Eastern or North American equity fund, although these funds can be quite volatile. Finally, unitised funds are simple from a tax point of view. Tax is deducted within the fund, and you don't have to declare investment returns to the Revenue Commissioners.

Direct investment is trickier. You must decide which share(s) to buy. It's harder to spread risk, unless you have a lot of money (£20,000 +) to build an equity portfolio consisting of at least four or five different shares. You can invest in foreign shares, since the lifting of exchange controls on 1 January 1992, but picking a German or French stock is an even bigger step into the unknown. Last but not least, you have to sort out your own tax affairs.

Investing in shares through a Special Portfolio Investment Account (SPIA) is far simpler and very "tax-efficient", but you usually have to commit at least £5,000. Profits from dividends and sales are taxed at a special rate of 10 per cent. Also, the stock-broking firm offering the SPIA handles tax and administration — for a fee. You can also buy a unitised version, see p. 46. SPIAs were very popular in 1995 and made investors a lot of money.

Which Share?

Stockbrokers usually advise small investors to choose "blue-chip" companies. These are called "blue chips" because they are well capitalised, earn healthy profits and have a strong core business activity (such as banking) or a diverse range of commercial interests (such as CRH). The downside is that the share price is usually high, and gains — both dividends and capital appreciation — tend to be modest.

Some investors treat share investment like a bet on the races. They may be quite happy to put £500 in a small exploration stock (sold by a company which is exploiting oil, minerals, etc.) and hope that it — and they — strike lucky. These shares can be cheap to buy and increase dramatically in value. But, as thousands of investors in Atlantic Resources found out in the 1980s, such shares can tumble in value overnight. You may lose your entire investment. The golden rule regarding speculative investments is never to invest money that you cannot afford to lose.

You can glean information on companies from stockbrokers' reports, the financial press and the business news on radio and

TV. Beware of tips given over a pint of beer in a hotel bar! Someone may be trying to "talk up" the share price.

How to Buy Shares

You can buy shares at a stockbroking firm, from an independent broker or from a financial adviser. A small stockbroker is probably the best bet. Large firms prefer to deal with people or companies who want to invest at least £10,000. They may be willing to arrange a share transaction, but may not give the time and attention that you want. (See Appendix for a list of small stockbroking firms.)

Stockbrokers usually recommend that you invest a minimum of £500–£750 in each company, preferably more. Dividend gains are very modest on small shareholdings, and it costs a lot to buy shares. Stockbrokers charge a minimum fee, which may be a cash sum or a percentage of your total share-purchase price. You also have to pay stamp duty of 1 per cent. Thus, buying £1,000 worth of shares at a small stockbroking firm will cost around £50. This includes a £40 minimum fee and a £10 stamp-duty charge. Note that this figure already represents 5 per cent of your investment. You will have to pay another £40 dealing charge when you sell your shares, but no stamp duty.

You can buy an exact number of shares, or invest a specific sum — usually a round figure. The stockbroker will give you a share certificate, bearing the date, your name and the number of shares that you purchased. It should be kept in a safe place, because it is your record of the transaction, and must be handed back when you sell the shares.

Tax

Shareholders are liable to both income tax on dividends and Capital Gains Tax (CGT) if they make a profit on the sale of shares. But they can claim an annual CGT "allowance" (£1,000 for a single person, £2,000 for a married couple) before paying CGT. They can also cancel out gains made on one share by losses incurred on another — but only if both were sold in the same tax year.

Here's an example:

Niall, who is single, sold his shares in Beara, an agricultural company, in February 1996 and made £3,500 profit. After deducting his £1,000

Capital Gains Tax allowance, Niall faces a CGT bill of £1,000 (£2,500 @ 40 per cent) for the 1995/96 tax year, which ends on 5 April 1996. But his other shareholding — the £5,000 he invested in ABC Mining — is worth only £2,000 by March 1996. Niall hasn't sold his mining shares yet, so he's only made a "paper loss".

He decides to sell just enough ABC shares to wipe out his CGT bill, but keep some in case they rise in value. But he has to sell the ABC shares before 5 April to keep both transactions in the 1995/96 tax year.

CGT is normally charged at 40 per cent. However, if you buy shares in a privately held company which is *not* quoted on a stock exchange, and valued at under £25 million, you qualify for a special 27 per cent rate. It is charged at 10 per cent on profits made in equities held in an SPIA.

LIFE ASSURANCE-BASED FUNDS

What are They?

When you take out an endowment mortgage, a pension or a school fees plan, you are usually doing the same thing — investing in the stock market through a life-assurance fund.

This is a simple way of dabbling in a risk-based investment. You can invest a lump sum — typically £3,000 or more — and then leave it there for several years. This is also called a "single premium" investment. Or, you can pay a regular sum — usually upwards of £30 a month — for 10, 15 or even 20 or more years. This is called "regular" or "annual premium" investment, because you are paying in a regular sum each year.

You can cancel a life assurance-based investment within 15 days of taking out the policy, thanks to the Irish Insurance Federation's "Code of Practice". But the chances are, you'll keep the investment policy for a few years until you get alarmed about news of falling stock markets. If you panic, you might enquire about the policy's current value and then decide to sell quickly to avoid more losses. This is called "early encashment". You will probably get less than you originally invested, even if the fund has performed well.

Many people encash their policies early, and lose money. You can avoid bitter disappointment by knowing *how* life-assurance investments work and how to pick a level of risk that suits *you.*

How Do They Work?

Life-assurance investments fall into two main groups: unit-linked funds and "with profits" funds. They work in quite different ways, but both invest heavily in the stockmarket.

In a unit-linked fund, you and thousands of other small investors are pooling your premiums to create a multimillion-pound cash reservoir. This huge pool of money is controlled by "fund managers" — usually the life-assurance company. The company uses it to buy various "assets", like company shares, government gilts (see Chapter 2), property and cash, which it will later sell in the hopes of making a profit. You also get life cover on your investment, which means that the policy pays a lump sum if you die.

Some unit-linked funds specialise in certain assets, such as North American equities. Others, like managed funds, contain a mixture of assets. In general, managed funds are less risky than highly specialised equity funds, as part of the fund is invested in "safe" assets, like cash deposits or gilts. As a result, managed funds (especially the "cautiously managed" variety) tend to show lower gains. But they are popular, and accounted for roughly 51 per cent of the £4.99 billion held in Irish unit-linked funds by late 1995.

Let's return to your investment. Your money buys a set number of "units" in this fund. If the fund makes a profit, the values of your units rise. But if the fund managers make a loss, the unit values fall. Life companies have many costs, including the controversial broker commissions. To recover these, they build a fee into the price of the units that you buy. This is called the "bid offer" spread. It is typically 5 per cent.

This is how it works:

Paul invests £10,000 in a "managed" fund. The units cost 100p each. The fund has a "bid offer" spread of 5 per cent, so if he sells his units the next day, they will be worth just £9,500. Sometimes life companies offer a special sales bonus, which reduces the effect of the "bid offer" spread. Thus, a 2 per cent bonus would allow Paul to buy a further 200 units in this unit-linked fund, boosting the "offer" value of his units to £9,690.

The performance of unit-linked funds is shown in the business sections of the financial press. Here's what the tables look like:

UNIT PRICES, 5 JANUARY 1996

UNIT PRICING WK ENDED: January 5 1996

COMPANY & FUND	BID PRICE	OFFER PRICE	Chgs 1 WK	Chgs YTD	Chgs 5 YRS Annualised
JAPANESE EQUITY					
Hib Life Hi-Japanese	90.60	95.40	0.63	2.47	11.89
New Irl Japanese Sec 1	167.10	175.90	-2.28	-0.90	NA
New Irl Japanese Sec 5	165.40	174.10	-2.25	-0.85	NA
New Irl Japanese Sec 6	88.60	93.20	-2.31	-0.85	NA
Irish Prog Japanese	103.90	109.40	-0.73	-0.73	9.37
MONEYMATE Category Average	—	—	**-1.38**	**-0.17**	**10.63**

Source: The Sunday Business Post, 7 January 1996.

Unfortunately, tables tell you little about the cash value of your policy. Also, the "bid offer" spread is only half of the charges story. If Paul encashed his units the next day, he would get a lot less than £9,500, because life companies also recoup costs by *not investing* some of the premiums you pay in the early years, and using them to pay the broker's commission and other charges. This is called the "nil allocation" period.

People who invest regular premiums, as opposed to a lump sum, suffer most heavily from these early charges. Between 30 and 60 per cent of their first year's premiums pay the broker's commission. Other charges, including the life company's own expenses, are "front loaded", which means that they are deducted from the first year's premiums. You may not even break even on the investment in the first seven years, let alone make a profit.

Lump-sum investors are slightly better off. The broker's commission is only 3.5 per cent of the cash you invest. This is built into the "bid offer" spread, along with other charges, but more of your cash is invested at the outset.

"With Profits" Policies

These are a bit different from unit-linked funds, although the commission charges are the same. Instead of paying a profit — or loss — related to the unit value of your fund, the life company agrees to pay "bonuses" on the money that you invest. Bonuses are paid each year (the "annual bonus") and/or when the policy matures (the "terminal bonus"). Once paid, the bonus cannot be clawed back.

This makes "with profits" investments a safer bet than unit-linked ones. Gains and losses are smoothed out by the life company, and each year the minimum amount that the company promises to pay you (the "guaranteed sum assured") rises. The snag is that most of the profit is often paid on the final, "terminal" bonus. Life companies have been cutting their terminal bonuses in recent years. Also, because most people encash their policies early, they miss out on this bonus anyway.

"With profits" investments always have a minimum value, however, which is based on the guaranteed sum assured, plus "attaching bonuses". The value is not based on units in a fund, which can fluctuate each day. Also, you can get a slightly better rate than the life company's early encashment value by trading them in. Several companies buy second-hand "with profits" policies. Beware of hybrid products called "unitised with profits" policies. They do not offer cash guarantees.

Where to Buy a Unit-Linked or "With Profits" Investment?

You can do this through an independent broker or a salesperson working for one insurance company (also called a "tied agent"). Fee-based independent brokers can reduce the commission bite if they charge a straight fee for their services instead, but you will still have to part with cash! This is not usually possible with a tied agent.

Commissions are set by the Irish Insurance Federation and dictated by the savings term. From 1 January 1994, they range from 30 per cent on a 10-year policy, to 60 per cent on a 20-year investment. Picking a shorter term cuts the commission. Typical savings terms include 10, 15, 20, 25, 30 years and "whole of life", which has no specified maturity date.

Chapter 9, Children, shows you how you can use a unit-linked or "with profits" policy to pay for special education costs.

Tax

Life-assurance companies deduct 27 per cent tax within the fund from any profits made. You pay no more tax. Also, you don't have to declare any gains to the Revenue Commissioners.

Consumer Warnings

Life-assurance funds are complicated. You can protect yourself by asking the salesperson or insurance broker key questions, such as:

- Do you offer fee-based advice? In other words, can I invest without paying commission? If not, how much will be invested in each of the first three years?
- Does this policy have any capital guarantee?
- What are the penalties for early encashment?
- Can I switch between other funds offered by the same life-assurance company? How much would that cost?
- What is the life of this policy (the term)? Does that suit my needs? (Tell the broker what those needs are.)
- How much life cover is there? Do I need it all?

WARNING!

If you choose a regular premium investment, commissions and charges can devour virtually all of your first year's premiums. You may get *no* money back if you encash the investment in the first two years, and very little between years 2 and 7. Aim to hold a unit-linked investment for at least 10–15 years.

With a regular premium investment, you have several options if you can no longer afford, or do not want, to keep paying money into the fund:

- Encash the policy
- Reduce the premiums
- Stop paying premiums, but don't encash the policy until it matures.

SPIAs AND SIAs

These are the equities-based equivalent of Special Savings Accounts. Profits are taxed (internally) at 10 per cent, instead of at 27 per cent, and the rate was unchanged in the 1996 Budget.

SPIAs sold like hot-cakes in 1995, thanks to their low tax rate and a bullish stock market. However, they remain a risk-based investment.

By law, at least 55 per cent of your money must be invested in Irish equities (15 per cent of which is "smaller companies"). Also, to buy shares directly through an SPIA, you may have to invest at least £5,000. The investment threshold is lower for life assurance-based SPIAs and at least one company, Ark Life, offers a "regular premium" alternative.

You can invest up to £75,000 in an SPIA (£150,000 for married couples). If you have invested £50,000 in an SSA, you can put a further £25,000 in an SPIA. Note that SPIAs, like SSAs, are not confidential investments.

UNIT TRUSTS (IRISH-BASED)

How Do They Work?

These are like unit-linked funds. They are also pooled investments, but are usually sold by banks, fund-management companies and other non-insurance institutions. Until recently, they gave returns without deducting tax first, which made them attractive to some investors. Investors were liable to Capital Gains Tax (40 per cent) on profits arising from their unit trust holdings. Since 6 April 1994, however, unit trusts have been taxed on the same basis as unit-linked funds. Fund profits are taxed internally at 27 per cent.

Ireland's unit-trust sector has always been tiny in comparison with its unit-linked cousin. The tax change has not boosted their appeal, but unit trusts have one big advantage. Unlike unit-linked funds, life insurance is not included as part of the package. This means that your investment should grow faster than an equivalent unit-linked fund since you are not paying life premiums.

Overseas unit trusts are taxed differently. They may appeal to more sophisticated investors because they still pay yields without deducting tax first. They also offer access to far-flung markets. See "Offshore Investments", p. 55.

PROPERTY

Pros and Cons

Investing in property is beyond the reach of many people with a mortgage to pay and children to support. Most of us — even if we have no dependants — can only afford to pay one mortgage, and it's unwise to treat your own home as a speculative investment. The property market is subject to booms and crashes. You may make a profit each time you sell your house to get a bigger one. But some people who "trade up" find themselves saddled with a huge mortgage if property values fall after they move. If the market value of your house falls below the size of your mortgage, you are said to have "negative equity" in your home.

It can be hard to move house if this happens, as the sale price may not be enough to repay the mortgage on your first house.

Because of the boom–bust syndrome, property is quite an "illiquid" investment. It can be difficult to sell your house or land when you want to, especially at a profit. The sale price is never guaranteed, although you can improve the chance of making a profit by trying to buy in an area where house/land prices are rising. Even the profit may prove illusory. You have to deduct buying and selling costs (which include legal fees, stamp duty, etc.), plus the money spent on maintenance and repair.

On the plus side, there are tax incentives for people who invest in the so-called "designated" areas, because the government wants to encourage urban renewal in these districts. Bricks-and-mortar also have an emotional appeal for some. Parents may like the idea of buying a house or flat in the city, where their children can stay during their college years.

How to Invest

As with equities, you can invest through a unitised fund or direct purchase.

There are several unit-linked and unit-trust property funds from which to choose. Each fund usually invests in a property portfolio, and aims to make a profit from rents/leases, and buying and selling various holdings. These funds have shown mixed returns, to say the least. Unit values in property funds rose strongly in 1994 and 1995, but they plunged in the late 1980s and early 1990s. Some fund managers refused to allow clients to withdraw their money.

Property funds are "illiquid", because the investors' cash is tied up in bricks-and-mortar assets. If a lot of people decide to cash in their units, the fund manager may be forced to sell properties in a weak market in order to raise the funds. This is why it can be hard to get out of a property fund. These funds invest in very solid assets, but because of the boom–bust factor, property funds are volatile and not for nervous investors or people who may need their cash in a hurry.

Direct investment is more clear cut, but you have to commit a larger sum and pick the property you want. You must also factor in the cost of:

- Legal fees
- Stamp duty
- Survey costs
- Mortgage finance
- Repair/refurbishment
- Insurance
- Letting costs (agency fees etc).

Draw up a list of these costs before buying an investment property. Your dream investment may cost more than you budget for, and deliver less income than planned. Rents are taxed as "Schedule D" income and must be declared to the Revenue Commissioners. They are liable for tax in the year in which they are earned.

Thus, rents received in the tax year ending 5 April 1997 will be taxed in the 1996/97 tax year. You can reduce the gross rents (i.e. the taxable income) by claiming the following "costs":

- Rents paid by you (the owner), such as ground rents
- Rates
- Goods and services provided in connection with letting the property, such as agent's fees
- Repairs and maintenance costs
- Insurance
- Interest on loans taken out to purchase, improve or repair the property.

You can also claim capital allowances on assets purchased for the tenants, such as furniture. You can write off 15 per cent of the total cost of these assets each year for six years, and then 10 per cent in the final, seventh, year.

There's a snag, however. You can't claim for any costs incurred before you start letting the property. This applies both to claims against income tax and capital allowances. Thanks to the government's "urban renewal" scheme, you can claim more generous reliefs if you buy a rental property in a so-called "designated area" — chiefly, the inner city.

Section 23-Type Reliefs

Property owners who buy a house/flat in a designated area can write off the building cost, refurbishment and/or conversion cost of a property for letting purposes against the rental income on this building and all other properties each year. If you're earning rents on non-designated properties, a Section 23-type house or flat may be a very good investment. The "building cost" — or purchase price in many cases — must exclude the site cost. The house or flat must also be below a certain size.

You must let the premises for 10 years after purchase, or all the tax reliefs will be clawed back. If you sell the property within that time, the new owner can claim reliefs until the period expires if they use it for rental purposes.

The "urban renewal" scheme was first launched in 1985. Under current legislation, only two areas now qualify for Section 23-type reliefs. These are:

- The Custom House Docks area (near Dublin's International Financial Services Centre). The deadline for investment was extended to 25 January 1999 in the 1995 Budget.

- Temple Bar area (which falls between Westmoreland Street, Dame Street, Lord Edward Street and the River Liffey, Dublin). The deadline for investment is 5 April 1996, unless extended further.

New Urban Renewal Scheme

In 1994, the government introduced a new system of urban renewal reliefs to replace those which had almost expired. This new system is complex, consisting of different reliefs for owner/occupiers and those letting their premises. It also introduced a new concept of "designated street" to encourage development in a very small geographic area.

The qualifying period runs from 1 August 1994 to 31 July 1997. You must invest during this period to qualify for relief (unless a particular scheme is extended). These allowances can be claimed by both private individuals and companies. The only exception is the owner/occupiers' residential allowance, which can only be claimed by individuals (see Chapter 11).

You can claim reliefs/allowances on the following types of property:

- Industrial buildings

- Rented residential accommodation

- Owner-occupied premises.

The size, duration and nature of the allowance may also be affected by other factors, such as whether the building is new, converted or refurbished. Premises must also be a certain size.

Last but not least, if you sell the property before the reliefs have expired, you may lose — or even have to repay — tax relief that you have already been granted.

You can get more information on urban renewal allowances from the estate agent or developer handling the sale of the property. Some mortgage brokers also specialise in this type of business.

The government's "Urban Renewal Scheme" offers very good tax savings, but the terms and conditions are complex. Get information from a number of sources before committing yourself to a major financial decision.

Buying a property for investment purposes can be tricky. Don't be swayed by a high-powered marketing campaign, or pressurised deadlines, like "Must sell in one week!" Look at the bottom-line costs, and talk to an accountant about tax. Finally, remember that Section 23-type reliefs will expire after 10 years. Some analysts warn that, when this happens, the market may be glutted by unwanted Section 23 properties. Don't be driven solely by tax-planning. Look for good value in a good area.

BUSINESS EXPANSION SCHEMES (BES)

BES schemes were due to be phased out on 5 April 1996, but the concept was renewed for another three years in the 1996 Budget. You can still invest up to £25,000 in any one year and claim tax relief at 48 per cent, but there are now tighter controls on how schemes are set up and run. In particular, BES projects which raise over £250,000 must get a special certificate and create jobs. Tax relief may be clawed back if they don't.

BES schemes suit high-income earners who want to cut their income-tax bill and make a speculative commercial investment. They allow you to invest directly in one company, or in a number of companies, through a designated managed fund. The latter spreads the risk, just like a pooled (unit-linked or unit-trust) investment. If one company in the fund does badly, these losses may be offset by gains on stronger companies in the portfolio.

BES schemes are marketed with gusto just before the end of each tax year (5 April), because tax relief is usually claimed in the year when the investment is made. So, if you invest in a BES scheme by 5 April 1997, you can cut your 1996/97 tax bill.

This can help to cut your preliminary tax bill, which is paid half way through the tax year by 1 November. Say you plan to invest in a BES venture by 5 April 1997, but haven't picked a suitable scheme yet. If you plan to pay 90 per cent of your 1996/97 tax bill, you can deduct this "planned" investment off your projected taxable income, and thus pay less preliminary tax.

If you don't make your BES investment by 5 April, however, you face an interest bill on the tax that you avoided paying the previous November. Here's an example:

It's October 1996. Mary is a hospital consultant and has a taxable income of £120,000.

	Without BES	With BES
Projected Taxable Income 1996/97*	£120,000	£120,000
Minus Planned BES Investment	N/A	- £20,000
Net Taxable Income	£120,000	£100,000
Tax Bill @ 48%	£57,600	£48,000
Preliminary Tax Bill (90% of tax bill)	£51,840	£43,200
Tax Savings	—	£8,640
Net Cost of BES Investment	—	£11,360

* After personal allowances, mortgage interest and other reliefs.

Mary had to pay "preliminary" income tax by 1 November 1996. Her tax bill would be £51,840 if she opted to pay 90 per cent of her liability for 1996/97 (see Chapter 12).

However, she can cut the preliminary tax bill to £43,200 if she reduces her taxable income to £100,000 by committing herself to investing £20,000 in a BES scheme. She must invest in the BES scheme before 5 April 1997 though, or she will pay a penalty on the unpaid tax.

Tax

You can still invest up to £25,000 per year in a BES-approved company/scheme and claim full tax relief at your marginal (top) rate of tax. This means that if you are a 48 per cent taxpayer with a £50,000 salary, you can reduce your taxable income by up to £25,000 in the chosen tax year. If you invest more than £25,000 in any given year, or the sum invested exceeds your income in that year — which might happen if you invest a windfall, for example — you can roll part of the relief into the next tax year.

Married couples can invest up to £50,000 per year in BES-approved schemes provided that each one has an income in their own right. The total (lifetime) threshold of £75,000 BES investments was abolished in the 1993 Budget.

BES schemes offering "bricks-and-mortar" guarantees — that is, schemes that invest part of your cash in property — are quite popular, because the assets are relatively secure. From 1996/97, investors will be able to pick music-industry projects, which will offer variety. Remember that all BES investments are risky. You *may* recoup the investment, but you may not. Making a profit is also uncertain. However, at least you are speculating with money that you would otherwise have given to the Revenue Commissioners.

Claiming BES Relief

You must give proof of payment to claim tax relief. This documentation is provided with your annual tax return. You must furnish either a RICT 3 Certificate (if you have invested in an individual BES company) or a RICT 5 Certificate (if you invest through a designated managed fund). If you invest directly into a BES company, relief is granted in the year when the investment is made. If you invest through a designated fund, you can claim relief in the year when the investment is made or when the shares are issued. Make sure that the BES scheme's rules meet the Revenue Commissioners' conditions. If they don't, your tax relief may be jeopardised. If in doubt, seek independent professional advice.

A BES investment must be held for at least five years. If you dispose of your investment any earlier — assuming that the BES scheme permits this — tax relief will simply cease. If the sale is made to a party that you know (in other words, is not made at "arm's length"), tax relief may be clawed back. You must claim the tax relief within two years.

FILM/SECTION 35 RELIEF

If you want to invest in film, as opposed to a manufacturing company, you can make a Section 35 film investment. These are now available until April 1999, thanks to a reprieve in the 1996 Budget.

You can still invest up to £25,000 per year in a qualifying film investment. This is on top of any BES investment, bringing the combined annual tax relievable sum to £50,000 per person each year. A married couple can avail of double relief — that is, invest up to £100,000 in BES/Section 35 projects — but each spouse must make the investment in their own right.

If you invest more than £25,000 (per person) in any given tax year, you can carry over the balance into the following year and claim tax relief on it then. Tax breaks on film were originally restricted to large corporate investors.

Section 35 investments are quite flexible. Unlike BES schemes, which are marketed early in each calendar year, Section 35 film investments are available on an ad hoc basis as the need arises. People who are interested in this sort of investment should contact a large accountancy firm for a current list of qualifying film projects. If you invest in a film by taking out share capital, you must hold these shares for one year, not five.

The 1996 Budget tightened up on Section 35 investments. Companies sponsoring these projects can only fund up to 60 per cent of the film's total cost with Section 35 funds, and the percentage reduces as the film's total budget rises. You can only claim tax relief on 80 per cent of your investment, and can only claim this benefit after filming starts. Other strict conditions apply, and if the project you pick fails to meet them, your tax relief may be lost. Get professional advice.

Aoife is a management consultant with a large disposable income. She is single, has topped up her pension contributions to the maximum 15 per cent threshold and has a Special Savings Account (SSA) and a "with profits" regular premium investment plan.

She wants to invest £10,000 in a business venture and claim tax relief in the process. She can't afford to invest in property, and doesn't want a second mortgage. Aoife thinks a film project will be more interesting than a BES company. She decides to put £10,000 in a Section 35 film project in July 1996.

Aoife may make a profit on this film investment. If she does, this income will be taxed in the usual way at the marginal rate (48 per cent), minus costs, etc.

Section 35 Film Investment	£10,000
Sum Qualifying for Relief	£8,000
Tax Relief at 48%	£3,840
Net Cost of BES Investment	£6,160

OFFSHORE INVESTMENTS

The lifting of exchange controls on 31 December 1992 created new investment opportunities for Irish people. You can open a Swiss bank account, own shares in BMW and invest in exotic offshore funds.

If you make a profit, you have to pay the Revenue Commissioners. Tax isn't deducted at source as is the case with many Irish-based investments. There's another big drawback. If the investment goes wrong, because you were badly advised or the business was fraudulently handled, you may lose everything. Expatriates who try to bury cash in shady offshore funds regularly lose their savings. Pursuing a bad investment through foreign courts is usually expensive and a waste of time. People who buy an Irish investment product have much more scope for redress if something goes wrong (see Chapter 16, Help!), although this, too, can fail them.

Legitimate, professionally managed offshore funds probably represent the safest and most exciting avenue for small Irish investors. Ireland is unusual in that the non-deposit savings/investment market is dominated by insurance companies that sell unit-linked funds. In the US, Britain and mainland Europe, the bulk of small investors' cash is poured into mutual funds, which are like unit trusts. These are non-insurance products. They are sold without life-assurance cover, and are taxed differently from their unit-linked cousins, but they are also "pooled investments".

Moreover, they give you access to a huge investment market outside this country. You can opt for one of three main alternatives.

UCITS

This stands for Undertaking for Collective Investments in Transferrable Securities. These are non-insurance-based pooled investment funds which can be marketed in any EU country. These funds are commonly registered in Luxembourg and are always regulated by EU law.

UCITS are sold in Ireland and throughout Europe by financial intermediaries who specialise in this market. Profits earned by UCITS are not taxed in Luxembourg. This means that gains accumulate faster than they would in an equivalent unit-linked fund marketed by an Irish life-assurance company. Irish unit-linked funds pay an internal government tax of 27 per cent.

An Offshore Fund

These are like UCITS, but are based in offshore tax havens, such as the Isle of Man, Jersey and Bermuda. Offshore funds are also marketed by our own International Financial Services Centre (IFSC) in Dublin, but these are not open to Irish investors. They are "pooled" (unitised) investments, which are sold by non-insurance companies. Unlike UCITS, they are not regulated by EU law, but by the "host" country where they are based. Profits earned within the funds also benefit from tax breaks. You must pay the tax bill if and when you make a gain on the investment.

Under current investment law, they can't be marketed in Ireland to Irish citizens.

Pooled Investments

There is a third option: "pooled investments" sold by foreign life-assurance companies. These are taxed heavily, however, which makes them less attractive than their Irish counterparts. Profits roll up tax-free but you must pay Capital Gains Tax (CGT) at 40 per cent, when cashing in your investment. Also, you cannot claim the annual CGT allowance (£1,000 for single people, £2,000 for married couples).

This applies to foreign life policies sold *after* 19 May 1993. Contact the Revenue Commissioners (tel: (01) 671 6777) for details.

Why Go Offshore?

UCITS/Unit Trusts

These are very like unit-linked funds in that they are pooled investments, which are professionally managed and invest heavily in equities.

If unit-linked fund values plunge, the chances are that a unit-trust fund won't do much better. There are two key differences — tax and the degree of specialisation.

UCITS/offshore funds are increasingly structured on a "single pricing" basis. This means that there is still a "bid offer spread" built into the buy/sell price, but charges for managing the assets are averaged. You also pay an up-front commission which is deducted from your lump-sum investment. The annual management fee is deducted from the "profit" on your units each year. If you get an income payment from the fund, from dividend earnings, for example, the annual charge may be deducted from this revenue. Otherwise, it's billed separately.

The giant offshore funds are priced daily. This means that you can phone the investment company and get an on-the-spot price, based on an auditor's valuation. This is the price you get if you sell. Unit-linked funds, in contrast, are priced weekly or monthly. This time delay can cause problems if you need to make a quick decision about switching into another fund. Also, you may get a price which is much less than the "valuation" if you encash a unit-linked investment. That's because of commissions and other charges.

Promoters of offshore funds claim that UCITS/offshore are much more "transparent" than their unit-linked rivals. You can also minimise the tax penalty by using professional advice (see "Taxation" section below).

From an investment point of view, offshore funds allow you to pin-point your choices. Fidelity Investments, for example, has funds specialising in Malaysia, Thailand and Singapore. An Irish unit-linked fund would lump all these countries together in a Far Eastern fund. Offshore funds are also marketed under an "umbrella" concept, which means that you can switch from one specialist fund to another at little cost and inconvenience. Irish unit-linked funds also provide this facility, but you often have more alternatives to choose from in an offshore unit trust/mutual fund.

The Drawbacks of Offshore Investment

- Less protection and information?
- Beware of unscrupulous salespeople and unreliable companies!
- Currency Risk.

Consumer advocates and the Irish Insurance Federation (IIF) argue that investors may get less protection and information than if they choose an Irish-based unit-linked fund or unit trust. This is partly true. There is no 15-day "cooling off" period with offshore funds, which allows you to cancel the purchase contract if you change your mind. Also, if you feel that you were ill-advised when you made the investment, you can't get help from the Insurance Ombudsman of Ireland or the Irish Brokers' Association.

Be wary of offshore funds that offer dramatic returns or advertise through box numbers in newspapers. Some are marketed by unscrupulous people, or individuals/companies lacking the necessary skills to handle your money. Sadly, the British financial press often tells stories of failed offshore funds.

Deal only with large investment companies, such as Gartmore, Fidelity and Mercury Asset Managers. These companies are well managed, employ professional fund managers and have a good track record on investment performance.

How to Invest in a UCIT/Offshore Fund

These funds are marketed in Ireland through local agents. The Taylor Investment Group is "master agent" for a number of international investment companies, and uses over 20 sub-agents. You can also invest through the personal finance section of a major accountancy firm, leading insurance broker, benefits consultant (like Irish Pensions Trust or Coyle Hamilton) or a stockbroking firm.

The minimum investment varies. You may be able to invest just £1,500 in a certain fund. You can get a "portfolio service", which manages your investment more actively and picks a fund that matches your attitude to risk if you invest larger sums — typically £5,000 or more. Customers pay an up-front charge of around 3 to 5 per cent, which is deducted from the lump sum invested, and a yearly management fee of around 0.5 to 1.5 per cent.

It's best to invest through an Irish intermediary, even if the offshore company/UCITS fund accepts direct investment. You will get professional advice on your investment from people with a more intimate grasp of Irish tax and investment regulations. They may also be of more help if you have a problem with the investment.

Taxation of UCITS/Offshore Funds

Yet again, this is complex. Irish-based unit trusts have been taxed in the same way as unit-linked funds since 5 April 1994. This means that all taxes are paid within the fund, and the investors have no further liability.

Offshore unit trusts/mutual funds fall into two groups for tax purposes: distributing funds and non-distributing funds.

- Funds with "distributor" status pass on at least 90 per cent of annual income to the customer each year, instead of rolling up profits and paying them when the fund matures. This income is earned from dividends paid by the fund's equity investments.

You are liable for income tax at the marginal rate (48 per cent for a top-rate taxpayer) on this annual revenue. When you encash the investment, you may have to pay Capital Gains Tax (CGT) on any earned profit. CGT is charged at 40 per cent, but you can claim a CGT allowance of £1,000 (£2,000 for married couples) and inflation relief before paying tax. As with other investments, you can limit the CGT cut by encashing only some of the units each year.

- Funds with "non-distributor" or roll-up status are treated differently. They pay dividends and profits when you encash the units. These gains are subject to income tax at the top rate, which is currently 48 per cent. You may also be liable to CGT if you took out the investment before 6 April 1990.

ALTERNATIVE INVESTMENTS

These can be a lot of fun. But they are not always rewarding.

They range from assets with a well-established value, such as gold, art and prized antiques, to off-beat items like telephone cards, comics, wine, old share certificates, toys and many others. The latter are also described as "collectibles". Prices are determined more by whim and collecting crazes than by anything else.

To make money on alternative investments, do your homework, find a source (preferably cheap) for the item you plan to collect and a market to sell it in. You can get useful information from specialist magazines, the media, auctioneers, antique dealers and other collectors. You can join a collectors' club — usually contactable through one of the above sources — but most members are enthusiasts who take a dim view of profit-driven collecting.

Read up about your chosen subject and haunt markets, car-boot sales and antique fairs for bargains. You may strike lucky. A "mint" (prime condition) first edition copy of Action Comics, which featured Superman, fetched stg£14,300 in a London auction house in August 1994. The seller made a handsome profit and the buyer, a British engineer, believes that the magazine will grow in value. For the record, that sum represented a 25 per cent annual compound return on the original 1938 cover price of 10 US cents.

The vast majority of people make little or no money on their collections, however. Collecting is more likely to become a passion — even an obsession — than a money-making venture.

Gains on alternative investment are subject to CGT at 40 per cent, but you can deduct your annual allowance, etc. Non-durable chattels with a normal life span of under 50 years, like cars, are exempt, as are items costing under £2,000.

INVESTING FOR AN INCOME

Strategic investment is not just about trying to make a good profit at little risk. Many people need an investment that will generate an income, preferably one that will also keep their lump sum intact. This applies to pensioners, widows who are trying to raise a family on a life insurance policy payout and people who want to eke out a living from a redundancy or disability cheque.

If the lump sum involved is very large, and surplus to your

needs, advisors may recommend that you earmark a portion — perhaps up to 20 per cent — for a high-yielding and high-risk investment. If you're lucky, this investment may replenish the cash fund as you start eating into the capital. Older people, and those who can't afford to take any risk, are better served by income-yielding deposit accounts at the bank or building society. Both offer Special Savings Account (SSA) versions, which take just 15 per cent tax (per annum) off the income you earn. They also offer a higher interest rate than regular deposit accounts. Meanwhile, your lump sum is safe.

Alternatively, you can opt for An Post's Savings Certificates. Savings Certificates pay a 40 per cent tax-free yield if you hold them to maturity (five years and nine months). But you can generate a tax-free income stream by cashing in some of the units every six months after interest is credited to your account.

Here's how £40,000 invested in An Post's Savings Certificates in January 1996 can produce a rising six-monthly income just by encashing units. Sums are rounded to the nearest £:

Encashment Date	Income	Amount of Money Left
6 Months	£880	£40,000
1 Year	£900	£40,000
1.5 Years	£919	£40,000
2 Years	£973	£40,000
2.5 Years	£1,023	£40,000
3 Years	£1,069	£40,000
3.5 Years	£1,145	£40,000
4 Years	£1,248	£40,000
4.5 Years	£1,341	£40,000
5 Years	£1,456	£40,000
5.5 Years	£1,527	£40,000
5.75 Years	£1,176	£40,000

Source: An Post.

Insurance companies also offer guaranteed products that pay an income. But make sure that you don't pick one that does so by eating into your capital. Also, you may lose a chunk of capital if you have to encash the investment. This doesn't happen with bank, building society and An Post products.

Other options include gilts (see Chapter 2) or an annuity — a yearly income sold by a life company in return for a lump sum.

Finally, beware of investments that promise a very high yield on your savings, even if the investment claims to protect your capital. Consumers in both Ireland and Britain have lost their life savings through these "high-income" bonds. If the yield seems too good to be true, it probably is.

CONCLUSION

Investment isn't a science, but it's certainly an art. No one can predict which asset will perform well, delivering a good, tax-friendly return. But careful study will reveal which investment is more suited to your needs and likely to perform as you would wish. The long-term saver — for example, a woman saving for her child's special educational needs or her own pension — may have to risk some of her capital, because a low return may not even protect her savings from inflation.

As we saw in Chapter 2, long-term savings can't be buried in a bank or building-society account. Conservative savers can put a big chunk in a Post Office investment product if they want to safeguard their capital, but they might put a very small sum in a riskier venture. The important thing is to understand the risk involved, and feel comfortable about it.

Equities may suit a person who can afford to lock up a modest lump sum for 5, 10 or even 20 years for their children or grandchildren. If you're lucky, a well-chosen stock can also deliver a good return in less than a year. The trick is to buy cheap and sell dear, not the other way around. Too many small investors pile into the equity market when prices are rising and then pull out in panic when they fall.

"Pooled" investments — including life-assurance funds, unit trusts and SIAs — spread your risk. But many people have lost money on them, especially those who ventured into unit-linked funds and then encashed their investment early. It's vital to understand *how* these products work.

Property is another long-haul investment, and far less "liquid" than most company shares. A lot of property investment is now tax-driven, because of the government's "urban renewal scheme", which gives landlords and owner/occupiers generous tax reliefs on their investments. These reliefs are complex, and subject to many conditions. As well as talking to the estate agent or mortgage broker — who have a vested interest in getting a sale — you should discuss the tax implications of these investments with a fully qualified professional. Unitised property funds offer a less complicated dip into the property market, but returns are volatile and your money could get locked away for longer than you think.

BES and Section 35 film investments are still available for affluent people who want to cut their tax bill and dabble in business at the same time. But they are subject to tight controls, thanks to successive Budgets. Make sure that the scheme you pick is fully Revenue-approved. Otherwise your tax relief — and capital — could be at risk.

Many investors, from the sophisticated to the plain curious, will find both pitfalls and opportunities in the offshore market. Offshore unit trusts can deliver good profits, but you'll have to spend more time on tax matters. If the investment goes wrong, you could lose heavily because of the weakness of cross-border consumer protection.

Last but not least, alternative investments may deliver a return for those who take them seriously and have luck with the market. But most collectors get more fun than money from their habit. Don't rely on your hobby to produce a nest egg in your retirement. Your faith in telephone-card investment may not be rewarded as well as you think!

4

BORROWING

"Money often costs too much."

**Ralph Waldo Emerson (1803–82),
US poet and essayist**

Borrowers had a good year in 1995. Mortgage and overdraft levels plunged to record lows, easing the cost of borrowed funds. Yet most people would still be shocked to learn the total interest bill on their mortgage, or car finance package. Interest-free loans are hard to get, unless you have a kind friend or relative, but you can shop around for cheap and flexible credit. This chapter looks at some basic choices available. It examines the pros, cons and costs of each. If you have already decided to take out a loan or finance deal, see p. 7 for a list of key questions to ask. Mortgage finance is covered in Chapter 5, Buying a House.

THE COST OF CREDIT

Firstly, a warning. To borrow cheaply, you have to know the *real* cost of a credit deal. In the past, consumers often relied on the Annual Percentage Rate (APR) to compare the price of rival loan products. The APR reflects the true cost of credit, because all fees and charges tied *directly* to the loan, and how you repay the loan, are factored into the interest equation. Thus, the APR can help you to find a "cheap" credit card rate. For example:

Ann's credit card has an APR of 28.7 per cent. Maintaining a £500 debt on the card for one year will cost £120.43 in interest. This assumes that she buys £500 worth of goods on the card on 1 January, pays the minimum payment each month, and clears the remaining bill on 31 December.

If she switches to a credit card with a 22.4 per cent APR, the credit cost falls to £83.07. Neither card is cheap, but one offers her (the borrower) a slightly better deal.

The APR is also useful if you are shopping for a mortgage or personal loan. Banks and building societies must state the APR on their advertising, but they sometimes quote an eye-grabbing *flat* rate, too, which does not include loan-related fees, etc. For example, they may use a flat rate to promote a fixed-rate mortgage. Interest repayments might be pegged at 6 per cent — or less — for a very short time, typically 6 months or a year. Thereafter, the rate will revert to a floating level and, often, a higher APR.

When shopping for loans, compare the *cost per thousand* as well as the APR. This reveals the monthly cost of borrowing each £1,000. It also helps you to work out the total cost of your loan (assuming that interest rates stay constant).

Suppose that you want to find out the cost of a £3,000 loan, taken out over 4 years. The "cost per thousand" is £26. Multiply £26 by 3. This gives you the monthly repayment on £3,000, which is £78. Now multiply this figure by 48. The result — £3,744 — is your total repayment sum over 4 years. Your loan is costing you £744. (See a comparative example, p. 68.)

CONSUMER CREDIT ACT

The Consumer Credit Act, which became law in 1995, sets tough new standards for the advertising, sale and supply of credit (including mortgage finance). Unfortunately, it is unlikely to be implemented until mid-1996.

When enacted, the law will:

- Give consumers a 10-day "cooling-off" period to cancel a loan agreement. Housing loans are not included, however, and customers can sign a form waiving this right.

- Force the loan intermediary (or institution) to record the full cost of the money borrowed

- Require intermediaries to be "authorised" by the institution they act for and/or the office of William Fagan, Director of Consumer Affairs.

This is just a sample of the new powers contained in the 75-page Act (further details are available from William Fagan's office (tel: 01 660 6011)). The legislation is welcome but it is up to you — the consumer — to be more vigilant.

Now what are your options for borrowing?

- Bank/Building Society
  - * Dial-a-Loan (from a "direct" banking service)
  - * Mortgage
  - * Overdraft
  - * Revolving Credit/Budget Accounts
  - * Term (Personal) Loan

- Plastic Credit
  - * Charge Cards
  - * Credit Card
  - * Store Cards

- Other Sources
  - * Assigning a Life Policy
  - * Credit Union
  - * Hire Purchase
  - * Car Purchase Plan
  - * Leasing
  - * Moneylender
  - * Retail Credit Deals

BANK/BUILDING SOCIETY

Dial-a-Loan

If you need money quickly, several large institutions offer a swift telephone-based loan application service. They advertise regularly in the press and on the radio, and can usually be contacted on a freephone number. Customers do not ordinarily have to visit an office, but give their details in a phone interview. Some lenders promise a response within 24 hours. To qualify, you must usually be in full-time employment and earning at least £12,000 per annum.

These products are consumer-friendly, offering insurance (as an optional extra), the choice of floating or fixed rates and a variety of loan terms. Don't be dazzled by the service, as these loans can be expensive. Unless you have a bad credit record, institutions will probably fall over themselves to lend you money so you don't have to grab the first offer that comes up. Again, check the monthly rate per £1,000 borrowed before committing yourself.

Mortgage

This is a long-term loan, typically 20 or 25 years, which is taken out to buy a house. See Chapter 5.

Remortgage/Top-up Loan

Mortgages spread your loan repayments over a long period. It's possible to get the same borrowing facility by increasing the size of your mortgage. This is called a remortgage, or top-up loan.

Mortgage finance has the advantage of being 3 to 4 per cent cheaper than standard overdraft and personal loan rates. It also qualifies for tax relief, provided that you inform the Revenue Commissioners in your annual tax return. On the downside, borrowing money over a long period can boost the interest bill.

Here's a fairly common dilemma.

Angela is 5 years into a 20-year £45,000 mortgage (current interest rate 7.5 per cent) and wants to build a kitchen extension which will cost £5,000. She is considering two finance options: getting a four-year £5,000 personal loan (11 per cent (APR 11.4 per cent)), or topping up her mortgage to £50,000 and repaying the extra £5,000 over 15 years.

The table "Which Loan is Best" on p. 68 shows how much the two options might cost (excluding extra administration/legal costs for the re-mortgage facility).

The four-year personal loan is a lot cheaper, as the projected interest bill is just £1,192 instead of £3,316. But can Angela afford to pay an extra £129 a month on top of her mortgage? If not, she might opt for the top-up mortgage but decide to pay a larger monthly repayment than necessary, or the occasional lump sum off the loan. This will eat faster into her borrowed capital, cutting both the term of the loan and the total interest bill.

WHICH LOAN IS BEST?

Loan	**£45,000 Mortgage Plus**	
	Option a) **£5,000 personal loan**	**Option b)** **£5,000 "top-up mortgage"**
Rate	11% (APR 11.4%)	7.5% (APR 7.9%)
Monthly Repayments	£129	£46.20
Total Projected Repayments	£6,192	£8,316.00
Total Interest Bill	£1,192	£3,316.00

Tax relief is not computed into these figures.
Source: An associated bank.

If you have debts — such as mortgage, car loan or special educational fees — remortgaging can repackage these borrowings into a single, low-interest loan. However, if you run into problems with this larger debt, your home may be in jeopardy. Beware of brokers who offer remortgaging as a "quick-fix" solution for financial trouble. Also, never agree to cancel an endowment mortgage policy in order to take out a larger one; you will lose heavily in commission and early encashment costs.

Finally, you can only claim tax relief on loans taken out to purchase, repair or renovate a property. You will not get a tax benefit if you remortgage your home to pay for a world cruise!

It's best to talk to a trusted independent advisor and your own bank or building society if you want to remortgage. Most lenders are quite flexible about this.

Overdraft

If you have a current account and a friendly bank manager, this is the simplest way of raising cash. It can be expensive, although the interest bill is calculated daily.

An overdraft facility allows you to go into the "red" (in debt) up to an agreed ceiling on your current account. The money can be withdrawn by cash card, cheque or any other method, and you only pay interest on the amount that you borrow. You must ask the bank manager in advance for an overdraft, or risk interest penalties and fees for going over the limit without approval.

The cost of "authorised" overdrafts fluctuates in line with other interest rates. You may take one out when the rate is around 11 per cent — as it was in January 1996 — and soon find yourself paying 2 or 3 per cent more for borrowed cash. The surcharge for an "unauthorised" overdraft is typically around 6 per cent each year (0.5 per cent each month) on the "unauthorised" sum.

Suppose that you go £100 overdrawn without permission. If the authorised overdraft rate is 11 per cent, and the surcharge is 6 per cent, you will be charged 17 per cent on this £100. You may also have to pay a referral fee (roughly £3.50) for each transaction that keeps you above your *authorised* overdraft limit. If the bank gets exasperated, and bounces a cheque presented to your account, you face another fee of around £5 (per cheque).

Overdrafts have other disadvantages. They can become a habit, because banks usually give this facility for at least 12 months and renew it annually thereafter. If you are overdrawn, you may have to pay for cash withdrawals, cheques and other transactions on the current account because you no longer qualify for "free banking". Bank charges can cost £70 or more a year on top of your overdraft interest bill, and AIB Bank and Bank of Ireland also charge an annual £20 fee for the overdraft itself. If you have an overdraft, you must bring the account back into credit for at least 30 days in the year, which may not suit some people. Finally, if you handle the overdraft badly or upset the bank manager, it can be withdrawn with little notice, leaving you badly in the lurch. That cannot happen as easily with a term loan, which is a financial contract between two parties.

Revolving Credit/Budget Accounts

Both offer flexible credit. With a revolving credit account, you have to pay a set amount into an account each month. This permits you to borrow a multiple of this amount. Budget accounts work like current accounts, in that they allow you to dip into the red to pay large bills during the year. See also Chapter 13, Budgeting.

Term (Personal) Loan

If you want to borrow over £1,000 and spread the cost over a few years, a term (or personal) loan could be a better choice.

You, the customer, agree to borrow a set sum from the bank or building society and repay it over a certain period — typically 1–5 years. Repayments are usually calculated on a level, monthly basis. This means that they do not fall as you repay the loan. Also, you must start the repayment schedule as soon as the bank or building society credits the money to your account, and not when you start spending the cash!

Remember to check the full cost of the loan by comparing the monthly repayment costs and/or the total repayment charge on offer from several lenders.

Here's an example:

Johnny wants to borrow £5,000 over 4 years to buy a second-hand boat. Bank A is quoting a rate of 11 per cent. Bank B's rate is 12 per cent, but it's giving away free petrol vouchers worth £100. Who's offering the better deal?

Johnny can find out by asking each bank what the monthly cost per £1,000 borrowed is. He should multiply this sum by 5 (for his £5,000 loan) and then by 48 (the number of months). This gives him the result below.

JOHNNY'S £5,000 BOAT LOAN

Bank	Rate	APR	Monthly Cost per £1,000	Monthly Repayment	Total Amt. Repaid	Interest Bill
A	11%	11.4%	£25.80	£129.00	£6,192.00	£1,192.00
B	12%	12.5%	£26.28	£131.40	£6,307.20	£1,307.20

Source: An associated bank.

Bank A is the most competitive, even when the £100 petrol vouchers are added to the equation.

Both banks and building societies give term loans. However, building societies may only lend you money if your mortgage is partly repaid and the outstanding loan is equal to less than 80 per cent of the property's value. Tell the lender if you want the cash for home improvements. You may get a lower interest rate, and can claim tax relief on your interest repayments.

PLASTIC CREDIT

Charge Card

This is a handy, safe alternative to cash. Charge cards can be used in a wide selection of restaurants, petrol stations and stores. The two charge cards in Ireland — American Express and Diners — are very prestigious, and offer good fringe benefits, like insurance for recently purchased goods. If you use either card to pay for a flight or holiday, you also get some free travel insurance for the trip.

Charge cards do not have a *revolving credit* facility. You must settle the bill very soon after you receive it, or face a hefty penalty. In effect, you can only "borrow" money for a short period before paying a surcharge. Here's a summary of the benefits/features of the two cards:

COMPARATIVE BENEFITS OF CHARGE CARDS

	American Express	**Diners Club**
APR*	N/A	N/A
Repayment Period	On receipt of bill	35 days
Late Payment Charge†	2.5% after 30 days, 3% after 60 days‡	3% after 45 days
Annual Fee	£37.50**	£37.50**
Benefits	Free travel insurance; automatic purchase protection; emergency "helpline"; cash on demand; accepted in 15,000 outlets in the 32 counties	Free travel insurance; "Get it home" insurance; access to Diners Club lounges in airports; accepted in 9,000 outlets in the 32 counties
Present Credit Limit	None	None

* Charge cards do not have an APR because the customer cannot use them as a loan facility.

† This applies if the cardholder does not pay the balance within the specified period. It is not an APR.

‡ The repayment period starts after the statement is issued.

** Does not include £15 government stamp duty each year.

Source: Amex and Diners, January 1996.

The late-payment penalty is severe and each card also carries a £37.50 annual fee, which is expensive. But there is no "preset spending limit" on an American Express or Diners Club card. You can spend as much as you like — provided that you can repay it!

Credit Card

Credit cards are also useful. They allow you to pay off a small portion of your debt and "roll over" the rest into the following months, which can help manage a temporary debt. The snag is, the APR on credit-card borrowings is roughly twice the standard overdraft rate. So when your overdraft costs 11 per cent, the APR on your card may be around 24 per cent.

The trick is to repay your bill in full each month — as half of cardholders do — or use the card for very short-term borrowing — at Christmas, for example. Most credit cards give you 25 days after issuing the statement to pay the bill. In theory, you can get a maximum of 56 days' free credit, depending on *when* you used the card to buy goods. You must pay at least £5 per month, or 5 per cent, whichever is the greater, and you accumulate interest on any unpaid sum.

Here's an example of how a credit card can help to spread the cost of borrowing:

Yvonne O'Reilly buys £500 worth of goods on her credit card in the fortnight before Christmas. This brings her up to the credit limit on the card. She is normally billed at the beginning of each month, and gets her first post-Christmas bill on 2 January.

YVONNE'S CREDIT-CARD BORROWING

Date	Action	Interest Paid
December	Spends £500 on the card	£0
2 January	Gets statement	
25 January	Pays £25 (min. balance)	£8.23
1 February	Gets statement	
25 February	Pays £475 (balance due)	£6.75*
Total Interest Bill		**£14.98**

* Interest charged at £0.27 per day, for 25 days.

Source: Adapted from *The Sunday Business Post.*

Broadly speaking, there are two main credit-card "families" — Visa and MasterCard. Access is the local brand name of MasterCard in Ireland; in continental Europe, it's called Eurocard. The cards offer similar benefits, and both can be used at 25,000 restaurants, shops and other outlets in Ireland. Visa is accepted by 12 million retailers worldwide, compared to 12.5 million for MasterCard. You can apply for a card at your bank or building society. Alternatively, shop around for one with a cheaper APR. For example, university graduates may be able to get an *affinity card* which charges a lower interest rate.

- Both AIB Bank and Bank of Ireland charge an annual fee (£10 and £8, respectively), which is on top of the government's yearly £15 charge. AIB Bank offers a no-fee option, but you have to pay your credit card bill within 10 days of the statement being issued. Gold cards have a high annual fee (typically £60+), but you get extra benefits.

You can also use your card to borrow cash. AIB Bank and Bank of Ireland both charge a "handling fee" of 1.5 per cent (minimum charge of £1.50 and £2, respectively). So, a £400 "loan" costs £6. This charge is waived if you pay the full bill within the 25-day period. If you miss the deadline, you pay the handling charge, plus interest (which can be twice the overdraft rate). Other financial institutions may start charging interest on your "loan" the day you take out the cash, which can be expensive. Avoid using the card in this way, if possible.

Debit Cards

The Laser Card, Ireland's first debit card, was given a trial on a pilot basis by AIB Bank and Bank of Ireland in late 1995. It is more an "electronic cheque" than a credit card, as it deducts funds directly from your account when you shop. Laser will start a nationwide launch in Spring 1996, but its usefulness will depend on the number of retailers that decide to accept it.

Store Cards

Store cards are issued by several major retail outlets, namely, Brown Thomas, Arnotts, Clerys and Best, the men's clothing store. They usually have a slightly lower interest rate than regular credit cards but, with the exception of the Brown Thomas MasterCard card, cannot be used outside the store chain which issues them. This may discourage cardholders from looking for better deals in other retail stores.

Store cards are useful for people who like to shop in one particular department store. You can use them like a credit card, to buy goods and then spread the cost over several months (with a revolving credit facility). Terms vary from one card to another but, typically, you have to pay at least 5 per cent (£5 or £10 minimum, depending on the card) each month. The maximum interest-free period range is roughly 2 months.

These cards can be used to buy sale or "special offer" goods. However, because the APRs are around 23 per cent, they are not ideal for purchasing expensive "white" goods, like fridges or washing machines. It is often better to get a "zero interest" or cheap cash deal (see p. 77). They can also be a disincentive to shopping around for better prices elsewhere.

OTHER CREDIT SOURCES

Assigning a Life Policy

You can raise money from a life-assurance investment policy by assigning it (writing it over) to another party. This can be a better option than cancelling it and losing a large chunk of money through early encashment costs. You can only assign a "with profits" policy, however, because these have a guaranteed minimum value, unlike their unit-linked cousins.

Credit Union

Your local credit union can be a source of cheap, flexible and consumer-friendly finance. The maximum APR is 12.68 per cent, which compares favourably with overdraft and personal loan rates. This rate is fixed, which means that it cannot rise like floating-rate term loans and remortgage finance. Some credit unions are even starting to offer cheaper rates, with an APR of about 10 per cent. Credit unions have other strong advantages. Interest is charged on a reducing balance, which means that the interest bill drops as you pay off the loan. Also, becoming a credit union member disciplines you into regular saving and sensible borrowing. And it can give you access to cheaper home insurance and VHI premiums through "group scheme" offers.

You can't walk in off the street and demand a loan. First, you have to join a credit union with which you can claim a "common bond". This means a credit union in your area, or one set up to serve your union, company or professional association. You then have to establish a track record by saving money on a regular (usually weekly or monthly) basis before you can apply for a loan. Each credit union sets its own lending criteria, which decides how much you can borrow. You may also have to prove your repayment ability by taking out a small loan (or several small loans) first. Each time you borrow, you get a loan repayment schedule stating the amount and frequency of your instalments.

Johnny decides to borrow the £5,000 for his boat from the credit union over four years. If his repayments are calculated over 48 months, he will pay £104.17 off the loan each month, plus interest. The interest bill falls each month, however, because it is being calculated on a smaller loan. Thus, the first month's repayment will be £154.17 (£104.17 capital repayment and £50 interest), but it will drop to £105.21 in the forty-eighth and final month (£104.17 capital and £1.04 interest). Johnny can pay off the loan early by increasing his monthly repayment or making extra, unscheduled payments. He should discuss this with the credit union first, however.

When you borrow from the credit union, your savings stay intact. These are called your "shares", and they are part of the pool of money which you have invested communally. Credit unions like their members to keep paying money into their share account, even as they are paying off their loan. You can withdraw money if you have no loan, and the credit union may also let you offset some of the shares against the loan in certain circumstances. Shares earn a yearly interest "dividend", usually 6 per cent interest, which must be declared to the Revenue Commissioners in your annual tax return. When they take out a loan, credit-union members are automatically insured against death or total and permanent disability. Ask at your local credit union.

Hire Purchase

HP differs from leasing in that customers hold title to the goods that they are buying. The interest rates are often high, and you have to pay VAT at 21 per cent on hire-purchase charges. As with lease contracts, there may be a heavy penalty if you want to repay early.

Car Purchase Plans

Most manufacturers offer finance packages based on the HP concept. These are cheap and proved very popular in 1995. Instead of paying interest on the full cost of the new car, you pay interest on the difference between the purchase price and the car's minimum market value when the "plan" ends — typically three years. When the time is up, you can either buy the car for that fixed projected value or start a new plan with a new car.

Leasing

This is another way of "buying" a car or other expensive items. It can be cheaper than a standard car-finance deal or a personal loan, because leasing companies enjoy certain tax advantages. Companies — including sole traders — can also claim tax benefits if they acquire a car through lease finance rather than direct purchase.

Leasing can be complicated. Lease agreements can include an extra monthly instalment as part of the payment schedule, bringing the total number of repayments to 37 over 3 years, or 61 over 5 years. The finance company may also make an extra charge to sell the car at the end of the term because, technically, the car still belongs to the leasing company, even when the customer is paying monthly instalments for it. These hidden costs can make it difficult to compare monthly charges, especially as leasing companies quote flat rates, instead of APRs. It's best to ask about repayment costs per £1,000 borrowed, or the total repayment cost instead. There may also be a "deposit" charge, equivalent to several months' payments, and heavy penalties for cancelling a lease agreement or repaying it early. It's vital to check the *real* cost of a leasing deal. You may face a hefty penalty if you want to repay early or cancel the contract.

Moneylenders

Much has been written about moneylenders. Suffice it to say that even authorised moneylenders charge an exorbitant rate for loans. Borrowing from the credit union is a far better option. If you get into trouble with a moneylender, contact an advice agency, such as the St Vincent de Paul Society or Threshold (see Chapter 13).

Retail Credit Deals

"Zero-interest" credit and low-interest credit deals should be treated with caution. These are commonly used to sell white and brown goods (fridges and TVs, etc.), and can be of benefit to cash-strapped buyers who have no other access to credit. The bottom line for anyone who can afford a cash purchase should be: "Is this item available more cheaply in other stores?" As with the other credit options, calculate the monthly and total repayment figures.

WHICH IS BEST?

✓ Good Option	? Be Wary	✗ Avoid
Budget Accounts Credit Cards (short-term borrowing) Credit Union Overdraft Term Loan Car Purchase Plans	Assigning a Life Assurance Policy Dial-a-loan HP Leasing Retail Credit Deals Remortgage Store Cards	Credit Cards (long-term borrowing) Moneylender

SHOPPING FOR A LOAN?

Five Important Questions for the Salesperson

- Affordability?
- Alternatives?
- Cost?
- Flexibility?
- Small Print?

Affordability

First, a question for yourself: Can I keep up my repayments if interest rates rise? If not, should I choose a more flexible option (the credit union, for example) or opt for a fixed interest rate?

Alternatives?

Can I take out a fixed interest-rate loan? How much does it cost, compared to a floating-rate loan? Do you offer an insurance policy to protect my loan repayments in the event of sickness, redundancy or death?

Cost?

What will my weekly/monthly repayments be? What is the "cost per thousand" and how much will I repay in total? What will my final interest bill be (if interest rates stay at the current level)? If interest rates rise by 5 per cent, what will my repayments be? Are there any other charges, such as insurance or arrangement fees?

Flexibility?

Can I repay this loan early? Is there a penalty? Can I suspend or alter payments if my financial situation changes?

Small Print?

What happens if I can't pay?

If You are Refused Credit

You don't have a legal right to borrow money. A lender will exercise its own commercial judgment when deciding whether to lend to you or not.

If you've never had a loan before, a bank may reject your application, even if you have had an account there and run it properly. This could happen because the bank has insufficient data about you, not because you are a "bad" customer.

If you are refused credit, it may be because the bank or building society has discovered information filed on you at the Irish Credit Rating Bureau. This might include details of court judgments, debts to the Revenue Commissioners or other gory details. For a £5 fee, you can access this data yourself and check that it is accurate. If it isn't, you can change it. If it is, you may be able to plead your case more honestly with the bank or building society manager. Under the Data Protection Act, you can also access computerised records held by financial institutions about you. Separately, you can take a case to the Ombudsman for the Credit Institutions (see Chapter 16, Help).

It is easier to borrow money from a lender with whom you have a relationship. Even people who stack up bad debts with moneylenders, and service providers like the ESB and Telecom Éireann, have been able to extricate themselves with the help of a credit union loan (see Chapter 13, Budgeting).

CONCLUSION

Most people have to borrow money at some stage or another, and the vast majority of us will carry a large debt (a mortgage) for 20 years or more. If you need to borrow, shop around and bring a calculator. If you compare only Annual Percentage Rates (APRs) and don't ask the monthly repayment cost or total interest bill, you could get an unpleasant shock. Don't overstretch yourself. Remember that circumstances can change, often at very short notice. If you are worried about interest rates rising, get a fixed-rate loan instead of a floating one. Take out insurance if you are afraid of being made redundant or getting sick and falling behind on your repayments. Read the contract terms carefully, as the cover offered may be quite restricted.

If you want flexibility and a cheap source of finance, go to the credit union.

Finally, be aware that you are entering into a contract when you borrow money. This gives you both rights and obligations. The Consumer Credit Act will help to protect you against unscrupulous lenders and bad industry practice. But by being an alert and careful consumer, you can do a lot to protect yourself.

5

BUYING A HOUSE

"Well! some people talk of morality, and some of religion, but give me a little snug property."

Maria Edgeworth, Irish novelist (1767–1849), ***The Absentee***

Buying a house is an experience — a mixture of fun, trauma and the unexpected. It's also the largest financial decision that many people ever make in their lifetime, with the possible exception of planning their pension.

House-buyers have to make big choices, often at short notice. You might spend months dreaming about your ideal home, but just 10 nerve-wracking minutes bidding at an auction for the house you finally buy. Or you could be smitten by a house at a viewing session, and then scramble for a mortgage to finance an offer on it. Buying a house, like any other aspect of personal finance, deserves time and thought. It can be very stressful. Planning can save money and ease the anxiety.

This chapter is about that planning process. It includes a step-by-step guide to buying a house, explains where you can shop for a mortgage and what the options are. It also looks at the chief pitfalls, including the hidden costs.

Each person will follow their own route to buying a house. A young, single professional on a good salary can often make a quicker purchase than a couple with children. The single professional can usually afford a deposit and is often buying a home for just three or four years, rather than 30. Married couples tend to seek greater permanence, and are less motivated by making a profit from their outlay — although some will also want to "trade up" (move into a more expensive home) within a few years. They must also weigh up other factors, such as access to schools, play facilities and public transport, for example. Nonetheless, the following checklist can be used by most buyers, be they young or middle-aged, married or single, affluent or struggling.

Here's the checklist:

(1) Do Your Sums (p. 82)	❑
(2) Pick the Right Mortgage (p. 86)	❑
(3) Find the House (p. 86)	❑
(4) Do More Sums (p. 88)	❑
(5) Complete the Transaction (p. 90)	❑

STEP 1: DO YOUR SUMS

It's important to work out your finances before getting down to serious house-hunting.

Saving the Deposit

Unless you are selling one house to buy another, you will probably have to save for a deposit. Most banks and building societies only lend up to 90 per cent of the house's purchase price, leaving the buyer to find the rest. Don't put your savings in any old demand account. Look for a lender that pays a high rate of return, and has either a competitive mortgage rate or a special discount for its own savers (also called the "qualifiers" rate). If you are in no hurry to buy, open a Special Savings Account (SSA). This pays better interest and deducts Deposit Interest Retention

Tax (DIRT) at 15 per cent, instead of 27 per cent. You must leave the money in for three months, and then give one month's notice before withdrawing it.

How Much Can You Afford?

Apart from the 90 per cent rule, lenders usually limit the amount they lend to a multiple of your income. Typically, this is 2.5 times the size of the main applicant's gross (pre-tax) salary. Thus, to qualify for a £50,000 mortgage, a single person would need to earn £20,000 per annum.

Lenders sometimes take regular overtime and bonuses into account. If the mortgage application is in joint names, they usually factor in a smaller percentage of the second person's salary. Here's an example.

How Much Can They Borrow?

Based on a joint mortgage application by Mr and Mrs McEvoy:

Customer	Salary	Multiple of Salary	Borrowing Threshold
Elizabeth McEvoy	£20,000	x 2.5	£50,000
Séamus McEvoy	£18,320	x 1.25	£22,900
Joint Mortgage Limit			£72,900

Source: An associated bank.

Each lender uses its own rules for working out how much it will lend. In this example, Mr and Mrs McEvoy can borrow a maximum of £72,900. Because of the 90 per cent rule, the dearest house they can get with their mortgage will cost £81,000. That will leave a gap of £8,100 for the deposit, plus transaction charges — say a further £1,500. If they buy a second-hand property, or a new one over 125 square metres, they will also have to find £4,860 in stamp duty costs for a house costing £81,000.

These charges quickly add up. The McEvoys may also have to spend money on their new home. It's not always wise to take the maximum that the bank or building society is prepared to lend. Many institutions quote cheaper rates for customers who borrow 80 per cent (or less) of the purchase price. Building societies also charge an extra fee for clients who borrow over 70–75 per cent of the purchase price (see Step 4), which is called the indemnity bond. You may have to pay a few extra pounds a month for the mortgage protection policy, too. This will repay the mortgage if you die. Last but not least, remember that your monthly repayments will go up if interest rates rise, unless you choose a fixed-rate mortgage (see "Which Mortgage?" section). Even people with fixed-rate mortgages could suffer when the period of level repayments ends and their mortgage reverts to a floating rate. Their repayment could rise substantially at that point.

The example below shows how repayments can surge on a floating-rate mortgage.

How Much Will It Cost Each Month?

MONTHLY REPAYMENTS ON A £50,000 ANNUITY MORTGAGE*

Interest Rate	Monthly Payments
7 %	£393.50
8%	£424.39
10%	£489.42
12%	£557.83

* Gross of tax relief. Based on yearly reducing balance.
Source: Mortgage Advice Shop.

Each 0.5 per cent mortgage-rate rise adds roughly £16 to your monthly repayments bill.

As a general rule, mortgage repayments should not exceed a quarter of your net (after-tax) monthly income. The personal budget planner on p. 85 will help you to calculate your monthly income (after tax) and monthly outgoings. The amount left over is the sum you can afford to spend on mortgage repayments each month (before other emergency expenses). It's a good idea to leave spare cash to cover yourself if mortgage rates rise. Also, if the mortgage is based on two incomes, remember that one partner may lose their job or decide to start working part-time if children arrive. Starting a family will also increase outgoings, unless you cut back elsewhere.

PERSONAL BUDGET PLANNER

Your Monthly Income

Salary (after tax and other deductions)	£.........
Guaranteed Overtime/Bonus (after tax etc.)	£.........
Payments/Commission	£.........
Income from Savings	£.........
Partner's Salary (after tax etc.)	£.........
Partner's Guaranteed Overtime/Bonus (after tax etc.)	£.........
Partner's Payments/Commission	£.........
Partner's Income from Savings	£.........
Total Monthly Income	**£.........**

Your Monthly Outgoings

Repayments on Personal Loans, Credit etc.	£.........
Repayments on Credit Cards	£.........
Regular Savings/Investments	£.........
Home Bills:	
Electricity	£.........
Gas	£.........
Other Heating	£.........
Telephone	£.........
House Insurance	£.........
Water/Refuse/Rates/Service Charges	£.........
Other Costs:	
VHI (or other medical insurance)	£.........
TV (licence, rental, repayments)	£.........
Holiday Expenses	£.........
Entertainment Expenses	£.........
Sports/Hobbies/Clubs	£.........
Food, Household Items	£.........
Car (repayments/insurance/tax, etc.)	£.........
Fares to Work	£.........
Clothing	£.........
Miscellaneous	£.........
Total Monthly Costs	**£.........**

Maximum Monthly Mortgage Repayment

Monthly Income, Less Costs	£.........

Source: Adapted from AIB Bank's housebuyers' guide, "A Place of Your Own".

STEP 2: PICK THE RIGHT MORTGAGE

Get "Approval in Principle"

You've decided how much you need, and can afford to borrow. Now you have to set up the loan. Most people do this by getting "approval in principle" for the amount they want. This is not a formal mortgage application. It is like an uncashable cheque, which allows you to shop for a house in your price range and put down a deposit in the knowledge that the lender should give you a mortgage in several weeks' time.

Pick the Right Mortgage...

See pp. 93–6 for the different mortgage options. It's vital to pick a mortgage that suits your personal attitude to risk and your financial circumstances.

... From the Right Lender

Most lenders can give "approval in principle" within 24 hours. Some will do it through a mortgage broker; others may ask you to visit the branch for a personal interview. Many sorts of institution lend mortgage finance (see p. 92).

Don't just pick the first that offers you a loan. Compare the Annual Percentage Rates (APR) on offer from rival institutions. The APR reveals the annual cost of servicing the loan, plus any fees related to the mortgage, but you get a clearer picture by comparing monthly repayment costs. If you get advice from a mortgage broker, ask to see a comparison of the monthly mortgage repayment for several banks and building societies. Ask what fees each lender charges and how flexible it would be if you wanted to repay the mortgage early, or extend the term. Then choose.

STEP 3: FIND THE HOUSE

Do Initial Research

Many people get a feel for the housing market before setting up their mortgage, to find out roughly how much to borrow. They can glean information from the property pages in the newspapers, estate agents and auctioneers. Some drive around the area where they plan to buy, asking how much houses have sold for.

The hunt can begin in earnest when Steps 1 and 2 have been completed, and you know how much you can actually borrow.

Get Down to Business

Don't waste time looking at unsuitable properties. It's a good idea to contact several estate agents and/or auctioneers, giving them a clear idea of the type of house you want and how much you can afford. Ask yourself some key questions:

- Do you want a new house (which is maintenance-free and may qualify for the £3,000 first-time buyers' grant), or an older house which might have more character and investment value but more potential problems (rising damp, woodworm, structural problems)?
- What size property do you need? Do you plan to start a family or have more children?
- Do you want to live near work, and/or family and friends, the sea, facilities such as shopping centres, a bank etc?
- What sort of neighbourhood will you feel comfortable in? Do you want a socially mixed area, an upmarket estate or a settled area where property prices may rise sharply?
- Do you want a garden, especially one that is south-facing and not overlooked? How important is a garage? Or a rear-entrance and back yard for bicycles, tools etc?

Do Your Homework

When you find a house that you really like, and at a price you can afford, do some final research before making a bid. Is the area "improving"? Are houses well cared for, and are values rising? Does the area have a low crime rate (check at the local Garda station or with the neighbours)? Are there any major development plans which could affect your quality of life, such as new housing estates, a nearby railway line or road-widening scheme?

STEP 4: DO MORE SUMS

Stop at this point, and make sure that you can afford this home. House-buyers incur many hidden costs. Some, like stamp duty on older properties, can be punishing. They are usually linked to the house's purchase price, market value or mortgage size. In most cases, this can boost the cost of an already expensive property by another 10 per cent.

Here's a list of these costs:

Valuation Fee

This is carried out to establish the house's market value. The charge ranges from £1.30 to £1.50 per £1,000 valued, to a flat fee of £75 to £100. VAT is charged at 21 per cent on top of this. The valuer may also add a travelling expenses fee.

Legal Fees

Charges vary. You must pay your own solicitor for the "conveyancing", or processing, of the transaction. The Incorporated Law Society no longer recommends a scale of fees. However, it suggests a ball-park figure of 1.5 per cent of the house purchase price, plus £100 and VAT at 21 per cent on the total. If you are selling a house, the percentage rate is 1 per cent, plus £100 and VAT. You can get a better deal by shopping around, and solicitors must reveal their fees at the outset — or at least an approximate figure. The lender may charge its own fee for legal costs. Ask before you take out a mortgage.

Stamp Duty

Buyers pay government stamp duty on the purchase deeds of second-hand houses and new homes over 125 square metres in floor area (1,346 square feet). The scale of charges is listed below.

Acceptance Fee

Banks and building societies often charge a fee. This is called an acceptance or arrangement fee. It is sometimes charged as a percentage of the loan (typically 0.5 per cent) or as a flat fee (generally, £100–£150). If you can afford to, pay these fees "up front" instead of adding them onto the loan. Why pay interest on this money for 20 or 25 years if you can avoid it?

STAMP-DUTY CHARGES

Purchase Price	Percentage Charged
Under £5,000	0%
£5,001–£10,000	1%
£10,001–£15,000	2%
£15,001–£25,000	3%
£25,001–£50,000	4%
£50,001–£60,000	5%
£60,000 or more	6%

Indemnity Bond

Building societies impose an extra charge if you borrow over 70 or 75 per cent of the property's value. It is used to buy an insurance policy which will protect the lender if you have difficulty in meeting repayments.

Future Costs

Think about how much this house may cost in the future, especially if you are stretching yourself financially. You may have to pay Residential Property Tax (RPT) if the house is valued at over £94,000 and you and other people living in the property earn over £29,500 (see Chapter 11).

Also, will you have to redecorate or refurbish the property? Sometimes a bank or building society will insist that work is done on the house — such as the removal of an illegal extension or putting in a damp-proof course — before it releases the full loan cheque. It may hold back several thousand pounds, leaving you to pay for the refurbishment and the cost of a bridging loan which you must take out to pay the seller their full amount. If the house does need extra work, get it fully costed by an architect or surveyor before you buy.

SAMPLE COSTS ON A £65,000 HOUSE (MORTGAGE £50,000)

Building Society Fee + VAT @ 21%	£121.00
Stamp Duty	£3,900.00
Conveyancing + VAT	£907.50
Valuation + VAT	£121.00
Total Bill	£5,049.50

Note: People who take out their first mortgage qualify for slightly higher tax relief on interest repayments (see Chapter 11). If you buy a new property, you may also get a £3,000 "first-time buyers'" grant.

STEP 5: COMPLETE THE TRANSACTION

This is the final, most nerve-wracking stage of house-buying, and can last over a month. Most houses are sold by private treaty. The process starts when the buyer makes an offer on the house, either through the estate agent who is handling the sale or direct to the seller. It ends with the finalising of the sale contracts.

Making the Offer

You don't have to match the seller's asking price. If the housing market is sluggish and the property has been on sale for a while, the owners may be keen to get rid of it. But if you are very interested, don't undercut too much. Your bid may be refused and put you in a weaker negotiating position.

It is customary to make a token deposit, usually £100 plus, at this stage as a gesture of good faith. This should not be confused with the real deposit, which is usually 10 per cent of the agreed purchase price. Both of these payments are held by your solicitor until the transaction has been completed.

Offers should be made "subject to contract and loan approval". This means that you agree to buy the house, provided that it passes a valuer's inspection and that you can get the necessary finance. A valuer who spots serious faults may recommend a lower purchase price or, in extreme cases, advise the lender that it is unsuitable for purchase. Even if you have paid a deposit, you are not legally obliged to buy the house until contracts have been signed and exchanged.

Getting a Valuation

Some lenders will insist that you use a valuer from their own "panel". Others allow you to pick your own. It is also a good idea to get an independent structural survey done of the house, especially in the case of older properties, and it is vital if you plan to buy a house at auction. This survey may cost £50–£100, but it can reveal serious problems, such as dry rot, subsidence and/or other structural defects.

The valuer submits a report to the bank or building society and sends you a copy. The lender then posts you a formal "letter of offer". This specifies the type of mortgage that you have chosen, the interest rate (if you have chosen a fixed-rate product), the term (length of the loan) and other details. When the Consumer Credit Act takes effect, this document must also show the total cost of your mortgage repayments. Read the small print on this document. As soon as you have signed it and sent it back to the lender, you are deemed to have accepted the terms of the loan.

Conveyancing

Your solicitor now prepares the documents and legal searches necessary for your part of the transaction. This process is known as "conveyancing" and can take up to several weeks. The solicitor must check that the seller owns clear "title" to the property (is entitled to sell it) and must search for other legal problems. When this process is complete, contracts are exchanged and the solicitor gives you a "closing date" for the sale.

Both parties sign the documentation and the bank or building society releases your cheque to the seller. The solicitor then wraps up the sale by arranging payment of stamp duty (this only applies to second-hand properties) and registering the title deeds in your name. The property is now yours.

Other Ways of Buying a House

Auction

This is a "sudden-death" method. The property is usually advertised for several weeks to allow people to view it. If you are keenly interested, you should have all your preparations done before coming to auction. That includes getting a valuation, other surveys and searches (on planning matters, for example) plus a cheque from the bank or building society. Most lenders will issue a cheque valid to a certain amount for this purpose.

Sellers usually set a minimum price called the "reserve", which is the least that they are prepared to accept. Houses which are being sold as part of a dead person's estate are sometimes sold without a reserve.

Auctions are not for the hot-headed. It is easy to get carried away and bid above a price you can afford. The sale is legally binding on the purchaser, so it is vital to stay within your financial limits and make sure that you are aware of any potential faults in the property. Houses are sold at auction to achieve a good price, but they can have defects or irregularities — such as an illegal extension, or some other planning problem — which can make them harder to sell by private treaty.

Sale by Tender

This is fairly uncommon. Instead of the house being sold by private treaty or by public auction, various parties are invited to make secret bids. The highest bidder who has their finances in place gets the property.

WHICH LENDER?

You can get a mortgage from three main types of lender:

- Bank
- Building Society
- Local Authority.

Banks and building societies offer very similar products. That means fixed- and floating-rate products, endowment and annuity mortgages and all the extras described in the section "Which Mortgage?" (p. 93). The interest rates tend to be similar, too. Traditionally, building-society mortgages have been slightly cheaper than bank mortgages, although this can change from week to week. Banks are competing strongly for new business, with cheap rates and special offers such as discounts or reductions for customers who save with the bank. So, if you plan to save for a deposit, it's a good idea to compare these incentives.

There is no great advantage in having a bank mortgage as opposed to a building-society mortgage — or vice versa. The important thing is to be satisfied with the mortgage itself: get a competitive interest rate, find out what fees the institution charges, and check the small print in the mortgage contract. Will the lender charge a hefty fee if you want to cancel a fixed-rate mortgage, or change the contract? One difference is that building societies request an indemnity bond if the customer's loan exceeds a certain percentage of the house's value. The extra cost is not great, however.

Local authorities also offer house-purchase loans, but only to certain people. You have to earn under £14,000 per year, and have had your mortgage application rejected by both a bank and building society. This refusal has to be in writing.

If there is a second salary earner in the house, you must multiply your own salary by 2.5 and add on the second person's income. If the total sum is less than £35,000, you are under the income limit. You must also have been in full-time employment for at least a year. For full details contact: Loans and Grants, Housing Department, Dublin Corporation (tel: (01) 679 6111).

County councils and corporations may also give house loans to people who rent local authority housing. This includes those who plan either to buy their local authority home or to move out to buy a private property. The interest rates are low, and repayments are also linked to the person's annual income. However, the loans tend to be very small — usually £27,000 maximum. Contact your local authority for details.

WHICH MORTGAGE?

A *mortgage* is a long-term loan, usually taken out for 20 or 25 years with a bank or building society to buy a property. The interest rate is lower than on a personal loan, because the house is used as security for the debt. If you have difficulty repaying the mortgage, the lending institution can repossess your home to get its money back. This only happens in cases of extreme bad debt, however.

A mortgage is tax-efficient because repayments on the interest portion of the debt qualify for tax relief. The bank or building society charges you the full repayment each month (gross of tax), but the Revenue Commissioners compensate by adjusting your Tax Free Allowance (see Chapter 11) and boosting your take-home pay. You must tell the Revenue Commissioners about your mortgage repayments to get this relief, and you can only claim it for a mortgage on your main residence. Holiday homes do not qualify.

Take out a "personal protection policy" if you want your repayment to be met if you fall ill, or become redundant or unemployed. This must usually be taken out with the mortgage. It costs about £2.25 a month for every £50 of benefit that you get.

There are two main types of mortgage to choose from: the *annuity* and the *endowment*. You can also decide whether you want to fix your mortgage repayments for a given number of years, or opt for a floating interest rate.

Annuity Mortgages

The annuity mortgage is the traditional repayment method, and the choice of most house-buyers. Each month, you pay interest on the loan and repay some of the borrowed capital. In the early days, interest accounts for a large part of these repayments; your mortgage will have shrunk very little if you move home within the first five years. As the mortgage *matures* (gets closer to the final repayment date), most of the monthly repayment is eating into the borrowed capital. You get far less tax relief, because the monthly interest bill is smaller.

Annuity loans are risk-free, provided that you keep up the repayments. There is no danger that the monthly instalments will fail to pay off the loan, but you have no opportunity to earn a tax-free lump sum, either.

Endowment Mortgages

An endowment mortgage is an investment product which is hitched to the repayment of your home loan. Monthly repayments are split in two. You pay interest on the loan for the full term, plus a separate premium into an insurance-based endowment policy (usually either *unit-linked* or *"with profits"*). When the loan matures, the proceeds of the endowment policy are used to repay the borrowed capital. If the investment performs well, you may get a tax-free lump sum. If it does badly, you may have to pay more into the endowment policy each month just to repay the loan. Most life-assurance companies review the performance of their endowment policies after five or ten years. They will write to you if there is any possibility of a shortfall, to ask for a premium increase. If you want a review of your endowment policy every year, write to the life company and insist on it.

Endowment mortgages written on a "with profits" investment policy are less volatile than unit-linked ones, because the investment grows as bonuses are added to the policy each year.

Which is Best?

Endowment mortgages have certain advantages. If you sell your house to *trade up* for a bigger home, you can transfer the endowment policy — complete with any profit — to the new loan. The prospect of a tax-free lump sum is also enticing, given the huge amount that house-buyers spend repaying their mortgage.

However, endowment mortgages must be treated with great caution. The key thing to bear in mind is that they involve a degree of risk. If you are uncomfortable with this and want to be in no doubt that the loan will be repaid, don't choose one. Above all, don't be pushed into taking out an endowment mortgage by an insurance salesperson, who earns a commission on each sale, and may not have your best interests at heart.

Fixed or Floating?

Opting for a fixed- or floating-rate mortgage also involves a degree of risk. With a fixed-rate mortgage, your monthly repayments stay level for an agreed period — typically 1–5 years. If interest rates rise or fall during this time, your repayments will stay constant. This is reassuring for buyers who want to protect themselves against sharp rate increases. On the other hand, they will remain locked into those repayments if interest rates fall. Customers should be aware of this downside, although mortgage rates were very low at the start of 1996 and many short-term fixed rates — one to two years — offered excellent value. If you cancel a fixed-rate mortgage contract, you face a penalty of up to six months' interest.

With a floating-rate mortgage, repayments fluctuate as interest rates rise and fall. House-buyers tend to choose floating-rate mortgages when interest rates are on a downward slide, and fixed-rate ones when interest rates seem to be rising again.

Clever marketing has made the standard mortgage almost unrecognisable, and there are now literally hundreds of different packages to choose from. Some, like the *capped-rate mortgage*, are quite useful. This is a hybrid version of the fixed-rate mortgage. It allows customers to benefit from falling interest rates but guarantees that rates will not rise above an agreed ceiling, or "cap". A *pension mortgage* resembles an endowment mortgage, but the house-buyer pays premiums into a pension rather than a life assurance-based savings policy. Self-employed people can get better tax relief on a pension mortgage because of this. However, a pension mortgage is not a substitute for a good pension plan. It's very important to spread risk, especially if you are self-employed and relying on your own income.

Don't be swayed by gimmicks when shopping for a mortgage, as many lenders offer discount rates or other features to attract custom. If a bank or building society is offering a 2 per cent discount on its standard mortgage rate for the first year, work out the real savings on a calculator. Check whether the lender offers a competitive floating rate, by comparing it with rival institutions. Remember that a mortgage is for 20 or 25 years, not just one year.

Comparative mortgage-rate tables appear regularly in the finance pages of the national press. You can get similar information from a good independent broker.

EARLY REPAYMENT

You can dramatically cut the total interest bill on your mortgage by either increasing your monthly repayment or paying a lump sum off the borrowed capital. This makes a lot of sense when interest rates are low, and you are paying less than you can afford. Ask your bank or building society about this.

CONCLUSION

Buying a house involves big decisions. Picking the right mortgage is just one of them. Remember that a mortgage lasts for 20 or even

25 years, unless you sell your house early. It's important to take out a mortgage that you feel comfortable with. Many people now regret having accepted an endowment mortgage, because they worry about whether the debt will be repaid. Other house-buyers still think that they offer excellent value.

Nobody can look into a crystal ball and predict that this type of mortgage or this bank or building society is really offering the best deal. But you can make an informed choice at the time.

Finally, remember that buying a house is one of the largest financial decisions you will ever make. It is also an investment. Doing your sums and other homework could save you a lot of money, time and upset in the future.

6

PROTECTION

"I don't want to tell you how much insurance I carry with the Prudential, but all I can say is: when I go, they go."

Jack Benny (1894–1974), US comedian

Sickness. Redundancy. Death. Few of us like thinking about these grim topics, especially the impact they could have on the quality of our life and/or the lives of our children and other dependants.

Sadly, they do happen. Thousands of people fall ill, are hospitalised and lose their jobs each year. One in five people will suffer serious illness, like a heart attack or cancer, by the age of 65. Each day, seven women and four men aged under 65 are widowed by the death of their partner. Coping with psychological strain is hard enough, but individuals and their families often face financial hardship when the main breadwinner's salary is abruptly halted. Savings may last only weeks or months, and social welfare payments can only provide bare subsistence. Friends and relatives may be able to help, but financial commitments will prevent most people from helping for long.

One solution is to take out an insurance policy which can act as a financial cushion. This is called a "protection" policy. Its main goal is to provide cash in the event of a claim, not to grow into a nest egg. Having adequate protection in place for you and your family is a fundamental, but often overlooked, part of financial planning.

This chapter will outline these policies, explain what they cover and suggest how to achieve maximum protection on a small budget. It also looks at social welfare entitlements in the event of sickness and redundancy (see pp. 107–9). The last part deals with house and motor insurance, and how to cut the cost.

DO A PERSONAL AUDIT

Analyse your needs before rushing out to buy cover. Salespeople usually work on a commission basis. They have a vested interest in selling because they make money on each sale. Your main goal is to buy what you need, and at the cheapest price, rather than be sold an insurance policy.

This checklist may help to clarify your priorities. Tick if you have the following:

A) Personal Details

A job?	☐
A spouse/partner?	☐
Children?	☐
Other dependants?	☐
A mortgage?	☐
Other financial commitments?	☐
Medical problems?	☐
Are you Separated?	☐
Divorced?	☐
Widowed?	☐

B) Existing Cover

- A pension plan? ☐
- Work-related cover? ☐
- Life assurance? ☐
- A mortgage protection policy? ☐
- Medical insurance? ☐
- An income replacement plan (PHI)? ☐
- Critical illness cover? ☐
- Insurance on loans? ☐

After you have ticked the relevant boxes in part A, add a few details. How much do you earn? How big is your mortgage? How many children do you have? Does your spouse/partner work? What other financial commitments do you have? This section should highlight your needs. Life assurance is a must for people who have children, but not for single people without dependants. On the other hand, single people rely heavily on their own earnings and may need protection against sickness or redundancy.

Part B shows what cover you have, and how to complement it. For example, many company pension schemes include a death benefit (life assurance cover) and income protection in the event of sickness. Most annuity mortgage holders have a mortgage protection policy which will repay the loan if they die, because banks and building societies insist on it. Endowment mortgages include life cover as part of the insurance contract. Most people have limited budgets. They need to prioritise and spend their money well.

If you are separated or divorced you may need expert legal advice before taking out protection policies. This particularly applies to people in second relationships and who have, or plan to have, children (see Chapter 7).

With a shopping list in hand, you can compare prices and products. It's best to consult an independent broker who is well qualified and a member of the Irish Brokers' Association (IBA). A broker will give you advice on a range of products, not just one sold by an individual life company. Also, members of the IBA are bonded and protected by an indemnity scheme. Avoid protection policies which include an investment element. You get a higher level of cover on a pure protection product, than on one which also promises an encashment value on your premiums.

LIFE ASSURANCE

This pays out a lump sum and/or income if you, the policyholder, die. This cash payout is not taxed by the Revenue Commissioners, but you can no longer claim tax relief on life-assurance premiums. The policy can pay your spouse or any other person who has an "insurable interest" on your life. Or, it can be "assigned" (ear-marked) to pay a specific bill, such as funeral costs or inheritance taxes.

Irish people are woefully unprotected, even though a 1995 Irish Insurance Federation survey revealed that life-assurance rates in Ireland are among the cheapest in Europe. Half of the families in this country have no life assurance at all, and the average cover is just £20,000. That is barely enough to keep one family for a year. Insurance brokers recommend taking out cover (called the "sum assured") equivalent to 10 times your salary, as this should allow your survivors to live off interest from the lump sum instead of eating into the capital. Also, life assurance is often taken out on the life of the breadwinner alone and not the home-based spouse. This is an omission, as the cost of replacing the child-rearing partner can be extremely high. In some cases, the main breadwinner may even be forced to give up their job to rear the children in the event of their partner's death.

- The cost of cover ranges widely from one insurer to another. You can save a lot of money by picking the cheapest quote. Also, if you are in a company pension scheme, check how much cover is provided by your employer.

There are three main types of life-assurance cover:

Term Assurance

This is the cheapest. It is taken out for a specific period or "term", usually when the children are young, and the family is most at risk from financial loss. If the policyholder survives this term, there is no payout or refund of premiums.

You can pick a required payout, or base the cover on the monthly premium that you can afford. Premiums remain fixed (level) during the agreed term, or rise in line with inflation.

Convertible

This is slightly dearer, but more flexible. It also covers you for a fixed term, but allows you to switch to "whole of life" cover (or make other modifications to the policy) with minimum fuss and no medical examination in the future.

Whole of Life

This pays out a lump sum whenever you die. It is more expensive than the above options. Beware of unit-linked whole-of-life plans which pay an investment-based return when you die instead of promising a fixed lump sum. If the insurance company's investment performs badly, your dependants may get a small payout.

CRITICAL ILLNESS INSURANCE

This pays out a tax-free lump sum if you or another named party (typically a spouse or partner) get a serious illness covered by an insurer. The "menu" of illnesses always includes heart attack, cancer, kidney failure, stroke, etc., but some insurers boast a longer list than others. It's a good idea to pick an insurer which includes permanent and total disability (PTD) as part of the package. Most policies include a hospital cash plan, which pays an agreed sum per night spent in hospital.

As with life assurance, the cost of cover rises steeply with age. Smokers also pay higher premiums. It pays to shop around, especially by using a member of the Irish Brokers' Association.

Critical illness insurance should not replace health insurance, and medical insurance, such as that provided by the Voluntary

Health Insurance (VHI), which reimburses you for costs arising from hospital and related expenses. Critical illness cover pays a tax-free cash benefit, regardless of any claim made on the VHI. It is fairly cheap, and strongly recommended for single people or families who are dependent on a single breadwinner.

Life assurance only pays out if you die. Many people survive major illnesses, such as heart disease or cancer, but are unable to work afterwards.

PERMANENT HEALTH INSURANCE (PHI)

This is also called income protection. It provides an income if the policyholder is ill or disabled and unable to work for a long period. The maximum cash payout is usually a percentage of your normal salary — typically two-thirds (minus any social welfare payments). It is treated as taxable income, but you can claim tax relief on premium payments totalling up to 10 per cent of your gross (pre-tax) salary.

PHI tends to be more expensive than life assurance or critical illness cover, even when the tax relief is taken into account. The cost of cover is largely determined by age, gender and occupation.

Premiums for people in "safe", white-collar jobs are far lower than for those in heavy manual trades, and some professions are barred from PHI cover. Read the small print before buying the policy. Some insurers insist that you are unable to take up any job, not just your own. Some policies may also refuse to pay out if the disability is caused by a dangerous hobby, such as hang gliding. Insurers usually defer payments for a set period — 13, 26 or 52 weeks. This means that the payment doesn't start until you have been ill for a certain period of time. You can reduce premium costs by opting for a long deferral period.

MORTGAGE PROTECTION

Mortgage protection policies come in different forms. All mortgage-holders have life assurance on their loan which repays the loan if they die. This costs just a few pounds a month.

People who take out new mortgages can also get accident, sickness and unemployment cover. This policy will cover their mortgage repayments for 12 months if they are out of work as a result of sickness or involuntary redundancy. There is no tax relief or tax liability on this payout; it simply meets the monthly repayment. It is 4 or 5 times dearer than the standard mortgage protection policy. Also, it is not usually possible to take out cover on an existing mortgage. Check with your broker.

MEDICAL HEALTH INSURANCE

This reimburses the policyholder for medical and hospital-related expenses. At present, only one company — Voluntary Health Insurance (VHI) — offers this cover, but its monopoly has been removed.

The VHI charges a set premium, regardless of your age, gender or medical history. This is known as "community rating". However, premiums rise if you opt for a higher level of service (a private bed in a private hospital, for example).

VHI premiums are tax-deductible, but relief has been cut back, and from 1996/97 will only be available at the standard rate (27 per cent). Consumers can get further cost reductions by taking out cover through a "group plan", for example at the credit union or their own professional body (see Chapter 11, Tax). Note that the VHI may not cover the full cost of your medical bill, as it may limit certain payments. You'll have to pay the balance yourself.

HOSPITAL CASH PLANS

These can be bought as part of a critical illness policy, or as a "stand-alone" product (on their own). They pay a tax-free sum per day if you are hospitalised, usually after a minimum period. Hospital cash plans are cheap, and offer useful cover for cash-strapped families, but they also have strict terms and conditions, which can exclude you from some cover. They are often marketed by mailshots through credit-card companies and insurance firms.

LOAN PROTECTION

Many financial institutions allow you to insure loan repayments against sickness, redundancy, death and other catastrophes. This insurance adds a few pounds to the loan repayment costs, and is often worth the extra expense.

TOTAL CARE

This is a new concept in Ireland. It is usually taken out by elderly people who want to be able to pay for nursing care in the home if they become disabled or very immobile because of sickness and/or old age.

WHAT'S THE BILL?

Protection cover is expensive, but you can achieve a lot on a small budget. Here's how three imaginary families solved their needs with an insurance broker's help:

The Young Marrieds

What Do They Need?

Julie and Andrew Daly are both aged 27. They have a 6-month-old baby, Sam, and plan to have another child soon. Julie earns £19,000 as a primary school teacher. Andrew works part-time as a graphic artist, and earns £6,000 p.a. They are in the VHI, but have no other protection cover. Andrew has just started a £30 a month unit-linked savings policy (with small life cover), and they have a £2,000 nest egg in the Post Office. NB: Julie smokes, Andrew doesn't.

Proposed Solution

The Dalys can convert their new £30 unit-linked savings plan into a protection policy. By paying an extra £21 a month, they can get £114,000 life cover for Julie (20-year term), and £60,000 for Andrew (same term). The policy includes £50,000 critical illness cover for both, plus a £50 per day "hospital cash" plan (same term). Income protection is probably a luxury here, as Julie has cover through her job. She already has some life cover through her pension, hence the need for only £114,000 extra.

The Single Mother

What Does She Need?

Karen O'Dwyer has just split up with her husband, Frank. She is aged 35, has a 1-year-old baby, Jack, and two older children, Martin (aged 5) and Róisín (aged 7). Karen does not work outside the home and lives on a tiny budget. She has no protection cover of any description. Karen is a non-smoker.

Proposed Solution

If Karen joins the credit union, she can get a 10 per cent discount on VHI cover. Critical illness cover is a luxury, but she could join a scheme that would allow her to take out a "stand alone" hospital cash policy very cheaply. Life cover (20-year convertible term for £100,000) would cost just £15.80 per month. The cost of both policies would be under £25 per month.

The Middle-Income Family

What Do They Need?

Gerry and Kathleen Ryan have one daughter, Maeve (aged 5). Gerry (aged 42) is a sales executive and earns £24,000 p.a. Kathleen (39) is an editor, and earns £21,000. Gerry's pension scheme has a "death-in-service" benefit equal to 4 times salary (i.e. £96,000 cover). He also pays £86.22 into a separate policy, which includes £100,000 life cover (him only), £50,000 critical illness for both his wife and himself and hospital cash of £75 a day. Kathleen has no separate life cover. Her pension scheme includes a "death-in-service" benefit equal to twice her salary (£42,000).

The Ryans are in the VHI. Do they need to boost cover? NB: both are non-smokers.

Proposed Solution

Kathleen could get extra life cover of £100,000. This would cost £27.54 a month for 15-year cover. Similarly, Gerry would have to pay an extra £16.30 a month to boost his total cover to £240,000, also for 15 years. Both quotes are for term assurance. The Ryans should check their pension schemes to see how much income replacement cover they have. They may need extra cover.

Note: For simplicity's sake, pension and savings needs were omitted from these examples. These are proposed solutions for imaginary cases, although the premium costs are real (based on quotes in January 1996). Quotes supplied by Finance Matters, independent insurance brokers and members of the IBA.

SUMMARY

What to Remember When Buying a Policy

- Be clear about your needs. Think them through.
- Avoid products that combine protection and investment goals. You get less protection for your monthly premium.
- Be honest when filling out your application form. The insurer may refuse to meet a claim if it learns that you withheld key information.
- Talk to an IBA member. Consult a solicitor and/or accountant if your marital status is complicated.

SOCIAL WELFARE/HEALTH BOARD PAYMENTS

Sickness

If you are a PAYE worker, and have made enough PRSI contributions, you are entitled to Disability (sickness) benefit. The maximum rate is currently £62.50 per week, plus £37.50 for an adult dependant (such as a non-working spouse/partner who is not drawing social welfare) and £13.20 for each dependent child. These payments go up to £64.50 and £38.50 from June 1996. The children's rate will not change. You must be out of work for at least a week to qualify, and need a certificate from your doctor. Your employer may pay your full salary, minus the social welfare benefit, for a certain period.

If you suffer from an occupational (i.e. work-related) injury, you are entitled to draw Occupational Injury Benefit, and the rate for this is the same as for sickness benefit.

You cannot claim both benefits. However, people on Occupational Injury Benefit may get other financial help, such as the "constant attendance allowance" or free medical costs. Contact the Department of Social Welfare (tel: (01) 874 8444 for details).

Disabled Person's Maintenance Allowance (DPMA)

This is paid by the Health Board to people who are permanently disabled. The rates and planned increases are the same as for disability benefit. This is a means-tested payment, so you must have a low income to qualify. Ring the Health Board's freephone number 1-800-520520 for details.

Rent and Mortgage Supplement

This is paid by the Health Board. You may qualify if you are in a financial emergency, and your family home is at risk. Ring the Health Board's freephone number 1-800-520520 for details.

Redundancy/Dismissal Payments

If you have worked over two years with the same employer for at least 18 hours a week (eight in the case of part-time workers), you are entitled by law to a redundancy payment if your job is terminated because of redundancy.

Your employer should pay you this directly as a lump sum. The amount you get will depend on your age, salary and length of time in the job. Some employers may give an extra payment, the amount of which may vary, but legally you are entitled to a *statutory* minimum, depending on your age and length of service. If your company goes out of business and is unable to pay the statutory minimum, this sum will be paid by the Department of Enterprise and Employment.

You should be given two weeks' notice before the redundancy is due to take effect. During this fortnight, you are entitled to "reasonable" time off to look for other work. Your pay should not be docked.

The minimum statutory redundancy lump-sum payments are not taxable; however, the taxation of extra lump sums can be complex. Contact your local tax office for advice. If you are being made redundant, you should contact your trade union and/or the Department of Enterprise and Employment (tel: (01) 661 4444), which has a special employment rights information unit. The Department of Social Welfare (tel: (01) 874 8444) will clarify your entitlement to unemployment benefit and other payments. If you get a large redundancy payment, seek good professional advice. A lump sum is easy to squander. You may even be at risk from fraudsters. See also Chapter 2 to research your investment options. There is a case study of a redundant worker on p. 33.

Several large firms specialise in advising employees about their benefits. Ask your credit union or the Pensions Board for details.

MOTOR INSURANCE

The cost of motor insurance is a huge issue with Irish consumers, although the arrival of "direct" insurers — who sell to the public via a telesales operation — has pushed down costs. Few other personal finance topics — with the possible exception of endowment mortgages — have generated as much heat and newsprint.

Motor insurance is still expensive, especially if you are young (aged under 25). However, surveys have shown that all consumers can cut their premium costs by shopping around for the cheapest quote. These savings can be quite dramatic for older drivers and women, who qualify for special discounts with some insurance companies.

How Motor Cover Works

There are three main categories of motor insurance:

- Third party only
- Third party, fire and theft
- Fully comprehensive.

By law, you must have at least third-party cover. It pays out if you cause damage and/or injury to another party, but will not compensate you for any damage to your own person and/or vehicle. However, you can claim against the other person's insurance policy if they are deemed to be partly responsible for the accident. Third party, fire and theft allows you to claim if your vehicle is damaged by fire and/or is either stolen or damaged during an attempted robbery. Fully comprehensive cover allows you to claim for any damage to the vehicle, such as anonymously inflicted scrapes in the car park.

How to Cut Premium Costs

The simple answer is, "shop around", but do it with your eyes open. A good independent broker can provide comparative quotes. You should then ring firms which offer a telephone-based quotation service. These include: Premier Direct, Celtic Direct (based in Galway), Guardian Direct, First Call Direct and Touchline Insurance. Other things you can do include:

- Increase the policy excess. This is the amount you pay on each claim before the insurer starts reimbursing you. It usually starts at £50.
- Consider not making small claims. You may lose some of your no-claims bonus and end up paying higher premiums.
- Pass your driving test. Many people still get their first insurance quote when they have a provisional licence.
- Get a vehicle with a smaller cc rating. Usually, the more powerful the car, the dearer the insurance.
- Fit an alarm. Only one company, Amev, currently gives a discount for customers who install one. It makes sense anyway, and may protect your car (and no claims bonus) against theft.
- Look for a group rate. Do you belong to a credit union, professional body or a trade union? Some offer special discount rates to their members. You may even be able to persuade your employer to get a group scheme for your company.
- Give up drink! Some companies offer discounts to non-drinkers, but the insurance application form must be validated by a member of the clergy, a total abstinence association or a relevant official.
- Drive carefully and maintain your car properly.

What's in the Small Print?

Don't buy on price alone, or you could short-change yourself in the future. It's important to check the small print and make sure that the policy matches your needs. Some of the following features can be worth a few extra pounds:

A No-Claims Bonus Protection or "Step-Back" Facility

A no-claims bonus is worth protecting, because it cuts the cost of your premiums if you don't claim on the insurance policy. Some insurers protect the bonus against certain claims, such as theft and non-third-party damage. Others allow you to insure the no-claims bonus for an extra premium.

Driving Other Vehicles

Some policies cover you automatically; others charge extra. Either way, it's a useful feature.

Windscreen Breakage

This may cost extra, or be part of the comprehensive cover package.

Assistance Package

This now covers you for breakdown/repair services in Ireland and/or continental Europe. It may include free car hire and accommodation.

- If you are refused insurance or get a quote which you feel is excessively high, you can appeal to the "Declined Cases" committee. However, you must get written rejections from at least five insurance companies. Ring the Irish Insurance Federation at (01) 478 2499 or the insurance section of the Department of Enterprise and Employment (tel: (01) 661 4444) for details. The Insurance Ombudsman's Scheme does not handle disputes over premiums, but will arbitrate in other cases (see Chapter 16, Help!, for details).

HOUSEHOLD INSURANCE

Similar warnings apply here. Shopping around can save a lot of money, depending on what you buy. Some of the issues to look out for are dealt with below.

Don't Underinsure/Overinsure Your House

The sum stated on the policy should reflect the cost of rebuilding your house — not its market value. If you underinsure either the property or contents, the insurer may invoke the "average" clause. This means, if you insure the house for £80,000 and the rebuilding cost is really £100,000, you are only insured for 80 per cent of its value. So, if you claim £50,000 worth of damages, the insurer may only give you £40,000. The Society of Chartered Surveyors publishes a useful leaflet each year which can help calculate rebuilding costs (see Appendix).

You can also find yourself "overinsured" if you have an index-linked policy which increases the "sum assured" each year. Check what your house is actually insured for.

Amount of Contents Cover

It's easier to overinsure here. Some companies give an automatic level of cover; others charge a rate per thousand.

"All Risks" Cover

This protects items if they are lost or stolen outside the home. It gives useful cover for bicycles, jewellery, cameras and other items at a cheap price.

Be wary of discounts. Installing a smoke alarm or burglar alarm may reduce your premium. But your claim may be disallowed if you fail to change the batteries or disconnect the unit.

- All insurance contracts are made with what the insurance industry calls "utmost good faith". If you fail to advise the insurer of a material fact — for example, that you suffer from an illness or have a drink-driving conviction — the insurer may dismiss your claim later as null and void.

Policy Excess

As with motor insurance, this exposes you to the first £50 or more of the claim. The excess for subsidence can be up to £1,000. Check that the policy excess figure is not too high.

Once again, go to an independent broker to get a comparative quote. If you belong to a credit union, ask about a group scheme rate but make sure the policy matches your needs.

CONCLUSION

Protecting you and your family against sickness, redundancy, death and other major catastrophes is a key part of personal financial planning. Sadly, it is often neglected.

Insuring your loan repayments costs just a few pounds per month. Term life assurance is extremely cheap, even for a substantial tax-free payout. Add a VHI subscription, which is still tax-deductible, and a hospital cash plan (another few pounds) and you have a basic protection portfolio. All it takes is a relatively small financial commitment and some planning.

Few people can afford to overinsure themselves. Whether you are single, married and/or a parent, the important thing is to identify your Achilles heel, and protect it.

7

DIVORCE — BEFORE AND AFTER

"Money is the sinews of love, as of war."

George Farquhar (1678–1707), Irish dramatist

Divorce — granted by Irish courts rather than foreign ones — will be a reality in this country by 1997, unless the legal challenge to the "Yes" vote in the 1995 Referendum succeeds. As we went to press, the outcome of Des Hanafin's High Court action, which began in January 1996, was unknown. Several things were clear, however.

First, marriage breakdown is a reality in Ireland, affecting tens of thousands of couples. Second, it is on the increase. Third, based on the number of applications for "judicial separations", a growing number of couples are seeking a formal end to their marriage. Even if Des Hanafin wins his case and the referendum is restaged or postponed, these trends will probably continue. And in the absence of divorce — which merely conveys the right to remarry — all the legislation is already in place to allow people to tie up their financial affairs.

This chapter looks at divorce and other issues. It explains how to adapt your financial planning to big "relationship" changes, like cohabitation, marriage and *either* separation or divorce. Your needs and priorities shift as you go through life, moving through different occupations and family circumstances. This is why "life-cycle" planning is vital.

The table maps some of these changes. It is very general, and ignores the fact that some people never marry or have children. Also, women's "life-cycle" needs are quite different from men's (see also Chapter 8, Women).

LIFE-CYCLE PLANNING

Age	Status	Financial Priorities	Solutions
Early 20s	Earning Independent	Personal Spending Mortgage	Savings/Loans Mortgages Personal Pension
Late 20s/ Early 30s	Relationships, Marriage/Cohabitation Young Family — tight budget	Children Household Mortgage	Savings (An Post, etc.) Term Assurance Other family protection plans
30s	Children growing up Women returning to work Some couples separated/divorced	Mortgage Pension interest starts	Pensions Savings for school fees (An Post or insurance-based)
40–50	More mothers in full-time work Teenagers at home	Pensions Investment of lump-sum inheritance Top-up pension	AVCs*, RACs†, Lump-sum Investments
60+	Retired/Widowed Children left home	Enough money for old age Wise investments for leaving to children	Annuities Income-generating Investments Inheritance Tax Planning

* AVC = Additional Voluntary Contributions.
† RAC = Retirement Annuity Contributions.

This chapter will highlight issues like taxation, cash management, investments and protection policies, for each phase in the "life cycle". Ultimately, each individual must make their own choices. Here is a list of the topics covered:

SINGLE

Being single does not preclude having children or other dependants. However, most adult single people are responsible for their own financial affairs.

Bank Account

For a young person starting college, the first priority is usually to get a bank account and ATM card, which you use to take out cash through the "hole in the wall". Banks compete fiercely for student custom, offering incentives such as interest on current account balances, cash or gift vouchers, or a free holdall. When you have grabbed the gifts and opened the account, try to build a good relationship with your branch manager: it may make them more sympathetic if you run short of cash! If you get a chequebook, don't abuse it. You risk a hefty penalty as well as interest charges if you run up an unauthorised overdraft. Ask the bank for a short-term overdraft instead, but bear in mind that you may be refused. You can apply for a student loan but the bank will look closely at your repayment ability. It may also ask your parents, or another person, to act as "guarantor".

If you don't need a chequebook, a building society savings account may be a good alternative. These pay interest (albeit very small) on credit balances, and allow you to access your money with an ATM card. Building societies don't give overdrafts, under any circumstances.

Savings/Loans

When you start your first job, you will have more disposable income to spend and save. You can apply for a credit card, and take out loans more easily. At this stage you don't need life assurance, unless you have dependants. But it's a good idea to build a savings habit. Opening a credit union account will give you access to cheap loans in the future, for holidays or buying your first car. It's important to start a savings account with a building society or bank if you plan to take out a mortgage. If you can't discipline yourself into regular saving, set up a monthly direct debit from your current account. Alternatively, invest in the Post Office with a view to creating a lump sum in 3–5 years' time. You can use this cash as a deposit on your first home.

Pension, etc.

Most single people in their twenties are more concerned with planning for holidays than for their retirement, but it's important to maximise your tax relief on pension contributions. If you are a 48 per cent taxpayer, putting an extra £40 per month into your pension scheme will cost approximately £21 net (after tax relief). You may find it easier to spare this cash when you are single and have fewer commitments. Remember, too, that the longer you save for a pension, the more cash you will accumulate.

In your thirties and forties, whether you are married or single, pay as much as you can comfortably afford. Sole breadwinners should consider taking out critical illness cover with a hospital cash facility. This will help to pay the bills if you contract a serious illness, such as cancer, and the hospital cash plan will cover the cost of short-term hospital stays. Health insurance, which pays medical and surgical fees, is also a must. If you get a mortgage, ask whether you can insure the repayments against sickness or redundancy for up to one year. This normally costs a few pounds a week, but can only be taken out with a new mortgage. If you buy a property, it's vital to make a will — whether you are married or not. Single people usually don't need life assurance, unless they have children or other dependants who rely on them financially. Save your cash for more pressing needs.

Getting married can cost several thousand pounds, excluding the cost of saving for your first home. When saving for a wedding, pick a high-yielding Special Savings Account (SSA) which taxes your interest at 15 per cent, instead of 27 per cent. Or pick an An Post product (see also Chapter 2).

Tax

Single people are treated as separate entities by the Revenue Commissioners, but they can claim extra tax reliefs. These "reliefs" and "allowances" are totted up, and you only pay tax on the balance of your income (before PRSI and other deductions). You can maximise your take-home pay by claiming all the permissible reliefs (see also Chapter 11 — there is a further list of allowances on p. 198 of that chapter.)

ALLOWANCES

	1995/96	1996/97
Single Person	£2,500	£2,650
Lone Parent* (deserted/separated/unmarried)	£2,500	£2,650
PAYE Allowance†	£800	£800
PRSI Allowance†	£140	scrapped
Age Allowance‡	£200	£200

* Single parents get a £5,300 allowance (£2,650 single person allowance, plus £2,650 lone parents' allowance), which is the same as a married person's allowance, provided that they have a dependent child. However, they do not qualify for double tax bands. Widowed people also get higher allowances, especially in the year of bereavement.
† These can only be claimed if the person is in PAYE employment.
‡ For people aged 65+.

Note: Single people may qualify for other reliefs if they have an incapacitated child, or another dependant. Check with your local tax office for details. For mortgage relief, rent relief and others, see Allowances table on p. 198 of Chapter 11.

Source: Department of Finance.

COHABITING

Marital breakdown and a weakening of social taboos have resulted in a growing number of cohabiting couples in Ireland.

Divorce may not stem this trend as many couples may continue to live in informal "second relationships". Some homosexual men and women also opt for "live-in" relationships. When people cohabit, they are regarded as "strangers in law" in terms of succession and inheritance rights. Though widely used, the term "common-law" wife or husband confers no legal rights on either party. It merely means that they are living together as sexual partners. Cohabiting couples can create closer ties through financial planning, but they can decide themselves whether they want this or not.

Bank Account

Suppose that you plan to move in with your boyfriend or girlfriend. You may decide to open a joint account because of the convenience of paying bills, rent and other living expenses. If so, ask the bank for "sole" authorisation, because this will permit either of you to sign cheques. Where there is "joint" authorisation *both* of you will have to sign each cheque. Total trust is needed if you opt for sole authorisation, because either party can clean out the account. Alternatively, you may prefer to retain separate current accounts and keep your financial independence.

In legal terms, anything that is held in "joint names" is deemed to be 50 per cent owned by both parties. Unfortunately, that also applies to debts run up on current accounts! If one person dies, their share will pass directly to the other person, even if a will states the contrary. There can be no other claims on this asset — be it a house or bank account — by another party, except in very special circumstances (such as by the children of the deceased person). As we shall see, joint ownership can be used to protect partners who are cohabiting with separated people in so-called "second relationships".

Savings/Life Assurance

When a couple start to live together, they rarely think about joint savings/investments accounts unless they are saving for a mortgage. Life assurance is also low on the agenda. However, if you have a child, or one party is financially dependent on the other, life-assurance cover can be very useful. Life companies allow you to take out a policy if you can prove an "insurable interest" in the other person's life. This can include partners in a live-in relationship, as well as parents of a new-born baby. The best choice is probably "term assurance" taken out on a joint-life basis. This is relatively cheap, and pays out a specified sum if either of the two insured "names" dies within a specific period (see Chapter 6, Protection).

Couples in gay relationships can also take out life assurance. Here's an example:

George (42) and Jim (35) are living together as a gay couple. They want to take out life assurance cover which would cover the surviving partner in the event of the other's death. Both are healthy, and non-smokers. As a cohabiting couple, George and Jim do have an "insurable interest" in each other's lives, but not every company may be prepared to quote for this business. Those that do will probably insist on a "lifestyle" questionaire, which may request information about their relationship. They may also need a private medical report and HIV test.

Pension

Cohabitation can affect pension planning. Many partners will continue to make separate pension arrangements, especially when they first move in together. Even people who have lived together for many years may prefer to keep that part of their finances separate, just in case they split up. However, you may want to make some provision for your partner. If you are in a company pension scheme, you can nominate your partner for the death-in-service benefit. This is a lump sum, usually a multiple of salary, which is paid out if the member of the pension scheme dies while still in employment. Unfortunately, pension scheme trustees have the power to override the member's wishes, and if this happens your partner may not receive the benefit. On the other hand, if there is a "spouse's pension" provision in the scheme, the trustees may decide to allot some for a partner — provided that that person can prove financial dependence on the deceased. The decisions of trustees are unpredictable, however, and it is simpler and more clear-cut to take out a life-assurance policy.

Tax/Social Welfare

From a social welfare perspective, cohabiting partners are viewed as a married couple. If a person claims social assistance, for example, their partner's income will be assessed by the social welfare officer. Also, cohabitation disqualifies an applicant for certain payments, such as lone parents' allowance. This even applies to means-tested payments.

Cohabiting couples are still treated as separate individuals by the tax authorities, although this may change if divorce is introduced. Each partner can claim all the single person's reliefs, but neither is eligible for the married person's allowance (which is double the single person's allowance).

The issue of property is complex. It is best illustrated by a few examples.

The Young Couple

Mary and Tom are in their early twenties. They decide to rent a flat together early in their relationship. For convenience sake, they open a joint bank account with sole signature status. Mary and Tom are jointly responsible for paying the rent. If either party leaves, the other person will have to fulfil the terms of the lease or negotiate with the landlord/lady.

The Middle-aged Couple

John and Susan are both in their early forties. John has a £60,000 mortgage on his £100,000 house, and he asks Susan to live with him. She may not have a direct claim on the house, even if she pays part of the mortgage after moving in, as this money is deemed to be rent (and is taxable, in theory). If they split up, she is entitled to nothing. Moreover, if John dies without a will, the house will pass to his next of kin.

If they have a child, or just a long-term, stable relationship, John will want to ensure that Susan is protected after his death. He can do one of several things:

- *Switch the house into joint names when he is still alive. They will have to pay a 4 per cent stamp duty (£2,000) on this transaction. Susan will also face a gift-tax bill for her half share in the property. When he dies, the life-assurance policy will automatically pay off the mortgage. The house will pass to Susan, even if there is no will, but she faces a tax bill on the remaining half (£50,000, or the current valuation) that she inherits.*

  John can help pay the second charge by taking out a Section 60 life-assurance policy. This is specially designed to pay off any duties and taxes arising from his estate if he dies. John may need to take out a "whole of life" policy, which is quite expensive, as this tax bill will arise whenever he dies (see also Chapter 15).

- *Leave the house to Susan in his will. Again, this will trigger an inheritance tax charge. Unless he covers this with a Section 60 policy, Susan may have to sell the house when John dies. His will may also be challenged by other family members, such as a former wife or children from a first relationship.*
- *Sell the house and buy another in joint names. The new purchase will also trigger a stamp-duty charge (if it is a second-hand property), but Susan's gift-tax bill will be smaller if she pays some cash towards the house. If John dies, the house will pass to Susan with the usual inheritance-tax burden.*
- *Set up a trust. This is a legally binding agreement which can ensure that John's wishes are carried out in the event of his death. He may stipulate, for example, that Susan can live in the house until she dies. Thereafter, the house will pass to any children from the first and/or second relationships. Trusts are complex, and can trigger serious tax and legal consequences. It is vital to consult a very competent advisor before following this route.*

The Older Couple

Margaret and Jack are pensioners in their late sixties. Jack never married, and Margaret is a widow, but romance has now blossomed between them. Margaret owns a house which she wants to leave to her three children. She has already written a will to this effect, but does not want Jack to be made homeless if she dies first.

Margaret can add a codicil (clause) to her will which gives Jack lifelong tenancy in the house. In effect, it means that he can live in it until he dies. However, Jack will have to pay inheritance tax on the value of his lifelong tenancy. This is calculated as a percentage of the actual value of the house, on a sliding scale (depending on his age and life expectancy). He will have the minimum inheritance tax exemption, because he and Margaret are "strangers in law". See also Chapter 15.

Note that John could also have chosen this option in the previous example.

MARRIED

This is a legally binding contract, which has a major impact on your financial situation — both present and future. A husband and wife commit themselves to support each other in sickness and health. Today, sadly, this commitment can also extend to separation and, in time, divorce.

Financial problems can cause a lot of friction, and it's best to minimise the potential for argument by discussing budgets, mortgage plans and other important issues before you marry. The question of who is going to pay bills or the childminder is not trivial, especially if both parties are earning different incomes. Taking a realistic look at your finances may also prevent you from taking out too big a mortgage and overstretching yourself.

Mortgage

If one partner already has a mortgage, think about what you will do with their property. You may prefer to keep it in their sole name and rent it. Or, you may want to sell it and buy another. In that case, think about whether you want the second property to be in joint names. Most married couples do put their family home in joint names, because if one spouse dies it ensures that the property will pass directly to the other. The Matrimonial Home Bill (1993), which automatically gave both spouses a 50 per cent stake in the family home regardless of their cash contribution, was rejected by the Supreme Court as unconstitutional. See the section, "Separated" (p. 126) for more information about property ownership after marital breakdown.

Protection/Wills

Many couples wait until they have children before taking out life assurance. In fact, it may prove cheaper to take out "convertible term assurance" on a joint-life basis early in the marriage (see Chapter 6, Protection). This can be switched to a "whole of life" basis, or the insured amount increased, with little fuss in the future. The life company will not usually insist on a medical examination. By taking this step now, you can avoid being refused life-assurance cover later in life. Other protection policies, such as critical illness and income protection plans, are a matter of personal choice. In the early years of marriage, many couples are financially strapped and unable to afford lavish insurance policies. Health insurance is vital, however, and still qualifies for tax relief. Critical illness cover is quite cheap, but is not tax-deductible. Whichever policy you take out, make sure that your spouse and children are also covered.

Write a will when you get married. Any earlier wills will no longer be valid unless a will states that it was made in *anticipation* of marriage. If you die intestate (without a will) your spouse may suffer unnecessary delay and hardship while your estate is being administered.

Pension

Pension planning is also important. Most company pension schemes provide for a spouse's pension. This is often equivalent to two-thirds of the scheme member's entitlement, and there may be a smaller sum for children. The maximum a scheme member can earn in a pension is two-thirds of their salary on retirement, so the spouse's share will be just under half of that sum (44.4 per cent of the deceased spouse's salary). A spouse's pension is usually paid in the event of a scheme member's death, not in addition to the scheme member's pension if both parties are living and together. However, if a married couple separate or divorce, the spouse can claim their share of this pension. See p. 136 for details. A spouse may also claim their partner's death-in-service benefit (see the section on Widowhood in Chapter 15).

Tax/Social Welfare

Married couples are treated as a unit from a social welfare point of view. If you apply for a means-tested payment or allowance, the income of your spouse will be taken into account, because it is viewed as household income. This does not apply to PRSI-based payments. If you have made the stipulated number of contributions, you are entitled to claim any contributory payment or benefit — ranging from sickness benefit to a pension — regardless of your partner's income.

When you marry, you should advise the tax office of your date of marriage and the RSI (Revenue and Social Insurance) numbers of both you and your partner. Both of you will continue to be treated as single people for tax purposes in the year in which you marry. However, if the combined tax bill is larger than the amount you would have paid as a married couple, you can claim a refund. This sum will be based on tax paid after your wedding date, and will be calculated after the following 5 April. The question of a refund normally arises if each person is on a different tax table during the year, or if one person can benefit from unused allowances, such as mortgage interest relief.

After the first year of marriage, you can choose one of the following methods of tax assessment:

- Joint Assessment/Aggregation
- Separate Assessment
- Assessment as a Single Person (Separate Treatment).

Joint Assessment

The tax office automatically puts you in this category, unless you request otherwise. Most couples prefer it, because it permits them to allocate the tax reliefs as they see fit. For example, if you are the only person with a taxable income, you can pay less tax by using up your partner's reliefs and allowances. However, you cannot take your partner's PAYE and expenses allowances, so the potential tax relief is quite limited. If you and your spouse are both working, you must decide who will be the "assessable spouse". This is the person who has to complete an annual return of income, and pay the tax bill on the couple's joint income.

You and your partner can decide who the "assessable spouse" will be, by completing a simple form and sending it back to the tax office before 6 July in the relevant tax year. Ideally, notify the Revenue Commissioners before the tax year starts. If you do not nominate an "assessable spouse", the Revenue Commissioners will pick the person with the highest income in the latest year for which details are known. If you were married before 6 April 1993, the husband will automatically be picked.

Couples can pick joint assessment even if one person is self-employed or unemployed.

Separate Assessment

If you choose this option, you are independent of your spouse for tax purposes. You normally submit your own annual return, but you can send in a single return which states combined income, if you wish. You can divide some allowances between you, such as the married allowance, age allowance (for people aged 65 or over). Each person retains their PAYE and expenses allowances. If one person is on a lower tax rate or has less income, some of their allowances may be transferred to the other.

Separate assessment must be claimed in writing, by either spouse, by 6 July in the relevant tax year. It cannot be backdated, and lasts until it is withdrawn.

Assessment as a Single Person (Separate Treatment)

This is different, in that both spouses are treated as single people for tax purposes. They are taxed on their own income, get their own allowances and must complete their own return. They cannot transfer allowances from one spouse to another. You can claim separate treatment by writing to the tax office, and will continue to be taxed on this basis until you withdraw the request.

You pay roughly the same tax if you opt for joint assessment or separate assessment. Separate treatment may not be as beneficial, because you cannot transfer used allowances from one spouse to another. If in doubt, ask an accountant.

SEPARATED

Divorce — when it is introduced — will be the very last step in the separation process. Many couples will shun it, whether because they can't afford to go to court, disagree with divorce on principle, or hope that their marriage will survive. But all couples whose marriages break down, regardless of whether they divorce or not, will have to face the trauma and the financial problems that usually come in its wake. Maintaining two households is more expensive than maintaining one and, almost inevitably, separated partners suffer a sharp drop in income. When the cost of legal action is added to the bill, the scenario may look bleak.

Financial planning can help. This section looks at the key issues you have to address when you separate — like the family home, maintenance payments, etc. — highlighting the legal, tax and social welfare implications in each case. "Divorce?" (p. 136) looks at the mechanics of seeking a divorce and the other available options.

Issues

Budgets

Budgets may be the last thing on your mind when you split up, but sorting them out can be therapeutic (although initially depressing). At best it will give you back a sense of control, help to restructure your life and — crucially — generate extra cash. At worst, it may minimise losses and prevent financial problems that could have serious consequences in the future, such as mortgage arrears or unpaid insurance bills.

The planning process will partly depend on whether the separation was amicable or not (see " Divorce?" on p. 136). In any event, it's a good idea if both parties sit down with pen and paper — together or separately — and work out a financial action plan. Assuming that you are the spouse — either husband or wife — who has custody of the children and is living in the family home, you need to work out the following:

BUDGET CHECKLIST: HOME-MAKING SPOUSE

- *Step 1*

  Draw up a basic budget. See Chapter 13.

- *Step 2*

  Check out the status of joint financial commitments with your spouse. Is your spouse still paying the mortgage, VHI, life-assurance policy? Consider closing any joint bank accounts, but discuss this with your spouse first (where possible). If you have a family business, seek professional advice.

- *Step 3*

  Ask yourself: what do I need to live on? What extra expense might I face as a result of separation, such as childcare costs, legal fees, etc?

- *Step 4*

  Contact Social Welfare, Free Legal Aid, etc. Find out what your entitlements are. Can you claim Deserted Wives' Benefit, Deserted Wives' Allowance, or Lone Parents' Allowance?

- *Step 5*

  Think about other income sources. Can you work part-time, or supplement an existing salary by letting a room, etc? If so, how would that affect your social welfare entitlements or tax situation?

- *Step 6*

  Work out how much financial support you need from your spouse. If you can't get this voluntarily, seek a Court Order.

The spouse who is the main breadwinner faces a similar exercise. Their calculations may look like this:

BUDGET CHECKLIST: MAIN BREADWINNING SPOUSE

- *Step 1*

  Draw up a basic budget. See Chapter 13.

- *Step 2*

  Discuss the issue of ongoing expenses — mortgage, VHI, life-assurance payments etc. — with your spouse. Don't let the house payments lapse.

- *Step 3*

  Ask yourself: what will I need to live on each month? Have I factored in all my costs, such as car maintenance, laundry, cigarettes, cost of outings/holidays with children, birthday presents, Christmas, etc? How much will it cost to run two households — mortgage plus rent, two ESB bills, gas, telephone, etc?

- *Step 4*

  Contact Social Welfare, Free Legal Aid. Find out what your entitlements are. Can you claim Lone Parents' Allowance (if you are caring for at least one child)?

- *Step 5*

  Get advice on tax. Can you cut your tax bill by availing of tax relief on maintenance payments? Can you claim other allowances? If your spouse is claiming deserted wives' allowance/benefit, find out if she's entitled to it in the long term. The Department of Social Welfare may pursue you for this money in the future.

- *Step 6*

  Think about boosting income and cutting costs. Can you supplement your existing salary? How? Can you reduce your outgoings, by selling a second car (with your spouse's consent) or restructuring loans. Might these decisions have a severe impact on you, your spouse or children?

Budgets are just the tip of the iceberg. Decisions about money rest on important underlying issues, such as ownership of the family home, custody of the children, etc. Both parents also need to think about how the children will be catered for in the event of either party's death. These decisions are personal ones, but it is wise to get professional advice from an accountant, solicitor and other professionals when considering budgetary and taxation questions. Working out your accounts, in the above example, may set other thoughts and decisions in train, like contacting your local welfare officer, seeking advice from voluntary agencies or obtaining free legal aid. You should also draw up a comprehensive list of your spouse's financial assets. These include lump-sum payments received as a result of redundancy, accident, etc., plus their pension assets. These may also be divided in the event of marital breakdown.

Custody of the Children

This is a key issue for separating couples to consider. It falls outside the scope of this book, other than to say that the court system (and society is general) is taking a broader view of rights of fathers in marriage breakdown situations. Fathers may fight for — and win — joint custody in court, but the children's welfare will be the prime consideration.

If your children are living with you (even on a part-time basis) you may qualify for additional Social Welfare payments and tax allowances. Get advice on this.

Family Home

The question of who owns and/or will live in the family home can be problematic. It is best resolved by negotiation. In the event of a deadlock, the courts decides. The Family Home Protection Act (1976) states that one party — even a person who has a 100 per cent stake in the property — cannot sell it or alter the mortgage repayment conditions without their spouse's consent. But whilst this gives each spouse a right of veto, it does not guarantee a stake in the property to a person who has not contributed financially to the mortgage repayments or purchase price.

The Judicial Separation and Family Law Reform Act (1989) permitted the courts to transfer "assets", including the family home and other properties, from one spouse to another. Typically, this was from a salary-earning husband to a wife who is rearing the children at home.

The Family Law (Amendment) Act, 1995, gives courts the same power. This legislation absorbed the key features of the 1989 Act, added extra powers (such as the authority of the court to divide a spouse's pension) and effectively paved the way for a future "Divorce" Bill.

If you go to court, seeking either a judicial separation or a full divorce, and have not agreed on who will live in the family home, the judge will decide for you. If the property is substantial, it may have to be sold to enable a "clean-break" solution. In this case, the home-based spouse will probably be given enough cash to buy a more modest property outright, or with a small mortgage. The breadwinning spouse may be entitled to the rest of the sale proceeds, after costs, to buy a second home.

Or, the judge may order the breadwinning spouse to pay the mortgage until the children are aged 18 (or leave college). The property may then be divided, and the proceeds split. If there are no children, the judge will probably order an immediate sale and a fairly even split of the proceeds.

Mortgage/Maintenance

A breadwinning spouse (usually the husband) can be obliged by a court order to continue the mortgage repayments, even though he no longer has a stake in the property. His earnings can also be attached to ensure that payments are made. This means that one spouse (usually the person who is working in the home, rearing the children) can apply to court for an "attachment of earnings order". It obliges the employer of the breadwinning spouse to deduct maintenance payments from that spouse's salary. Note that this only succeeds if the breadwinner is in regular employment, not the "black economy". If you are deserted by your spouse and left with custody of the children, a mortgage and no means of support, you can apply to your local health board for help with the mortgage repayments.

In theory, you should contact the mortgage lender (bank or building society) if you face difficulty with the repayments. However, the lender may seek to repossess the home if you have fallen into arrears. It is probably better to contact a voluntary agency first, such as Threshold, the housing advice service, or the Society of St Vincent de Paul (see Appendix). These organisations may be able to help negotiate on your behalf. You may also be able to resolve a short-term cash crisis by letting a spare room in your house, for example.

The Family Law (Amendment) Act (1995) gives the court more power to attach earnings, even when the errant spouse has moved overseas. In such cases, a deserted spouse can ask the Department of Equality and Law Reform to seek maintenance payments from a foreign jurisdiction. However, it remains to be seen if this will prove workable. If maintenance is awarded by the courts, some may be allocated for the children and the rest for the spouse. In this case, the payment may stop when the children leave home or complete their education.

- **Note:** A breadwinning spouse who is paying two mortgages can claim tax relief on both. Talk to an accountant about this.

Social Welfare

If your spouse has deserted the family home, has not lived there for three months and does not plan to return, you may qualify for either Deserted Wives' Benefit or Deserted Wives' Allowance. The former is based on PRSI contributions, and the maximum rate is £66.10 per week, plus £17 per dependent child. The main payment will go up in June 1996 to £68.10. Your entitlement to payments may be affected if your income exceeds a certain threshold and you may not be eligible if your income exceeds £14,000. Check at your Social Welfare office. Deserted Wives' Allowance is means-tested, and you will get less money if you have an alternative income. The maximum rate is £62.50 per week (rising to £64.50). If you have a child, you claim Lone Parents' Allowance instead. This pays the same adult rate, plus £15.20 per child. Fathers are also eligible.

The Department of Social Welfare plans to merge the deserted wives' and lone parents' payments by January 1997 into a new "one-parent family payment". This will make them equally accessible to men and women, and remove the need to prove desertion. The distinction between means-tested and PRSI-based payments may remain, however. Separated people who start to cohabit in a second relationship risk losing these payments. Also, until the schemes are revamped, some will continue to discriminate between men and women. If in doubt, contact your local Social Welfare officer.

- **Note:** If divorce is introduced, the government has promised that the spouse's Social Welfare entitlement will not be affected if their partner divorces them and remarries. Such ex-spouses may still be entitled to a share of a State contributory (PRSI-based) pension, or a Deserted Wives' payment, for example. A separated husband may also claim entitlements, such as Family Income Supplement, for a divorced wife if he is supporting her financially.

Tax

Tax is also an important issue for separated couples, as it can affect maintenance payments and both partners' living standards.

If a couple agree to separate on an amicable basis, without entering into a legally enforceable agreement, maintenance payments are deemed to be voluntary. These are ignored for tax purposes. The person providing them cannot claim a tax deduction, and the recipient is not assessed for tax on this income. This situation changes if the parties end their marriage with a rule of court, and order of court, a deed of separation or a trust. In this instance, the spouses can choose to be taxed in either of two ways:

- Separate Assessment
- Joint Basis.

Separate Assessment

Seán and Rita have got a court order to give their separation agreement legal standing. They have no children. Seán pays Rita £5,000 maintenance per year, but he can deduct this from his taxable income. Rita, on the other hand, is liable to pay both tax and PRSI on this income if it exceeds a certain sum. Apart from that, both spouses are treated by the tax office as separate people. They both have a single person's allowance, but neither can claim the married person's allowance. If Seán and Rita had had a child, his maintenance payments for that child would not be tax-deductible.

Joint Basis

Mary and Jim got a judicial separation in the Circuit Court. Jim has been ordered to pay Mary £10,000 per year for the maintenance of herself and their three children. This payment will supplement Mary's part-time income. They have decided that they still want to be taxed on a joint basis.

Because they are being taxed jointly, Jim will not be able to write off the full £10,000 he gives Mary each year. In the first full tax year after the separation, both parties retain their separate allowances, and neither can claim the married person's allowance. However, Jim can *claim the part intended specifically to go towards Mary's support. Mary can continue to claim her PAYE and PRSI reliefs for as long as she works, but this income will be assessed for tax. The portion of the £10,000 maintenance used for the support of the children will not be taxed, but the portion used for Mary's support will be taxed.*

Mary can also cut her tax bill by claiming Lone Parents' Allowance (an extra £2,650 in 1996/97). This reduces the amount of income on which she can be taxed. It can be claimed by any single parent who is deserted, separated or unmarried. If Mary and Jim decide effectively to share custody of the children, they can both claim the lone parents' tax allowance separately.

Tax on Assets

Provision in the Family Law (Amendment) Act (1995) may eventually ensure that a divorced couple will be able to transfer property and assets to each other without triggering the tax charges normally faced by single people. This is intended to facilitate property settlements in the wake of divorce. It will initially only apply to couples with foreign divorces, but will be extended to Irish divorce if, and when, it becomes legal.

Pension

Unlike the Judicial Separation Act, the Family Law Act also permits the courts to allocate part of the main breadwinner's pension to their spouse. This is called a "pension adjustment order", and can happen if neither party seeks a divorce. It either splits the pension of the spouse who belongs to the pension scheme or earmarks part of it for the other person's benefit in the future. In each case, the trustees of the pension scheme are asked to report on the member spouse's interest in the pension scheme. Suppose that you are the main breadwinner, and the court decides to "split" your pension. It orders the trustees to allocate part of your pension fund to the spouse. Your former spouse can remove the cash from the fund and invest it in another scheme and it would then be subject to the rules of that scheme. Alternatively, a bond could be purchased in the name of the non-member spouse. This entitlement to the pension will not be affected if either of you remarries.

Alternatively, the court can "earmark" part of the fund for your spouse's benefit. In this case, your spouse can only draw a pension when you retire yourself, or thereafter. This does not permanently split your pension, and your spouse may lose their share in the event of remarriage. In order to ensure that the children are cared for in the event of your death, the court may also order that you take out a life-assurance policy.

Life Assurance

As we have seen, life-assurance policies can also be used creatively to protect partners in second relationships. If you separate from your spouse, and have children in a second family, life-assurance policies can help to provide for both sets of off-spring, but planning can be complex. Here's one example. Suppose that you split up with your wife, and cede ownership of the family home to her. If you do this through a "Deed of Separation" (i.e., through negotiation), it is customary — but not obligatory — for her to waive succession rights. In practice, many partners prefer this because it creates a clean break and prevents either spouse from claiming on the other person's estate in the future. If you are unable to reach an amicable settlement, and go to court for a judicial separation, her succession rights will probably be "extinguished" in that process.

You may still wish to provide for both your (ex-) wife and children, even if you have waived automatic succession rights. This can be achieved by taking out additional life-assurance cover which will benefit your "first" family when you die.

Succession Rights

These will be affected if divorce is introduced. Under the existing family law legislation, a court can "extinguish" the inheritance rights of both spouses when it grants a judicial separation. This is to ensure a "clean-break" situation for both spouses when the marriage property is duly divided by the court.

If these rights are not waived or dissolved, a wife (dependent spouse) can claim all of your assets if you have no children, and two thirds if there are children. In the second scenario, the children are entitled to one third. A "wife" cannot be written out of a will, unless her succession rights are extinguished by court.

Divorce will extinguish those rights. However, to compensate for this future loss, the government has promised that any court granting a divorce can (through "property adjustment orders") make sufficient provision for a dependent spouse (usually a wife). Secondly, if a "judicial separation decree" has already been granted before the divorce, and if adequate provision had not been made for the spouse, she (if she has not married in the meanwhile) can claim on her dead ex-husband's estate. This must be done within a limited time.

Your children do not have automatic succession rights. However, Section 117 of the Succession Act (1965) permits them to write to court if they feel that they have been unfairly treated. You can provide for them with a life-assurance policy, but the cost of even basic-term assurance cover rises sharply with age. Financial and tax planning after marital breakdown is complex. It's very important to base your decisions on good advice, both legal and financial.

DIVORCE?

Until divorce is introduced in Ireland, couples have to use other mechanisms to put a final seal on their marriage.

In cases where the separation is mutually accepted or fairly amicable, the couple may simply agree to separate. This will probably include an informal agreement on maintenance, access to the children (if there are any), ownership and access to the family home. Though non-confrontational, this approach may deny the non-breadwinning spouse access to important assets, such as pension rights or lump-sum awards. In short, she (for it usually is a she) may short-change herself. However, an amicable separation does not prevent her from going to the District Court at a later date to claim maintenance or to take out a barring order against her spouse. Nor will it stop her from filing for divorce and tying up financial matters in the future. See Appendix (p. 295 for useful addresses.

Mediation

Couples who separate in an amicable manner can still put their agreement on a more legal footing. The customary route is to go to a mediator — either a private individual or the free State-run service — and work out the terms on which they will separate. The mediator helps them to draw up a document with the "heads of agreement" which decides such crucial issues as ownership of the family home, custody and access to children, maintenance, succession rights and pension arrangements. This is usually achieved in about six sessions. The couple then ask a solicitor to translate the "heads of agreement" into a "Deed of Separation". This can be given extra legal clout by a Deed or Rule of Court if it is not being adhered to.

Judicial Separation

If mediation breaks down, or the couple cannot negotiate in the first place, they may have to let solicitors handle the dispute. This is expensive and time-consuming. The solicitors may be able to agree terms between the two parties. If not, the spouses can go to the Circuit Court or High Court for a Judicial Separation. These cases can take between 12 and 30 months to reach court. When the day finally arrives, it is the judge who decides the key issues of maintenance, custody, ownership of the family home, etc. The judge's opinion will be based on the testimony of each spouse, expert witnesses and the views expressed by the children. The latter do not have to give evidence in court, and may be interviewed separately by a child psychologist who prepares a report for the judge.

As we have seen, the Family Law (Amendment) Act (1995) gives the court a lot of power to decide on the division of assets, and awarding of maintenance. Going for a fully fledged Judicial Separation can achieve a clean break after years of bitter wrangling. Also, thanks to recent legal reforms, these hearings are held in a relatively informal atmosphere to make the process as unintimidating as possible. However, a Judicial Separation is expensive, and can cost both parties over £3,000 apiece in legal costs. If you are on a low income, you may qualify for free legal aid, but there is a long waiting list and a breadwinning spouse may not qualify.

Some experts argue that mediation is better, because it is non-confrontational, cheaper and quicker. Partners of wealthy spouses may find themselves better served in court, however.

COST OF SEPARATION

	Min. Cost per Spouse (approx.)
Legal Separation	£725
Judicial Separation	£3,025–£4,250*
Divorce	£3,000 upwards
State Annulment	£4,850
Protection Order	£180
Barring, Maintenance, Custody, Access Orders	£365 each
Any Combination of the Four Orders Above	£800
Application for Variation or Enforcement of an Order	£180
Making a Will	£50–£60†

* This is an estimate for Circuit Cost costs (High Court costs are higher). The Decree of Separation includes maintenance, and custody/access orders.

† This is a simple will — more complicated wills needing tax advice, or the setting up of trusts, are dearer.

Note: Civil Legal Aid (for a nominal fee) is available to those who pass a means test. In a family law case, each partner is assessed on their own income (not including housekeeping money), not on their spouse's income.

Source: Consumer Choice magazine, April 1994.

Divorce

As stated earlier, this is the final phase in the separation process. It will probably be taken by people who either wish to put a total seal on the end of their marriage, or want to re-marry.

If — as appears likely — the "Yes" vote in the Divorce referendum stands, the government will introduce a Divorce Bill. It will be debated in the Dáil, and probably passed by mid-1996. The terms for granting divorce will be strict: while it will be given on a "no-fault" basis (with no requirement to prove adultery or another cause), couples must have been separated for at least four of the previous five years. They can (in certain circumstances) have continued to share the same family home, however.

The process of "filing" for a divorce will be very similar to that of seeking a judicial separation. You will have to apply to the Circuit or High Court, where a judge can adjudicate on any disputed matters. If the court feels that the dependent spouse has not been properly provided for, the judge can refuse to grant a divorce. The fees will probably be similar, starting at at least £3,000 per party for very quick, simple cases.

Expensive and protracted divorce settlements, especially those taken in the High Court, may prove extremely costly — in the region of £50,000 per spouse, as can be the case with some judicial separations.

The waiting process will be long, probably at least 12 months. This means that the earliest Irish divorces are unlikely to be granted before mid-1997. However, more judges are due to be appointed, which may alleviate the clogged family court system. If you already have a judicial separation, the court may grant a divorce quite automatically and the cost may be modest. However, it has the power to review any arrangements made by the first court to ensure that the dependent spouse is properly provided for. This may also apply to people with foreign divorces — legal or otherwise.

It was not clear, at the time of going to press, if parties who have already applied for a judicial separation can change their application as it moves through the court system.

CONCLUSION

Like life itself, personal financial planning cannot be a static thing. Your age, gender and family status will strongly influence your needs at any given time.

Cohabiting, marrying or losing a spouse through separation, divorce or widowhood each creates a different set of circumstances. It's best to review your finances before any of these events, and discuss their implications with your future or current partner. Many decisions — about bank accounts, ownership of the family home, pension planning etc. — should be decided in consultation, and not unilaterally.

Even if divorce is not introduced yet, the rate of marital breakdown seems likely to rise in Ireland. This chapter maps out a practical and fair approach to dealing with the financial challenge of separation. Some couples will seek the final solution of divorce, but they should do it with their eyes open. Divorce, like separation itself, is a costly and traumatic business.

8

WOMEN

"From birth to age fifteen, a girl needs good parents. From eighteen to thirty-five, she needs good looks. From thirty-five to fifty-five, she needs a good personality. From fifty-five on, she needs good cash."

Sophie Tucker (1884–1966),
Russian-born US entertainer

Women have special financial needs. That's because their life cycle is quite different from that of the average man.

In general, women live longer, earn less and take more career breaks than men. If a woman marries and starts a family it's usually she — not her husband — who gives up work, or starts working part-time. In the past, these factors made a woman very dependent on her partner's income. Modern women still face the problem of how to spread a smaller income over a longer life span. However, many are now financially independent in the first place, having either stayed single or split up with their husband or partner. Others are making more financial decisions within their marriage or relationship.

Today's woman is also marrying later and deferring motherhood until her late twenties or thirties. In the 1970 census, over half of all "new" brides (52.3 per cent) were aged 20–24. Women aged 25–29 or 30–34 made up 23 per cent and 6.8 per cent, respectively — less than a third of those who had recently married. But in 1991, 56.1 per cent of women tying the knot were aged 25–34 (CSO Statistics).

Nowadays, a woman is often the sole breadwinner in a one-parent family, because of the rise in marital breakdown and births outside marriage. Census statistics show a 2 per cent increase in marriages between 1986 and 1991, but a 48 per cent increase in marital breakdown (desertions, legal separations, annulments, informal separations and foreign divorces) during the same period. The number of births outside marriage has risen from just 3 per cent in the mid-1960s, to over 20 per cent in the first half of 1995 — or one in five births.

Meanwhile, a growing number of women now have their own bank account, credit card, mortgage and separate pension plan. Women are buying more financial products in their own right.

There is still a strong case for joint financial planning by a woman and her partner — for example, if they plan to take out a mortgage or life assurance. However, one in ten marriages now ends in separation, according to the Divorce Action Group, and women face the prospect of planning for their own financial future. The "yes" vote in the Referendum to lift the Constitutional ban on divorce will also facilitate those who want to, or must, end their marriage. Some independent planning is now crucial for women.

This chapter offers guidance on this topic. Some issues are also covered in Chapters 7, 9 and 15.

WHO'S COVERED?

A 1993 survey by Lansdowne Market Research suggests that married women are more likely to have some type of financial cover — such as life assurance or a savings plan — than married men. For example, 57 per cent of customers surveyed who had an educational savings plan were married women. Table A shows the sort of products where married females made up the largest single group of policyholders. Table B, in contrast, shows where married and single women lag behind their male counterparts.

Surveys can mislead. Married women make up a surprisingly high percentage of policyholders in Table A. However, the survey appears to confirm that few single women have a savings/investment plan, a pension plan or critical illness cover. This tallies with

UK research, which showed that less than a quarter of working women, or 10 per cent of all women, have made independent pension arrangements (outside the State system).

TABLE A: PERCENTAGE OF TOTAL POLICYHOLDERS, BY GENDER

	Life Cover	**PHI Cover***	**Savings/ Investment Plan**	**Educational Plan**
Women				
Married	43%	42%	39%	57%
Single	6%	6%	10%	2%
Men				
Married	41%	40%	32%	36%
Single	10%	13%	19%	5%

* Permanent Health Insurance. This replaces your income if you are unable to work through sickness or disability. Figures in this column total 101 per cent due to rounding.

TABLE B: PERCENTAGE OF ADULTS WITH A POLICY

	Personal/Company Pension Plan	**Critical/Serious Illness Cover**
Women		
Married	32%	34%
Single	9%	5%
Men		
Married	50%	41%
Single	9%	20%

Source: Lansdowne Market Research.

The Cost of Cover

The fact that women live longer than men is not just academic. It has a key bearing on the cost of life assurance, pension planning and protection cover. You should be aware of these cost factors when shopping around.

At age 40, the average woman can expect to live until she is 79.2 — 4.8 years longer than her male counterpart (see also life expectancy table in Chapter 10). Hence, she pays cheaper premiums for life-assurance cover, because there's statistically less chance that the insurer will have to pay out on her policy. On the other hand, saving for a pension will cost her a lot more.

When people retire, they use most of the proceeds of their company or personal pension plan to buy a yearly income (also called an "annuity") from a life-assurance firm. This is your pension, and it's paid at least until you die (longer, if your spouse or other dependant is entitled to payments or if the contract is guaranteed for a certain minimum time). Because women live longer, the life company has to pay their pension for a longer time, on average. Hence, companies give women a smaller pension in return for their lump sum. To get the same pension as a man, a woman needs to invest more (see also below).

Here's an example:

Siobhán and Jim are both aged 30. They earn the same salary — £20,000 per annum — and both want to take out a personal pension plan. Ideally, they'd like to draw a pension equivalent to two-thirds of their salary when they retire. This salary will be a lot bigger in 35 years' time, so they have to "fund" for a pension of £75,363 which they will start drawing down in the year 2030.

Because she's a woman, Siobhán will have to pay 14 per cent more into her pension plan each month to achieve the same basic pension as Jim. This is not taking into account any career or maternity break that she might take. If Siobhán doesn't take out a pension plan until she's 40, her premiums will rise sharply. How much will they have to pay?

SIOBHÁN AND JIM'S GROSS MONTHLY PENSION PREMIUMS

	Starts Plan at 30	**Starts Plan at 40**
Siobhán	£237	£370
Jim	£208	£324
% Difference	14%	14.28%

Source: Kathy Dillon, LifeWise Ltd., insurance brokers, Dublin.

Note: *These are the "gross" premiums. Thanks to tax and PRSI relief, both Siobhán and Jim will pay less than half of this amount. These* *figures assume that their pension fund will achieve an average growth rate of 8 per cent each year, and that their salary and contributions will increase at a rate of 5 per cent per annum.*

Finally, although women live longer than men, they are more prone to sickness in general, and to specific illnesses, such as cancer in the 20–54 age group. As a result, women pay roughly 50 per cent more for Permanent Health Insurance (PHI) than men pay. This cover replaces your income if you are unable to work through illness or disability. Women may also face higher premiums for critical illness cover, because of the higher cancer risk, but this will partly depend on the life company's pricing structure and the woman's age. The risk of heart attack rises sharply as men get older — particularly after the age of 45 — and their premiums go up as a result.

How Does This Affect Your Financial Planning?

Quite a lot. Premiums for protection policies (life cover, PHI and critical illness) rise sharply with age, but companies often guarantee the premium for a fixed period. So if you want cover, it's best to take it out when you're as young as possible.

HOW THE MONTHLY COST OF PROTECTION RISES

Woman's Age	Life Cover	Critical Illness	PHI	Total Cost
25	£9.80	£15.00	£29.35	£54.15
35	£12.30	£18.01	£36.80	£67.11
45	£29.70	£39.00	£65.05	£133.75

Notes: * The woman is a non-smoker in all examples.
* *Life cover* is for a 20-year term. The policy will pay £100,000 if the woman dies within the 20-year period. Premiums are "level", i.e. will not rise for the life of the policy.
* The *critical illness* policy will pay a £50,000 lump sum if the woman contracts a disease/illness covered by the insurer. It includes a "hospital cash" payout of £50 a day (with some conditions).
* The *PHI* policy will pay two-thirds of the woman's £20,000 annual salary, less her Social Welfare entitlement, after a deferred period of 26 weeks, if she is unable to work because of illness. This payment is also subject to many conditions.

Source: Kathy Dillon, LifeWise Ltd.

PHI cover is expensive, and particularly so for women, so it is important to take it out early. But remember that you might not need PHI cover if you don't have children or other financial dependants, or you can be supported by your family. For example, a 22-year-old starting her first job is unlikely to need a PHI policy. On the other hand, a single professional woman with a mortgage may need one.

Make sure that the cover is appropriate for your needs. Also, pick a company that guarantees the same premium rate for a long time. Critical illness cover and life assurance (notably, term assurance and convertible cover) are a lot cheaper than PHI. But both become quite dear as you get older.

Retirement Planning

Pensions

Women need to pay special attention to pension planning. As we've seen from the Lansdowne survey (p. 143), fewer married women than married men have a pension plan. When they retire, women also end up getting a smaller pension (annuity) for the same lump sum as a man.

Here's an example:

John and Mary both went shopping for an annuity in January 1996. Both had a £100,000 lump sum, were aged 65 and wanted a pension that would continue to be paid, in full, for 5 years if either of them died. They did not want other fringe benefits, such as a spouse's pension. John got a yearly pension of £10,547 (before tax and after charges). Mary's pension was £9,736 (before tax).

Mary would have needed £108,304 to buy the same pension as John. Unfortunately, her nest egg would probably be smaller.

Source: Irish Pensions Trust.

Sex discrimination is illegal, but most women still earn less than men. This means that any contribution (made either by them or their employer) which is based on a percentage of their salary tends to be smaller than in the case of men. Also, women interrupt their careers more often because of child rearing and other family obligations.

A woman aged 25 needs to pay at least 10 per cent more into her pension fund to achieve the same benefits on retirement as a male colleague, research by Scottish Provident (UK) has shown. If she takes a five-year career break, she must contribute 50 per cent more.

The solution is to boost your fund through Additional Voluntary Contributions (AVCs). Remember that you qualify for tax relief on premiums equivalent to 15 per cent of your salary.

Excluded from Your Pension Scheme?

In theory, pension schemes should not discriminate between men and women. Although life companies are free to quote whatever annuity rate they wish, the Pensions Act, 1990 prohibits pension schemes from giving better benefits to male or female members. Discrimination still exists and is legal in old pension schemes, however. A European Court ruling in mid-1994 also forbids schemes from keeping out part-time workers if this would constitute sex discrimination. In other words, a company whose staff primarily consists of male full-time workers and female part-time workers can't prevent the latter from joining the scheme.

Most part-time workers are female, and the ruling should benefit them in particular. But it is very complex. You should contact the Pensions Board (tel: (01) 676 2622) or your union to see if you have been wrongfully excluded from your company scheme.

Wills

If you have children, both parents — whether married or not — should have a will. No one likes thinking about death, but it's important to get your affairs in order. Say, for example, that your partner has left his possessions to you in his will. If both of you are killed in a car crash, his wishes cannot be carried out. It may take your dependants longer to get the proceeds of your estate.

> **Note:** Marriage automatically invalidates a will. This does not apply if the will is made in *anticipation* of marriage to the (named) spouse. (See also Chapter 15, Wills and Inheritance Planning, pp. 267–70.)

Single women with a substantial asset, such as a house, should have a will. But you can have one just for prized belongings, such as books, clothes or a pet. A simple will costs barely £50 and is good psychological housekeeping. You can update it by adding "codicils" as you get older or your circumstances change.

PRE-FAMILY PLANNING

In 1994, the *Sunday Telegraph* argued that British working mothers-to-be needed a "stringent" financial check-up. This is equally true of Irish women.

Firstly, any parent needs a ready pool of cash in a bank or building society to cope with extra costs when the baby arrives. Parents should also make sure that they have adequate insurance cover — especially life — to cope in the event of disaster. As a general rule of thumb, you need to insure your life for roughly 10 times your combined income. Term or convertible insurance is the cheapest option, and cover should last until the youngest child reaches 20 (see also Chapters 6 and 9), or later if they enter third-level education.

Working mothers should also consider their own needs. A career break can decimate your pension prospects, as we have seen. You can avoid this in two ways: by starting your pension contributions earlier, or increasing them by making Additional Voluntary Contributions (AVCs) when you return to the labour force. Ideally, you should also review the performance of your fund as often as possible, to avoid future problems.

Few people, either men or women, reach the threshold for tax relief on pension premiums. This rule states that you can pay up to 15 per cent of your salary (or net relevant earnings in the case of self-employed people) into your pension scheme/plan and claim tax relief on your top rate.

Women who can't join a company pension scheme, or who are self-employed, should make sure that their personal pension plan is flexible. For example, if you have a regular premium contract, which commits you to paying premiums each month or year, check whether it allows you to stop paying premiums for a certain period. This is called a premium "holiday" facility. Some plans do not allow this until the contract has been in force for at least 2 years, so pick one with a shorter minimum investment period. Also, ask if the pension allows you to vary the premium without penalty.

If it doesn't, shop around for another pension. LifeWise, a Dublin-based firm specialising in products for women, has its own customised flexible product, called WomanWise. You can also pay into several pension plans, provided that the combined premiums do not exceed 15 per cent of your gross (pre-tax) salary, if you are a PAYE worker, or 15 per cent of "net relevant earnings" if you are self-employed. This means that a woman earning £10,000 per year can pay £1,500 p.a. (before tax relief) into a personal pension plan.

It's bad value to take out two regular premium plans, however, because you will lose up to 60 per cent of the first year's premiums in commissions and charges on each pension contract. Single-premium (lump-sum) investments are more flexible, because the upfront commission is around 3.5 per cent on each policy. On most single-premium pension policies, this and other charges will be built into the "bid offer spread", which is typically 5 per cent. It means that if you put £1,000 in a pension plan, £950 will actually be invested (after charges).

Ideally, opt for a low-cost regular premium plan — which obliges you to save each month but is affordable — and a series of single-premium contracts when you have a lump sum available. You can either take out single-premium policies with the same company, or with different ones. The latter spreads your risk.

Maternity Benefit

If you have a job, you will probably qualify for Maternity Benefit. It is paid for 14 weeks, by cheque every week.

The weekly rate is 70 per cent of your average "reckonable" earnings in the relevant tax year. The minimum and maximum benefits are £75.70 and £162.80 per week (These did not rise in the 1996 Budget). In other words, even if your salary is £25,000 a year, you will only get £162.80 per week from Social Welfare. Your employer may top up your income, but don't bank on it! You qualify for benefit at the maximum rate if you earn £11,350 or over.

Thanks to a 1994 EU Directive (Protection of Pregnant Workers), low-salary earners are entitled to get the equivalent of Disability Benefit (DB), instead of the Maternity Benefit payment, if their income is so low that the 70 per cent rule would give them less than £74.20/£75.70 per week. Disability Benefit is £62.50 per week, increasing to £64.50 in June 1996, plus £13.20 per child. You do not have to claim this payment. Social Welfare will assess your income automatically, and pay you the DB figure if it brings you above the £75.70 threshold. The payment is still called Maternity Benefit, however.

You may also be able to claim an extra £37.50 per week (rising to £38.50) for your husband/partner if he is an "adult dependant". He must be either:

- Earning less than £60 per week, before tax, or
- Unemployed, and not claiming a Social Welfare or Health Board payment.

Women who are on a widows' pension, or drawing Lone Parents' Allowance or Deserted Wives' Benefit/Allowance, get reduced Maternity Benefit. Self-employed people cannot claim Maternity Benefit at all.

You should apply for Maternity Benefit on an MB10 form at least 10 weeks before the baby is due. You must meet the following conditions to qualify:

- You must have paid at least 39 PRSI contributions in the 12 months immediately before the first day of your maternity leave, or

  Have paid 39 weeks since you first started working and have 39 weeks' PRSI paid or credited in the relevant income-tax year. The relevant income-tax year means the last complete income-tax year before the calendar year when you start drawing benefit. So, if your maternity leave starts in March 1997, the relevant tax year is 1995/96 (which ended on 5 April 1996).

  If in doubt, ask your employer or Social Welfare.

- You must stop work at least four weeks before the baby is due, or else risk losing the benefit.

Mothers can take further unpaid leave of four weeks. Thanks to a recently approved EU accord, both fathers and mothers will be able to take up to three months' paid "parental leave". Income will be based on Social Welfare levels, however, and this is unlikely to be introduced before 1997.

Note: Even if you qualify for maximum Maternity Benefit of £162.80 per week, your finances may be in shock. Do a few sums before leaving work. Can you afford to keep up extra pension payments for three months? Can you put aside money before you get pregnant to help with mortgage repayments?

Lone Parents

People, both men and women, who are bringing up a child without the support of a partner may qualify for Lone Parents' Allowance. This is a means-tested payment — in other words, your income is assessed and the allowance is paid on a sliding scale. However, you can deduct childminding and travel costs from your earnings when calculating your income for the test. To qualify, you must be one of the following:

- Widowed
- Separated
- Deserted
- Unmarried
- A prisoner's spouse.

You cannot be cohabiting, however, and must meet other conditions. Lone parents are entitled to a maximum payment of £62.50 per week (rising to £64.30 in June), plus £15.20 per child up to the age of 18 (or 21, if the child is in full-time education). You are still entitled to Child Benefit for any qualifying dependent child (see also Chapter 9).

- The government plans to merge Lone Parents' Allowance and Deserted Wives' Benefit into a One-Parent Family payment from January 1997. Both men and women are eligible.

TAKING A CAREER BREAK

If you plan to take a career break, don't let it damage your PRSI record. Your state contributory pension could suffer, because this is based on the frequency of your PRSI contributions. Women can now take a career break of up to 12 years per child, without affecting this record. This was extended from five years in the 1995 Budget, but it cannot be back-dated to include years spent child-rearing in the past. Eventually, the Department of Social Welfare plans to give home-based working women their own PRSI credits. In the meantime, women who spend longer than 12 years outside the labour force can keep their PRSI record intact by making voluntary payments.

You will get a P45 form from your employer when you leave work. This will let the Revenue Commissioners know that you are no longer earning a salaried income. Because the tax and Social Welfare systems are interlinked, you don't — in theory — have to tell Social Welfare that you are taking a career break. But it might be advisable to keep a personal record of the dates when you stop and resume work, just to be on the safe side.

Details of the 12-year child-rearing break may be advertised in the media in 1996. Contact your local Social Welfare office or the Department's information service, at (01) 874 8444, for details.

Remember that you can keep your PRSI contributions after leaving the labour force. This is useful for those who want to stay at home for over 12 years (per child), or others who want to study, travel or simply opt out of employment. If you are made redundant or become unemployed, PRSI credits will be paid for you.

You must meet two conditions to make "voluntary" PRSI contributions. These are:

- You must have been in the PAYE net for at least 156 weeks, but not in the same job or continuously.

- You must apply within 12 months of the end of the tax year when you last worked. For example, if you left your job in January 1996, you have until April 1997 to apply.

To apply, or get further details, contact the Department of Social Welfare's Voluntary Contribution section (tel: (01) 704 3767). Making the payment will allow you to maintain your PRSI record for the state Old Age Contributory Pension, the Retirement Pension and Survivors' Pension. It will not entitle you to Sickness or Unemployment Benefit.

The size of the contribution varies. Full-time employees pay 6.6 per cent, which is based on their last year's salary, during the first year out of the labour force. Civil servants pay a lower rate (2.6 per cent), but this reduced payment disqualifies them from some benefits.

Here's an example which predates the 1996 Budget:

Margaret left her job to start a college degree. She had been earning £19,000. In the first year after work, she has to pay 6.6 per cent of her previous salary — or £1,254 in voluntary PRSI contributions. Margaret can pay this yearly, half-yearly or every three months directly to the Department's Voluntary Contribution office. Her bill drops sharply in the second year, however, because she has no income. Her PRSI payments will now be assessed on a "floor" salary of £4,750, so she'll have to pay £313.50.

The upper ceiling on voluntary PRSI contributions was set in the 1995 Budget at £1,419 for PAYE workers, and £230 for self-employed people earning under £2,500. It may rise in 1996. Remember that if you are made redundant and/or are claiming unemployment benefits, PRSI contributions will be paid on your behalf by the State. You can keep your entitlement to the "reckonable credits" even if you stop claiming unemployment benefit. For details contact the Department of Social Welfare (tel: (01) 704 3767).

CARERS

The 1996 Budget increased the "Carers' Allowance" — which can be claimed by any live-in person who is looking after a person in need of constant care — from £62.50 to £67.50 (from June 1996). The previous year, Carers' Allowance was extended to people looking after pensioners aged 66 and over and who are receiving non-Social Welfare pensions. This removed the anomaly whereby people on Social Welfare pensions could claim an allowance, but those on low occupational pensions — such as retired civil servants — could not. Thanks to a relaxation of the means test, the first £150 of the earnings of the carer's spouse (if appropriate) will be excluded when calculating the benefit. Finally, carers also avail of free travel when accompanying the person they are looking after.

WOMEN'S GROUPS AND CO-OPS

The Department of Social Welfare provides a number of grant schemes to support voluntary and community activity. See Appendix for details.

CONCLUSION

Women have similar needs to men, but they often need to plan for them more creatively.

If they marry and have a family, women are still more likely than their partner to give up their paid job or work part-time. This reduces their independent income and can have a devastating impact on their pension planning. At the very least, women should have a financial "audit" when they start their family. Better still, they should plan in advance just by starting their pension contributions a few years earlier, perhaps in their early twenties instead of when they are aged 30 or over. Pensions can now be carried from one job to another, and you get valuable tax relief on pension contributions. A monthly pension premium of £50 costs a 48 per cent taxpayer just £26, excluding the fact that she avoids PRSI on her pension contribution. A 27 per cent tax-payer would pay £36.50, before PRSI relief.

Women also need to take stock of a few other realities. Because they live longer than men, they get smaller pensions than a man would from the same nest egg. If they also plan to take career breaks, they need to put much more into their pension scheme than a man would, just to get the same income when they retire.

Research suggests that very few single women are in a company pension scheme, or have a private pension plan. In the past, women often relied on their husbands and families for financial support. Today, at a time when women are marrying later and a growing number of marriages will end in separation or divorce, woman need to plan more for their own financial future. Women who make their own choices can take more control of their lives.

9

CHILDREN

"Saving is a very fine thing. Especially when your parents have done it for you."

Sir Winston Churchill (1874–1965), British Statesman

You have a new baby. Or, maybe you're planning a family. Perhaps you have children already but worry about school fees, life assurance and general financial planning. There seem to be hundreds of products to choose from. Deciding which one to pick, and what you really need, is hard.

This chapter will help. It covers financial planning, social welfare and tax — all in relation to children. It may also be useful for grandparents or close family friends who want to "help out" financially. You may have a nest egg which you want to invest for a growing child. Where's the best place to put it? Can you protect your money from fraudsters, inflation or just bad investments?

These pages will touch on issues covered by other chapters. To avoid repetition, some topics will simply be highlighted here and the reader referred to other parts of the book where they are dealt with in greater detail.

We'll start with the basics: the cost of rearing baby and how to start planning for the future.

HOW MUCH?

It costs a minimum of £1,875 a year to feed and clothe a child. *The Cost of a Child*, published by Combat Poverty in May 1994, estimated the basic cost of rearing a child at £1,500 a year and inflation has boosted this sum by at least 2.5 per cent. It excludes the cost of any special needs.

Here's the estimated weekly bill for 1994:

Food	£12.90
Clothes	£ 5.60
Education	£ 2.90
Personal Care	£ 2.30
Presents/Toys/Pocket Money	£ 1.80
Outings/Holidays	£ 1.30
Household Durables*	£ 1.10
Fuel*	£ 0.70
Total Weekly Cost	£28.60
Total Annual Cost	£1,487.20 (circa £1,500)

* These represent the portion of the overall household cost accounted for by the child.

The Total Cost figure is a basic minimum. Add a more varied diet, extra toys and presents, extra educational opportunities, such as preschooling and a trip to the Gaeltacht — the cost rises by a further £10 a week. This brings the total bill to over £2,000 per year. Some sources put the cost far higher, estimating a total bill of up to £100,000 until the child finishes college. Ultimately, it depends on your life-style and whether or not your child has special educational needs.

Whatever the final bill, it's vital to take stock of your personal finances when baby arrives. Low-income, unemployed and/or single parents can boost their income through claiming more social welfare allowances, if possible (see below). Parents with larger incomes are in a better position to take out protection or investment plans for the future. Here's a useful checklist:

Do You Have?	Yes	No
Life Assurance		
Health Insurance		
Hospital Cash Plan		
PHI (Income Replacement Cover)		
Long-Term Savings		
A Will		

What Do You Need?

The list is not as daunting as it seems. *Term life assurance,* which pays a lump sum if you or your partner die within a specified period, is inexpensive (see Chapter 6, Protection). Typically, the parents of a new baby could take out a 20-year joint life policy. This will pay a tax-free sum in the event of either of the two named parties dying within the 20-year period. Term assurance is far cheaper than "whole of life" cover, which pays a lump sum whenever you die, and offers good value for low- and middle-income families. Quotes vary greatly, but a young couple (aged, say, 29) can get cover of £100,000 on both lives for 20 years for around £20 per month. This is purely insurance, and does not have an investment value. The cost of cover rises steeply with age, and smokers pay higher premiums.

It is vital to have cover for both "lives", even if only one of the two partners is a breadwinner. One UK insurance company estimated that it would cost £370 per week to replace the home-maker's work with paid helpers.

Health insurance is another priority, if you can afford it (see Chapter 6, Protection). Credit unions and employers sometimes provide group rates for Voluntary Health Insurance (VHI) plans. Group schemes offer a discount of about 10 per cent on regular premium costs. Remember that you can also claim tax relief on your health insurance contributions.

Hospital cash plans are different. They pay a tax-free lump sum if the policyholder or others named in the policy — such as a wife or children — are hospitalised. You may have to spend a minimum period in hospital to qualify for the benefit, perhaps 3 days, but you can use the money as you wish. Hospital cash plans can be bought as "stand-alone" products (without any other cover attached), from Cigna Insurance Company, AIG Europe and other institutions. The cost varies, depending on the size of your required daily hospital cash payment, your age, and number of family members covered, but tends to be cheap. A whole family can get basic cover for around £10–£15 per month. A 29-year-old couple with two children would get £50 daily cover for under £20.

Critical illness cover pays a lump sum if the policyholder gets a serious illness, such as cancer or heart disease. As part of the package, policyholders can also get cover for total disability. Most life-assurance companies offer a hospital cash plan as well. Critical illness cover is quite expensive, starting at around £26 per month for a young couple (aged 29, non-smokers). Premium costs can rise dramatically with age. You can't claim tax relief on premiums paid into hospital cash plans or critical illness policies, but the benefit is paid tax-free (see Chapter 6, Protection).

Permanent Health Insurance (PHI), also known as income replacement plans, is expensive, and beyond the reach of many families. It pays up to two-thirds of the salary of a policyholder who is unable to work through illness or disability. For families supported by a single, high-earning breadwinner, such as a doctor, barrister or self-employed businessperson, PHI can be invaluable. It is less crucial for two-income families or those with other means of support. See also Chapter 6.

Long-term savings plans are a good way of saving for your child's special needs. A few options are described below.

A *will* is a "must" when you become a parent. Most people put off writing a will, but it can be a reassuring experience to sort out your possessions and make provisions for family and friends. Remember that if you die "intestate" (without leaving a will) your partner and child could face unnecessary financial hardship. Even a bank account, held in one partner's name, cannot be touched and the proceeds go directly into the dead person's estate. Go to a solicitor if you want to write a will, as DIY wills can cause a lot of problems. Most solicitors charge barely £50 to write a simple will.

- See Chapter 6, Protection, for examples of how three families meet their protection needs.

SOCIAL WELFARE PAYMENTS

Child Benefit

After the baby is born, mothers are entitled to tax-free Child Benefit until the child is aged 16 — or 18 if the child is in full-time education, on a FÁS course, or is physically or mentally handicapped. This is £27 (£29 from June) a month per child for the first two children. You get £32 (rising to £34 in June) for any subsequent children. It can be claimed on the first Tuesday of the month after the baby arrives. Thanks to the 1996 Budget, parents of twins will get a £500 "grant" when the children are born, plus an extra £500 when they reach 4 and 12.

Child benefit is not means-tested (based on your income). If you are a low-income family, you may be entitled to other Social Welfare benefits, such as Family Income Supplement (see Chapter 13, Budgeting). Ask at your local Social Welfare office, or ring the Family Income Supplement helplines (01) 704 3482, (01) 704 3483 or (043) 45211. See also "Single Parenthood" below.

In future, the Department of Social Welfare plans to boost the income of low earners and families on social welfare through a discretionary Child Benefit Supplement.

CHILDMINDING

The Budget gave no tax relief for childminder costs. However, single parents who work can deduct childminding costs from their earnings when applying for the means-tested Lone Parents' Allowance.

EDUCATION COSTS

The 1995 Budget announced plans to abolish college fees by 1996/97, but only partly addressed the issue of education costs. These start with primary school, or even earlier, in nursery school. The Department of Education calculates the annual cost of primary school books from £10 to £60, depending on the child's age. The average cost in of kitting out a child for school is over £50 for a boy and over £60 for a girl. At secondary school, book costs now total roughly £150 per year, and the uniform costs on average a further £65 for a boy and over £75 for a girl. These figures do not include the cost of shoes. Fees in private schools can cost £1,000 plus per year for primary school, and more for secondary.

Parents will get some relief when their children go to college, however. Undergraduate fees on full-time courses at state-funded colleges have been abolished for the 1996/97 academic year. Part-time, post-graduate and specialist courses (at the Royal College of Surgeons) will not benefit, however. Also, living costs may remain a problem for some. The Union of Students calculates that it costs £3,193.50 per year to maintain a student at home, and £5,497.50 for students living away from the family in the 1995/96 academic year.

Paying the Bill

The government's "free fees" scheme does not help with living costs. A handicapped child may have special educational needs. You can still help to meet these costs with a long-term savings plan. That may seem a tall order if you are financially strapped. What about your £29 child-benefit cheque? Can you save it? Better still, can you afford to top it up with an extra £1 or £11 a month?

Most parents will have to take out a regular savings plan, unless they can afford to lock up a lump sum for 15 years or more. Regular savers have three basic options.

- An Post's National Instalment Savings
- "With Profits" plans
- Unit-linked investment plans.

Think about your attitude to risk and return when deciding which one to choose. An Post's plan gives a cast-iron guarantee on your capital, and the prospect of a good, tax-free return. "With profits" plans guarantee your capital, plus a small growth, and may produce quite high returns. Profits from unit-linked investment plans can be dramatic — but your capital is rarely guaranteed.

A brief description of each product follows. It includes a sample "quotation", based on a £30 monthly regular premium. The quote was given to John and Anne (both aged 29) who want to take out a savings plan for their new baby, Jimmy.

If you are taking out a plan for older children (aged 10 or older), think before opting for a unit-linked plan. These products can give very volatile returns on short periods. If you have more than one child, you might consider spreading the investment risk by splitting your savings between An Post and a unit-linked or "with profits" plan.

An Post

An Post's Educational Savings Plan is based on its National Instalment Savings (NIS) scheme. But instead of saving for a year and locking up your money for 5 years, you save the same amount each month for as many years as you wish. Your savings can be drawn down as a single tax-free lump sum when your child starts college. The plan can be "encashed" early, if you need the money.

An Post cannot quote an interest rate for longer than the first 5 years. The quotation below is based on a £30 monthly instalment. It also assumes that the current interest rate (50 per cent after 6 years) does not change. The premium can be paid on any day in the month, but missing a payment may jeopardise the savings plan. To avoid this, you can pay in one of two ways:

- Pick up the child benefit each month, add £1 and pay £30 into the NIS plan.
- Join An Post's electronic funds transfer scheme, and arrange to have the benefit paid directly into the savings plan. You would have to take out a second NIS plan for any extra cash, however. The minimum is £10 per month. Check your bank statements to ensure that the money goes through.

John and Anne open an NIS account when Jimmy is born in February 1996. They pay in £30 a month for each year until Jimmy's eighteenth birthday. Their total outlay is £6,480. They will get £13,064 back — tax free — in a single lump sum after 18 years in the year 2014. If inflation rises sharply, this sum will also rise.

"With Profits" Plan

These are also sold by life-assurance companies. They offer some capital guarantees, because the investment grows as bonuses are added to the policy each year (reversionary bonuses). Once paid, bonuses cannot be taken away. However, the bulk of the profit often comes from the terminal bonus, which is paid at the end. You won't know how big — or small — that is until the policy matures, and life companies have cut these bonuses in recent years.

The life company's quote will include a "guaranteed sum assured". You are certain to get this amount if you keep the plan going until it matures.

You can invest either a lump sum (single premium) or make regular payments, usually each month. Before taking out the policy, decide whether you want it to include life assurance, which will pay a death benefit if either or both parents die. This type of policy has a slightly lower investment value, but may suit single-parent families or those who are dependent on one bread-winner. Savings plans pay out a small sum — usually the premiums paid in, plus some investment return — if one of the policyholders dies. These plans give a higher investment return if you hold them to maturity, however.

What happens if you can't afford to pay the premiums? Investors who stop payments within the first two years probably won't get any money back. After that, you have three options:

- Cash in the policy. Its value will probably be small, however.
- Sell it to another investor, or Irish Policy Exchanges (see Appendix for contact number).
- Freeze it, or make it "paid up". The policy will continue to grow, albeit at a slower rate, and you can cash it in later.

After Jimmy is born, John and Anne take out a 30-year "with profits" savings policy in both names, with a leading life-assurance company. There is no extra life-assurance cover, but the policy will pay the premiums (plus any investment return) if either parent dies. They pay £30 a month for the first 17 years. The premium drops to £18 and eventually down to zero in the final, thirtieth year. Their total outlay is £6,552.

This plan gives them the flexibility of cashing in "segments" (or portions of the policy) when they need money. Typically, parents encash segments at the start of each academic year. The amount they can draw down will depend on the plan's investment performance. Life companies quote two projected "investment returns", based on a 7 and 9 per cent annual growth rate (before charges). Here's John and Anne's quote:

JOHN AND ANNE'S QUOTE FOR "WITH PROFITS" SAVINGS POLICY

A	B	C	D
End of Year	**Guaranteed Sum**	**7% Yield**	**9% Yield**
17	£4,947	£9,375	£11,327
18	£5,238	£10,334	£12,649
19	£5,529	£11,357	£14,086
20	£5,820	£12,446	£15,646
30	£8,730	—	—

Let's say the investment return on John and Anne's policy is very bad — under 5 per cent annually. They are still guaranteed to get the figure in column B from the entire policy at the end of the year shown in column A. At the end of year 17, for example, the total return would be £4,947. (Note that this is less than they paid in). If the investment grows by 7 per cent, their policy will be worth £9,375 at the end of year 17 (see column C). If it grows by 9 per cent, they will get £11,327 (see column D), which is less than the likely return at An Post. Each year, they may only want to encash a quarter of this amount. If they do, the rest of the policy will continue to grow.

If they don't encash any of the policy and keep it for 30 years, their guaranteed minimum return will be £8,730.

Unit-linked Plan

Unit-linked plans invest heavily in the stock market, and have the potential for strong growth. They can easily outperform an An Post savings plan, but if stock market values drop before your child starts college, the investment may pay far less than you hoped.

If you have to stop premium payments after two years, you can either encash the policy or make it "paid up". You will probably not be able to sell it to a third party. The policy is unlikely to have any value at all in the first two years because of commissions and other costs.

When you get a quotation from a life-assurance company, remember that it is not a guarantee. The figures are estimates, based on projected growth rates.

John and Anne start to invest £30 a month in a savings policy for 18 years. If one of them dies, they will get their premiums back, plus some investment return. Their total outlay will be £6,480.

By boosting monthly payments to £31.49, John and Anne will get extra cover of £10,000 on both lives, but the return on their savings will also be a bit smaller. This table is not like the "with profits" example. It shows how much they can withdraw from the policy each *year if it achieves the growth rate shown in columns B and C:*

A	B	C
End of Year	**7% Yield**	**9% Yield**
18	£2,766	£2,766
19	£2,766	£2,766
20	£2,766	£2,766
21	£2,766	£2,766
22	£250	£3,261

The amount they can draw may fluctuate each year, depending on the policy's performance. The figure quoted in column B is the amount they can withdraw from the policy each year if the investment has achieved an annual growth of at least 7 per cent (before charges). It is not the total value of the policy. John and Anne may have to take a smaller sum if the policy grows by less than 7 per cent. If the investment performs well, John and Anne may have money left in their policy after paying fees in the fourth year. This could be £250, if the fund averages a 7 per cent yield, or £3,261 if it grows by a yearly average of 9 per cent over the full investment term.

> **WARNING!**
> With profits and unit-linked savings plans are risky. You may lose money, instead of making a profit, and put your child's future plans at risk. Think carefully before picking an insurance-based investment plan. You may feel safer earning a secure return with An Post. Alternatively, split your savings between a low-risk deposit and a higher-risk insurance policy.

Lump-Sum Savings

Some people choose a single premium investment instead of a regular savings plan. This means that they lock away a lump sum for their children for several years, instead of saving on a monthly basis. In the above example, Jimmy's grandparents or uncle may decide to help out in this way.

So where should they invest? Both "with profits" and unit-linked investment plans are available to lump-sum investors. The minimum amount a life company will accept is usually £3,000. The advantage of single premium investment is that the broker commission is lower, typically 3.5 per cent of the total lump sum at the outset. You can also encash a single premium investment slightly earlier, as less is sliced off in commission at the start.

Before making a lump-sum investment, it is vital to get good, independent financial advice. That doesn't mean visiting a life-assurance company and speaking to an agent. That agent will be a tied agent of that company and will promote its products. It's a good idea to speak to a life-assurance company, a broker who is a member of the Independent Brokers' Association (IBA) and an accountant. The first can tell you about unitised (life assurance) investments, the second about other options, and an accountant can advise you about tax. This will help you to make an informed decision rather than an impulsive one.

Deed of Covenant

The 1995 Budget severely restricted the use of covenants taken out for educational purposes, but some still qualify for tax relief.

Here's how they work:

John earns £45,000 per year. He agrees to covenant £2,000 a year to his eldest daughter, Sarah, who is mildly incapacitated. He "gives" Sarah £2,000 in July 1996, but withholds 27 per cent tax — which is £540. Sarah can reclaim the missing money by completing a Form 54 (which states her annual income), and sending it to the Revenue Commissioners.

Meanwhile, John also contacts the Revenue Commissioners. He sends in a copy of the Deed of Covenant, an R185 form and a Form 12 (annual return). The Revenue Commissioners will boost the monthly relief on John's Tax Free Allowance (TFA) form. This means that John's salary should rise each month by the amount of tax withheld on the covenant. Because he is claiming tax relief at 48 per cent, giving Sarah £2,000 will cost him only £1,040 in 1996/97.

Tax relief on educational covenants already taken for children aged over 18 will be abolished in 1996/97, unless the child is incapacitated. Also, the rule permitting a person other than a parent or grandparent to covenant over 5 per cent of their income to a child has gone, and tax relief was restricted to just 5 per cent in 1995/96. Tax relief on covenants to children aged under 18 has been abolished (both on new covenants taken out after the 1995 Budget and on existing covenants from 6 April 1995).

OTHER WAYS OF PAYING COSTS

If you can't afford a savings plan and are dismayed by the removal of tax relief on covenants, don't worry. Many students get through college by accessing other sources of income. These include:

- Grants. Contact the Higher Education Grant Section of your local authority, or the Department of Education.
- Part-time work.
- Bank/Credit Union Loans.

CHILDREN'S SAVINGS ACCOUNTS

It's a good idea to encourage your children to start saving when they are still young, even though the pressing need to save for college fees has gone.

Several financial institutions have child-friendly savings accounts.

They include Ulster Bank's Henry Hippo Super Savers Club, which comes with a money box, savers' pack and even a wall calendar. The Irish Permanent has three products for young savers: "Beanstalk" (for 0–8 year olds); "Savings Scene" (8–13 year olds); and Pace (13–18 year olds). An Post's young saver's product is called Cyril the Squirrel.

These accounts tend to pay very low returns, barely more than the regular demand deposit account. Profits are also liable to Deposit Interest Retention Tax (DIRT) at 27 per cent. They are not a good place to park large sums of money for long periods. It's a better idea to withdraw chunks of money (say sums of £100 or more), and invest them in An Post Savings Bonds or Savings Certificates. These pay higher rates.

CHILDREN'S TAX-FREE ALLOWANCE

There is scope for quite sophisticated financial planning if you use your child's tax-free allowance. Basically, this means choosing products that produce an income. Because your children can "earn" up to £3,900 per year without paying tax, they will not have to pay tax on income-generating investments that yield under that amount.

There's a snag. Tax avoidance legislation forbids parents to transfer assets to children in order to avoid tax. Also, if the child is aged under 18, the income is viewed as belonging to the parent. However, a grandparent can buy a gilt, shares or some other income-generating investment. Gilts pay a twice-yearly interest income, and shares pay dividends (if the company performs well). Children do not have to pay tax on these profits. This area is complicated, and best discussed with an accountant.

DISABLED CHILDREN

Financial planning is crucial if your child is either born with or develops a disability. Take out enough life-assurance cover on the lives of both parents. A mixture of "term" assurance and "whole of life" cover may be appropriate. Set up a trust to ensure that this money is handled wisely, by "trustees", in the event of your death. Typically, parents nominate a younger family member and at least one "professional" trustee, perhaps a family solicitor, to oversee the trust. Setting up a trust costs £500 to £2,000 or more, but it can ensure that your child is looked after. It is possible that your child may qualify for some state support too. Trusts are complex and have major tax and legal implications. Get expert advice. Parents of an incapacitated child can also claim an extra tax allowance of £700 in 1996/97.

SINGLE PARENTHOOD

There are at least 50,000 single parents in Ireland, the vast majority of whom are unmarried women. In November 1995, 45,401 people were claiming Lone Parents' Allowance. Over 20,000 people claimed allowances as separated or deserted spouses.

Most single parents qualify for Social Welfare payments, and some are completely dependent on them. The following are the main payments to which you may be entitled. Note that men, as well as women, are entitled to claim Lone Parents' Allowance (see also Chapter 8, Women). Thanks to EU legislation and the Treaty of Rome, it is now illegal for Member States to discriminate between men and women when allocating Social Welfare payments.

The more common problem is that people fail to claim payments to which they are entitled. Here is a list of them:

Non-Means-Tested

CHILD BENEFIT

Number of Children	Monthly Allowance	
	1995/96	**1996/97**
1	£27	£29
2	£54	£58
3	£86	£92
4	£118	£126
5	£150	£160
6	£182	£194
7	£214	£228
8	£246	£262

DESERTED WIVES' BENEFIT

	1995/96	1996/97
Maximum*	£66.10 per week	£68.10 per week
Each Dependent Child	£17 per week	£17 per week

WIDOWS'/WIDOWERS' CONTRIBUTORY PENSION

	1995/96	1996/97
Maximum*	£66.10 per week	£68.10 per week
Each Dependent Child	£17 per week	£17 per week

Means-Tested

LONE PARENTS' ALLOWANCE

	1995/96	1996/97
Adult	£62.50 per week	£64.30 per week
Each Dependent Child	£15.20 per week	£15.20 per week

WIDOWS' NON-CONTRIBUTORY PENSION

	1995/96	1996/97
Adult	£62.50 per week	£64.50 per week
Each Dependent Child	£15.20 per week	£15.20 per week

DESERTED WIVES' ALLOWANCE

	1995/96	1996/97
Adult	£62.50 per week	£64.50 per week
Each Dependent Child	£15.20 per week	£15.20 per week

SEPARATED WIVES' ALLOWANCE

	1995/96	1996/97
Adult	£62.50 per week	£64.50 per week
Each Dependent Child	£15.20 per week	£15.20 per week

PRISONERS' WIVES' ALLOWANCE

	1995/96	1996/97
Adult	£62.50 per week	£64.50 per week
Each Dependent Child	£15.20 per week	£15.20 per week

FUEL BENEFIT

	1995/96	1996/97
Mid-October to Mid-April	£5 per week	£5 per week

RENT ALLOWANCE

Paid by Health Board	Discretionary

MEDICAL CARD

Provided by Health Board	Free hospital accommodation, medicines, and GP service

Note: The 1996/97 increases will apply from June 1996. People aged over 65 or 80 may get higher payments.

Social Welfare payments fall into two main categories.

Benefits are not means-tested, and are based either on your PRSI contribution record or automatic entitlement — such as the Child Benefit. If you have been in regular employment and have a long PRSI payment record, you may be entitled to additional benefits. *Allowances* are means-tested. You may qualify for the full payment if your income is below a certain level, or you may get a part-payment. You may qualify for other benefits, like a free fuel allowance or butter vouchers, if you are receiving social assistance (non-PRSI-based) payments or are over 66 and getting a Social Welfare pension. Your local Social Welfare or Health Board officer may also be able to make extra, discretionary payments.

Contact your local Social Welfare office or citizens' advice bureau to find out if you are entitled to draw additional benefits/ allowances. They could boost your income.

CONCLUSION

Having a baby changes your life, in more ways than one. It's an important time to review your personal finances and make sure that your child is financially secure. That means making a will, taking out life-assurance cover and — if you can afford it — starting a savings plan.

There are many choices to make. Work out your priorities, and try to get real value for your money. Your child's future is at stake.

10

YOUR PENSION

"The older you are, the more slowly you read a contract."

Leonard Louis Levinson (1905–74), US writer

Retirement can be a golden age, a time for hobbies, travel, a new career or just relaxation. It can also last a long time. The average Irish man and woman now live until the age of 72.3 and 77.9, respectively, and life expectancy rates are climbing, thanks to improvements in health, housing and nutrition. Instead of a few short years, retirement can stretch into decades. The snag is, you probably won't have a salary to live on.

Here's the average life expectancy of a man and woman once they reach the following ages:

Current Age	Male	Female
40 Years	74.4	79.2
50 Years	75.2	79.8
65 Years	78.4	82.1

Source: CSO (Health Statistics, 1993).

Sadly, too few people make adequate plans for a long, fulfilled retirement. Some rely totally on the state (or their family) to support them when they get older. Others pay a small sum into a pension fund/plan and hope to get a "full" pension at age 65. A minority — usually self-employed people and company directors — pay large sums of money into pension products. But because of poor planning, their cash can be swallowed up in commissions and charges.

This was highlighted in a *Sunday Business Post* pensions survey of December 1995.

Most of us, if we want a decent income in retirement, will have to save for it. That usually means paying into a life assurance-based pension fund/plan. Over the long term, 20 to 30 years, these can give excellent value. But you have to stick the course. Switching jobs, making erratic pension contributions or picking the "wrong" product can decimate your nest egg.

It's vital to inform yourself, get good advice and shop around. This chapter will help, but it is just a start. (See also Chapter 12, Self Employed and Chapter 8, Women).

WHAT WILL YOU LIVE ON?

If you are 25 or 30, retirement can seem a long way away. In fact, the earlier you start saving, the more chance you have of saving an adequate nest egg.

As a mental exercise, try thinking about the following:

- Inflation
- The Cost of Delay
- What Income?

Inflation

This eats into your savings. Every year, inflation erodes the real value of your money, which means that £100 in 1996 will buy far more goods or services than in 2026. Here's how inflation can push up the cost of basic foodstuffs:

Year	Price of Milk (1 litre)		Price of Bread (large sliced loaf)	
1996	60p		82p	
	5% inflation	10% inflation	5% inflation	10% inflation
2006	£0.98	£1.56	£1.33	£2.13
2016	£1.59	£4.04	£2.17	£5.51
2026	£2.59	£10.47	£3.54	£4.30

Source: Adapted from *You and Your Pension*, Which Books.

The Cost of Delay

Based on January 1996 estimates, a male (non-smoker) who starts paying £100 per month level premium into a personal pension plan at the age of 30 will gross £153,161 if his fund grows by a yearly average of 9 per cent until he reaches 60. If he waits until he is 40, he will accumulate just £54,611 in the next 20 years. The longer you wait before starting your pension fund, the more you have to save.

What Income?

People have different sources of income when they retire. These include a state pension — contributory or non-contributory — their own company and/or personal pension(s), investments, earnings and other income (such as rent). It's dangerous to assume that a certain asset, such as a business or commercial property, will give you a pension in the future. You may lose your business. Rents on commercial properties may plunge, or you may have to spend most of this income on repairs or refurbishment.

There are generous tax incentives for people who save for their own pension. It makes sense to take advantage of them, and help secure your own future. So what are the different types of pension, and how do they dovetail with each other?

TYPES OF PENSION

There are five main categories of pension:

Your "pension" may come from one or more of the above sources. PAYE workers who also contribute to a company pension scheme in their working life should be entitled to both a state *and* a company pension (size of contributions permitting). People who change jobs several times in their career may accumulate cash in different company pension funds. These are usually amalgamated into one large fund when they retire. Some people work abroad, building up social welfare "credits" in other countries which can boost their Irish state pension or may entitle them to a pension from that country. Self-employed people usually set up a personal pension plan, or a series of them. Directors of limited companies also have the option of an executive pension plan or starting a Self-Administered Scheme.

Non-contributory State Pension

A non-contributory pension is provided by the state for people who have little or no other income. If you have savings, or any property other than the family home (such as a farm or shop), this will be taken into account by the social welfare officer assessing your claim, and your payment may be reduced accordingly.

Even the full non-contributory pension is meagre. It's certainly too small to allow a life of travel and leisure in retirement. If her husband dies, a woman can claim a Widow's Non-contributory Pension, which has a slightly higher payment for dependent children (£15.20 per week). Or, she may be entitled to a Survivor's Contributory Pension, depending on her own or on her husband's PRSI contribution record. In fact, both widows and widowers can claim this, and the maximum rate is £66.10 a week (£68.10 from June), plus £17 for each dependent child. You get the same "living alone allowance" (£6 from June) and "old age allowance" (£5 from

June, if you are aged 80 or over), as you would on the regular non-contributory pension. Widowers also qualify for this higher rate.

NON-CONTRIBUTORY STATE PENSION

Weekly Benefit	Payment	
	1995/96	1996/97
Personal Rate		
Aged under 80	£62.50	£64.50
Aged over 80	£67.50	£69.50
Adult Dependant Allowance	£37.50	£38.50
Child†	£13.20	£13.20
Living Alone Allowance	£4.90	£6.00

* Increase in rates will take effect from June 1996.
† You can claim for each child aged under 18 (living at home) and for any child up to three months after finishing third-level education (normally until age 21), also living at home.
Source: Department of Social Welfare.

Contributory State Pension (PRSI-based)

If you started making PRSI contributions before the age of 55, you may be entitled to a state contributory pension. This applies to PAYE workers, state employees and self-employed people. The latter were only required to start making PRSI payments after 6 April 1988, so few will have built up enough credits yet. There are two types of contributory pension: the Retirement Pension and the Old-Age Contributory Pension.

To qualify for a Retirement Pension you must retire at the age of 65. To qualify for a minimum pension, you must also have built up an average of at least 24 weeks' PRSI credits for each of your qualifying working years before retirement. People who want to continue working — energy and opportunities permitting — and have accumulated fewer PRSI credits can claim the Old-Age Contributory Pension. This is payable at the age of 66, but you don't have to retire. You need an average of 20 weeks' PRSI credits per working year to qualify for a minimum pension.

A yearly average of 48 weeks is required to get the maximum pension (for both the Retirement Pension and Old-Age Contributory

Pension). Neither of these state contributory pensions is means-tested, but you might pay tax if your income exceeds a certain threshold.

The size of your pension will depend on the number, frequency and size of the PRSI contributions made during your working life. As with the non-contributory pension, you may be entitled to a higher pension if you have dependants (a spouse and/or children) or are living alone. There is a means test for dependants.

Here are the maximum weekly rates for both the Retirement Pension *and* the Old-Age Contributory Pension. They are based on a full PRSI payment record:

STATE CONTRIBUTORY PENSION

Weekly Benefit	**Payment**	
	1995/96	**1996/97**
Personal Rate		
Aged under 80	£72.80	£75.00
Aged over 80	£77.60	£80.00
Adult Dependant Allowance		
Aged under 66	£48.10	£49.50
Aged over 66	£52.30	£53.90
Child (full rate)†	£15.20	£15.20
Living Alone Allowance	£4.90	£6.00

* These rates take effect from mid-June 1996.

† Same conditions apply as per non-contributory pension.

Source: Department of Social Welfare.

Career breaks and unemployment can greatly reduce your state contributory pension. Luckily, women who take "time out" to rear a family are no longer penalised. They can spend up to 12 years at home per child, so that when their PRSI credits are calculated, these will be averaged over a shorter number of years (see Chapter 8, Women).

If you stop work for other reasons, you can also damage your state contributory pension. This can be avoided if you continue to make PRSI payments on a voluntary basis. If you are sick, or made redundant, the Department of Social Welfare will pay your credits for you. You cannot make back payments of PRSI to fill a gap in your contributions record, so it's important to keep payments up to date (see Chapter 8, pp. 152–3, for details).

If you have worked abroad, you may be able to boost your state pension or even claim a separate pension from that country. Ireland has reciprocal agreements with many countries, including the EU states and the US. See "Flow Chart 2: How to Claim Your Pension", p. 191).

State contributory-pension payments are only slightly larger than the non-contributory pension. If you want a decent income on retirement, it's important to create a future revenue stream by means of an investment/savings plan (see p. 183), or privately funded pension. You can join a company pension scheme (if your employer has one), or start your own personal pension plan (if your employer has no scheme, or if you are self-employed). PAYE workers who take up either of these options will get a dual income when they retire — that is, from their PRSI-based pension *and* from their other pension. This revenue will be taxable as income, but not means-tested. A person who leaves PAYE employment to set up their own company, and then starts a personal pension plan, may even be able draw on three pensions on retirement.

Your employment history can complicate how your pension is calculated. Public-sector pensions are based on your "reckonable service" — in other words, the length of time you have worked for the state. These pensions are not described in this book, but you should contact your employer or trade union for information. If you have worked in both the public and private sector, you will have paid PRSI at different rates, so you may qualify for a "mixed pension". For details on any of the above, contact the Department of Social Welfare's information service (tel: (01) 874 8444).

Company and personal pensions are usually built around life assurance-based investments, but company directors can also set up a Revenue-approved Self-Administered Scheme (see p. 184). These are becoming a popular alternative.

Company Pensions

Some people resent having to pay money into their employer's pension scheme each week or month. In fact, it's a tax-efficient way of saving for your pension, and some schemes also provide extra benefits, such as sickness and redundancy cover and a death-in-service payment. Buying this protection through separate policies can be expensive.

How Do Company Pension Schemes Work?

In a typical scheme, employees pay a percentage of their salary into a pension fund each month. The employer may also make a contribution.

Pension schemes are supervised by trustees. They make sure that the scheme is run in accordance with the rules and regulations which set it up. They must pass information about the scheme to its members and/or their trade union (see also Appendix), and report any suspected case of fraud or mismanagement to the Pensions Board. Trustees can agree to change the trust rules and improve benefits under the scheme. Trustees usually ask an insurance broker to shop around for a firm of pension fund managers. A large brokerage may take on administrative tasks, such as sorting out your tax reliefs, and can usually give useful advice (free of charge) to the scheme members. The fund managers handle the growing pool of pension cash, investing it in assets like equities, property, cash deposits and government stocks.

When you retire, your savings, plus any share of the investment profits, can be removed from the main fund. You can take up to 1.5 times your final retirement salary as a tax-free lump sum (see below). The remaining cash in your pension fund must be used to buy a compulsory purchase annuity from a life-assurance company. This will lock up your capital, but give you a yearly income (or pension) for life.

Tax relief greatly reduces the real cost of saving for a company pension. Under present legislation, you can claim full relief on up to 15 per cent of your gross (pre-tax) earnings This means that a payment of £100 per month costs a 48 per cent taxpayer just £52. Over a year, your £1,200 contribution will set you back £624. The real savings are slightly higher, because you are exempted from paying PRSI and other levies, which total 7.75 per cent, on this £1,200 premium. So you save another £93 *provided that* the contribution is docked directly from your pay. If the combined premium from you and your employer is less than 15 per cent of your salary, you can make up the difference through Additional Voluntary Contributions (AVCs). The rules of your pension scheme must permit this, however (see "Improving Your Company Pension", p. 181).

Company pension schemes fall into two main categories. The crucial difference is that one guarantees a certain income when you retire. The other doesn't.

Defined Benefit

Most older schemes fit into this category. They promise you a specific pension. If there is too little cash in the pension fund to meet this obligation, the company pays the shortfall (in theory, at least). The size of the promised pension will vary from one scheme to another. Here's a typical example:

John has worked in a company for 40 years and is on an £18,000 salary before he retires. He is promised 1/60th of his final pensionable salary for each year of service, up to a maximum of two-thirds of his final pay.

What will he get?

Final Pay	£18,000
Service	40 Years
Pension Fraction	1/60th
Pension Entitlement	£18,000 x 40/60th = £12,000

Source: Adapted from *Understanding Pensions*, by Paul Kenny.

Your "final pensionable salary" may be less than your gross annual pay. If benefits from your company pension are integrated with the Social Welfare pension, your employer may base your pension on a lower salary. The size of your lump sum will also affect your yearly "pension", because your yearly income will be drawn from a smaller savings pool. For example, if John takes a £27,000 (£18,000 x 1.5) lump sum, his pension will be far smaller than £12,000 per year.

Defined Contribution Scheme

Most newer schemes are of this sort. The size of your pension is not guaranteed. It will depend chiefly on the amount you and your employer have saved over the years, and the net (after cost) profit on this investment. If the pension fund has performed badly, or your contributions are very small, the company won't make up the difference. As with defined benefit schemes, you can take up to 1.5 times your final salary as a tax-free lump sum. You must use the rest to buy your compulsory purchase annuity.

Improving Your Company Pension

First, check out your scheme. Irish pensions law is quite progressive, and company employees are entitled to a lot of information about their pension scheme — that information is summarised in the section "Your Rights under the Pensions Act (1990)" in the Appendix. Look at the benefits provided by your scheme. Do they include the following:

- Maximum benefits of two-thirds salary? How many years do you need to qualify for a maximum pension?
- Provision for an index-linked pension? Some schemes allow you to buy an annuity which is index-linked. This means that your pension will increase gently each year, and provide some protection against inflation.
- A widow's or dependant's pension? Does the scheme provide this automatically, or will you have to take a smaller pension to give your spouse one?
- Death-in-service benefit? Most schemes provide this, but it can be quite small.
- Early retirement? Some schemes are more flexible than others. You may want to stop work early, because of ill-health or personal choice. It's important to find out how soon you can draw a pension.
- Portability? Again, schemes differ. Some allow you to claim both your own contributions and those of your employer if you have been in the job for under five years, which is the minimum statutory requirement. Most workers can expect to switch jobs many times in their career, so pension portability is very important.
- Additional Voluntary Contributions (AVCs)? You can use these to top up your pension fund, but not every scheme has an AVC option.

If your pension scheme falls short, you can lobby for improvements. Some, such as permitting you to make AVCs, just require a simple rule change. Others, like providing extra benefits, may be resisted because they cost money. You cannot change the scheme from a defined contribution to a defined benefit one!

Your fellow staff members may also want changes, so it's a good idea to reach some consensus before approaching the pension scheme's trustees or your employer. You may also get vital backing from your union in this. The Pensions Board (tel: (01) 676 2622) can provide information and guidance, too. It may also investigate any concerns that you have about the scheme, such as suspected irregularities, or underfunding.

Boosting Your Pension

You may not want to campaign for improvements, or be able to achieve them. The other option — boosting your pension contributions — is just as effective, but it costs money. You have two main choices: to increase your pension premiums or to create another nest egg.

AVCs

In most company pension schemes, members contribute a fixed percentage of their earnings. By boosting payments to a maximum of 15 per cent of your salary, you can claim full tax relief (either at 27 per cent or 48 per cent, depending on your earnings). If you pay tax at the 48 per cent rate, paying £100 extra per month will only cost £52, because the tax relief will boost your take-home pay. A 27 per cent taxpayer will pay £73. These extra payments are usually made as Additional Voluntary Contributions (AVCs). If you have the choice, it's a good idea to pay your AVCs to a second life-assurance company, instead of the one that manages your pension fund. This helps to spread risk, and can help to compensate for a poor return on the main fund. Pick a fund that has achieved a good investment record for the past five years.

Your company pension scheme may not allow you to invest with another life company. However, you may be able to decide which "fund" you want to invest in, however, ranging from an ultra-safe (but low-yielding) cash fund, to a more adventurous (and risky) aggressively managed fund. Most people take the middle road, and pick an ordinary managed fund.

AVCs should be paid on a regular basis, and are usually deducted from the company payroll. Some schemes will allow you to pay in a once-off lump sum before the start of the tax year on 6 April. Paying AVCs should boost your final pension, and may allow you to get a higher tax-free lump sum, but try not to stop and start AVC contributions. Remember, if you pay £1,000 gross extra per year in a regular premium AVC, all of this may be lost in charges and commission in year one.

Other Savings/Investments

Your scheme may not allow you to pay AVCs. Or, you might want a more flexible investment option, because AVCs made after 31 December 1990 are locked away until you retire. You can get a refund of AVCs made before that date (minus 25 per cent tax) *provided that* you have been with your employer for less than five years (see also "When You Leave your Job" in the Appendix).

The main alternative is to start your own unit-linked or "with profits" investment plan. Instead of paying £52 net into an AVC, you can pay £52 per month into a life-assurance plan that will mature when you are near the age of 60 or 65. Because you are getting no tax relief, your £52 is not equivalent to £100 gross of tax. Both AVCs and unitised investments carry a commission charge. On an AVC, the commission is determined by the length of years to retirement, while on unitised savings it is decided by the length of the investment (typically, 10–30 years). The maximum commission in either case is equivalent to 60 per cent of your first year's premiums. Insurance brokers who set up pension schemes are sometimes prepared to negotiate commission rates.

You can avoid commission costs by investing with An Post or a building society. This is a good option for people approaching retirement who can't risk losing any capital, but the returns may be low. Equitable Life is the only life-assurance company that never deducts a commission charge. It also offers flexible investment options.

Life companies warn against early encashment, but you can get your investment back, with some loss, in an emergency. You pay no tax on a lump sum from a unitised investment, and are not restricted in the way in which you use that money on retirement (unlike the AVC, which forms part of your pension fund).

So how do AVCs and a separate life-assurance savings plan compare?

	AVCs	Unit-linked or "With Profits" Plan
Tax?	Tax relief on premiums.	No tax relief on premiums.
Income from Annuity?	Proceeds are taxable.	Payout is tax-paid.
Investment Time Frame?	Limited access to funds.*	Access after roughly five years, but with early encashment penalty.
Flexibility?	Very little. Investment is locked up for years.	Some. Depends on investment choice.

* See "When You Leave Your Job" in Appendix.

Self-Administered Scheme

This is a special type of private pension scheme for directors of limited companies. Instead of putting your cash in life assurance-based investments, you can opt for high-yielding deposits, property and other alternatives — but still qualify for tax relief and tax-free profits in your fund.

The Finance Act, 1972 allows you to set up either a Small Self-Administered Scheme (companies with under 12 members) or a Self-Administered Scheme (companies with over 12 and/or those where the directors hold at least 20 per cent of the share capital).

Small Self-Administered Schemes must be supervised by a "pensioneer trustee", who in turn reports annually to the Revenue Commissioners. Investments, such as property, are also subject to stricter controls. Setting up an SSAS or an SAS can cost £1,500–£5,000, plus a yearly management charge. But they suit company directors who want a fund that avoids life industry charges and is under their control (even if they cannot withdraw the money until retirement). This is particularly true for older executives who need the safety of a deposit-based product.

There are roughly 50 Revenue-approved "pensioneer trustees" at present. Contact the Revenue Commissioners' Retirement Benefits section ((01) 679 2777) for details.

Personal Pension Plan

If you are self-employed, or your company does not have a pension scheme, you can take out a personal pension. As with a company pension scheme, you can claim tax relief on up to 15 per cent of your gross (pre-tax) income on pension-fund contributions, but to benefit from this tax break you must inform the Revenue Commissioners.

Directors of limited companies can claim even higher relief. The 1972 Finance Act entitles a limited company to full tax relief against corporation tax on payments made into a pension fund for its directors. The tax ceiling rises progressively with the directors' age, and is expressed as a multiple of their salary (see Chapter 12, Self-Employed, for details).

What is a Personal Pension?

This is essentially an investment contract taken out with a life-assurance company. You can opt for a regular premium investment, in which you pay a set sum (usually monthly or yearly) into your pension policy. Or, you can pay a series of once-off single premium (lump-sum) investments, each of which is an individual contract. Single premium investment is more suited to people who have an irregular income, because you may get penalised for breaking the conditions on a regular premium contract.

On a regular premium policy, the maximum commission is equal to 60 per cent of the first year's premiums, plus a yearly management charge. On a single premium investment, there is a once-off charge, which is roughly 3.5 per cent of the invested lump sum. You can sometimes avoid this charge by paying the insurance broker a fee, instead of commission.

Personal pensions are either based on a "with profits" plan, which gives some guarantee on your money, or a "unit-linked" plan, which doesn't (see also Chapter 3, Investments).

People with personal pension plans can draw their pension anywhere between the age of 60 and 70, and do not have to stop work before they retire. They need approval from the Revenue Commissioners to retire earlier.

How to Buy One

Speak to a good accountant and an independent broker before taking out a personal pension. The accountant will explain how to maximise tax relief on your pension investment. The broker will help you to shop around for a life-assurance company which has a good investment record and offers a flexible product that suits your needs. If you pick a broker who will charge a fee for their services instead of deducting a commission from your pension premiums, more of your pension premium will be invested in the fund. You may lose tax relief on the fees paid, however.

Seven Questions to Ask the Salesperson/Broker

(1) Does this pension plan carry any guarantees? What are they?

(2) Do I incur penalties if I:
  - Retire early?
  - Alter my premium payments?
  - Stop/start my premium payments?

(3) Is a single premium or regular premium contract better for me?

(4) Does this pension plan have an "open market" option? (in other words, can I shop around for an annuity when I retire?)

(5) If I add benefits to my plan (life assurance etc.), how will it reduce my final pension?

(6) How can I maximise my tax relief?

(7) How much should I pay in?

Don't fall for glossy brochures or the first life-assurance salesperson that you meet. All life-assurance products are basically the same, in that they fall into the "with profits" or unit-linked camps. But some pension plans are more flexible than others, and permit you to halt or alter your premium payments, for example. Equitable Life, which was mentioned earlier in this chapter, deserves a special mention because it does not charge commissions and offers a flexible product. Other life companies have achieved better investment results, however.

Remember that procrastination costs money. It's important to take out a pension early.

Improving Your Personal Pension

Making erratic regular contributions is wasteful, because you can lose a big chunk of money in broker commissions. Opt for recurring single premiums instead. Be wary of building life cover and other "protection" into your pension. You'll get tax relief, but it will eat up your premiums too. Insist on clear, regular statements from the life company.

Drawing Your Pension

You can take a quarter of the final accumulated fund as a tax-free lump sum, but must use the rest to buy an annuity. Many people with personal pensions take the annuity offered by their own life-assurance company. It's best to pick a personal pension that has an "open market" option, however, because this will allow you to shop around for the best annuity rate when you retire.

Buying an Annuity

Under Irish pension law, you must use a large part of your pension fund to buy an annuity. This applies to people who have a personal pension or a defined-benefit company pension.

To get an annuity, you must pay the life company a substantial lump sum. In return, you will get an agreed income for the rest of your life. It is usually paid monthly, and treated by the Revenue Commissioners as taxable income (see table, p. 184). The annuity is your "pension". Several factors decide the amount you get:

Your Age and Gender

The older you are, the larger the annuity rate (in general). Women get lower annuity rates than men, because they usually live longer than men.

Interest Rates When You Retire

Suppose that the life-assurance company quotes you an annuity rate of 9.95 per cent. Your £100,000 lump sum will buy an annuity of £9,950 per year (before charges) for as long as you live. A quote of 12.5 per cent will yield a £12,500 pension from the same lump sum. Ideally, you should buy an annuity when interest rates are high, but you may not have a lot of control over this. Self-employed people can retire between the age of 60 and 70, under the Revenue Commissioners' rulings. PAYE workers can usually only work past the age of 65 with their employer's consent.

The Size of Your Lump Sum

It stands to reason that £200,000 will buy twice as big a pension as £100,000.

Which Company You Pick

Some life-assurance firms quote better annuity rates than others. That's why it's good to be able to shop around.

What Sort of Contract You Want

You can pick an index-linked annuity which pays a slightly larger sum each year (and protects you against inflation), but this buys you a smaller pension at the outset. You can opt for a guaranteed contract, which will pay your pension for five years, even if you die shortly after retirement. Most married couples choose an annuity that pays a spouse's pension in the event of the annuity holder's death. This is in contrast with a single-life annuity, which ceases to pay any money after the guaranteed term expires. The life-assurance company keeps the proceeds from the lump sum.

Think about your annuity long before retirement. Otherwise, you may find that the lump sum will not stretch as far as you hope. Ideally, get professional advice and ask a reputable accountant or benefits consultant (at one of the large brokerage firms, such as Irish Pensions Trust or Coyle Hamilton) to shop around for your annuity. They will get the best rate for you.

To summarise, follow the steps in Flow Chart 1 on p. 190 to help maximise your pension income.

PREPARING FOR RETIREMENT

The process of actually claiming your pension(s) is shown in Flow Chart 2 on p. 191.

It's worth considering other points, like income. Income from your pension and other sources is taxable. It's important to keep filing an annual tax return (by 31 January of each year for the previous tax year) and to put away money for your tax bill, if necessary. Otherwise, you might accumulate a big debt. The Retirement Planning Council (tel: (01) 661 3139) can give valuable guidance, and refer you to specialists in the area of tax, social welfare and other topics, if necessary.

Do you want to remain in the family home? If not, don't sell in a hurry. Sheltered accommodation in purpose-built retirement "villages" can lead to complications. In addition to buying your new home — typically a bungalow or flat in a complex — you may have to pay up to thousands of pounds each year in service fees. Can you sustain that? Another option — signing over your house to a relative in return for care and accommodation — can create other difficulties, such as tension in the family. You may not get the level of care that you need. Hiring a live-in carer, on the other hand, will give you an extra £7,500 tax allowance in 1996/97, which can be used to reduce tax on income earned by you or your spouse.

If you are financially strapped, and need nursing-home care, you may get a means-tested subvention from your local Health Board. The three maximum rates of subvention are: £120, £95 or £70 per week, depending on the degree of care you need. If you have savings over £20,000, these will be taken into account when assessing your "means". Private nursing-home care is expensive, and can cost over £500 per week. Contact your local Health Board for details.

Weigh up your needs and options long before retirement. Seek professional advice, but don't act hastily, and try retain control of your affairs.

CONCLUSION

Saving £40 a month (or more) in your company or personal pension plan each month is a start, but it is not good pension planning. If you want a financially secure retirement, it's vital to invest enough money — and invest it well.

FLOW CHART 1: HOW TO IMPROVE YOUR PENSION

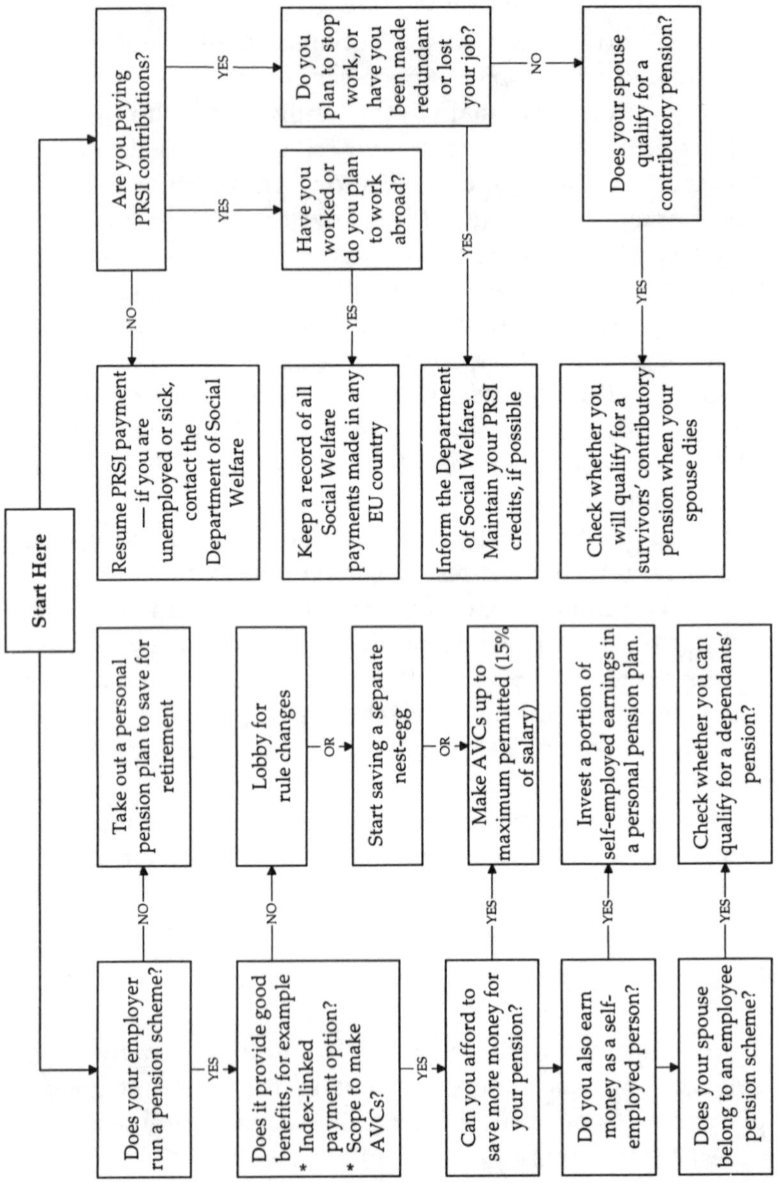
Start Here
Does your employer run a pension scheme?
NO
Take out a personal pension plan to save for retirement
YES
Does it provide good benefits, for example
* Index-linked payment option?
* Scope to make AVCs?
NO
Lobby for rule changes
OR
Start saving a separate nest-egg
OR
YES
Can you afford to save more money for your pension?
YES
Make AVCs up to maximum permitted (15% of salary)
Do you also earn money as a self-employed person?
YES
Invest a portion of self-employed earnings in a personal pension plan.
Does your spouse belong to an employee pension scheme?
YES
Check whether you can qualify for a dependants' pension?
Are you paying PRSI contributions?
NO
Resume PRSI payment — if you are unemployed or sick, contact the Department of Social Welfare
YES
Have you worked or do you plan to work abroad?
YES
Keep a record of all Social Welfare payments made in any EU country
YES
Do you plan to stop work, or have you been made redundant or lost your job?
YES
Inform the Department of Social Welfare. Maintain your PRSI credits, if possible
NO
Does your spouse qualify for a contributory pension?
YES
Check whether you will qualify for a survivors' contributory pension when your spouse dies

FLOW CHART 2: HOW TO CLAIM YOUR PENSION

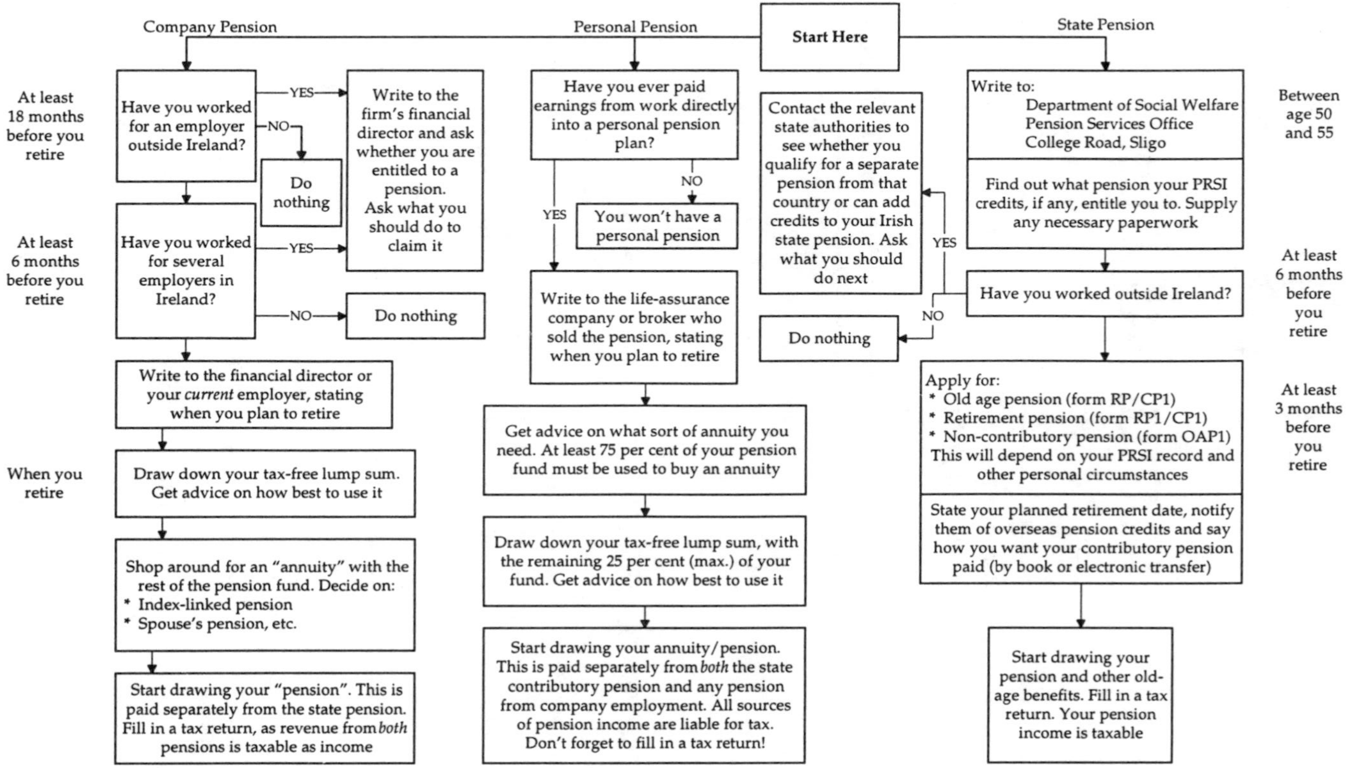

11

TACKLING TAX

"Tax reform is when you take taxes off things that have been taxed in the past and put taxes on things that haven't been taxed before."

Art Buchwald (b. 1925), US humorist

The 1996 Budget added almost £4 a week to a wage packet of a single person earning £15,000–£20,000. A married person, earning the same salary, gained roughly £2.50 (see Appendix, p. 304). However, their gains were nearly wiped out by the progressive erosion of tax relief on mortgage interest and VHI premium payments.

Overall, most people were confused by the tax and income implications of Ruairí Quinn's Budget. Most welcomed his efforts to help the long-term unemployed and low-income workers, but were unclear as to how the rejigging of PRSI changes, tax bands and other allowances affected them. This chapter explains the impact of the 1996 Budget on key *reliefs* and *allowances* claimed by ordinary company workers. A table showing how different income groups were affected by the Budget is also shown in the Appendix. This chapter is not just a Budget résumé, however. It explains how the Pay As You Earn (PAYE) tax system works, and offers tips on how you — as a PAYE worker — can boost your take-home pay by claiming all the reliefs and allowances that you can. It also introduces other taxes, and offers tips on how to pay less *and* keep the Revenue Commissioners happy. See pp. 203–8 for other taxes and tax-cutting tips.

THE PAYE SYSTEM

The tax year runs from 6 April to 5 April of the following calendar year. So the 1995/96 tax year ends on 5 April 1996, and the 1996/97 tax year starts the following day.

Reliefs and Allowances

You aren't taxed on your full income. All taxpayers get personal allowances, which exempt part of their earnings from tax. These allowances are determined by your marital status, employment status and age. Most single working people get the following allowances:

	1995/96	**1996/97**
Single Person's Allowance	£2,500	£2,650
PAYE Allowance	£800	£800
PRSI Allowance	£140	scrapped
Total	£3,440	£3,450

Broadly speaking, this means that the first £3,450 of your income is not taxed. Thereafter, the next £9,400 of earnings is taxed at 27p in the pound. Earnings above this are taxed at 48p in the pound. This is a simplification, however, as people on low incomes may be exempt from tax, or be taxed at a slightly lower rate than other taxpayers (see section, "Low-Income Earners", p. 201). Married people also get higher allowances (see p. 198). A married person who is the sole breadwinner now pays 27 per cent tax on the first £18,800 of their income, after allowances.

All income earners can also reduce their tax bill by claiming reliefs. These are not like allowances, which protect the first block of your income from tax. Reliefs are granted by the Revenue Commissioners if you decide to make certain investments. Tax reliefs reduce the amount of income that is taxed, but you have to spend money to get them. They include relief on mortgage interest repayments, VHI subscriptions, pension premiums and investments in Business Expansion Schemes (BES). Relief is usually given at a certain tax rate (27 or 48 per cent or a mixture of the two), and there is often a threshold or ceiling on this tax-relievable contribution.

For example, Joe earns £20,000 a year. An insurance salesman has said that he can invest up to 15 per cent of his gross salary in a pension in the tax year ending 5 April 1996 (1995/96 tax year) and claim tax relief at the marginal rate. He can put up to £3,000 per year in a pension scheme and claim tax relief. So his premiums will only cost £1,560.

For other reliefs, see "How to Cut your Tax Bill" below.

Note that government levies (such as the 1 per cent income levy which was scrapped in the 1994 Budget) and other mandatory contributions are docked from your gross (pre-tax) salary, rather than from your net (post-tax) salary. The most important of these is Pay Related Social Insurance (PRSI), which is used to fund state benefits, including your future pension. This is charged at a rate of 5.5 per cent on the first £22,300 of your income in 1996/97. The 1996 Budget scrapped the PRSI "allowance" of £140, a move which cost the 48 per cent tax-payer £67 per year. It also raised the amount of the salary on which you pay PRSI by £800 to £22,300. But it raised the amount of your weekly earnings that are exempted from PRSI from £50 to £80. Overall, 48 per cent tax-payers gained a maximum of £86 per year. Two other charges are still deducted from your total "gross" (pre-tax) salary. These are: the health levy (1.25 per cent on your total income) and the employment and training levy (1 per cent). This brings the total deductions to 7.75 per cent.

Because different parts of your salary are taxed at different rates, the Revenue Commissioners need to smooth out the impact. Otherwise, you'd be taxed at just 27 per cent at the start of the year, but leap to 48 per cent when you pass the £9,400 threshold. This is achieved with the help of *tax tables*. They permit your employer to deduct tax at a level rate throughout the year. Each month, you get one twelfth of the sum of your total allowances/ reliefs for the 12 months in the tax calendar.

HOW TO CUT YOUR TAX BILL

We've seen how maximising reliefs and allowances can cut your tax bill. So how do you claim these reliefs and allowances?

Around February each year, each PAYE worker gets a Tax-Free Allowance (TFA) certificate from the Revenue Commissioners. Your allowances and reliefs for the next tax year (starting 6 April) are listed on this certificate.

Here's an example:

Jane Smith works as a salesperson. She has a gross salary of £18,000 but gets Benefit-in-Kind (BIK) of £4,500 through the use of a Toyota Carina (value: £15,000 on which she does no business mileage). She pays a £250 premium to the VHI. Her mortgage is £35,000 and her estimated mortgage interest bill is £2,625 (based on a 7.5 per cent interest rate). The TFA certificate issued to her is shown on p. 199 (Source: Ernst & Young).

Here's what to do when you get your TFA certificate:

- Check whether your allowances are correct. A list of allowances is shown on p. 198. Which can you claim?
- Check whether the figures given for your tax reliefs are correct (see below).

If there are mistakes on the form or other allowances you can claim, fill in the "tax allowances" claim form which accompanies the TFA and post it to the Inspector of Taxes named on the TFA certificate. If you beat the 5 April deadline, the Revenue will send you an amended TFA certificate. This should boost your May salary cheque. If you send off the tax allowances claim form later in the year, you'll get a tax rebate.

Working out the reliefs is complex. The main ones are explained below. Cross-check them on the TFA certificate on p. 199.

RELIEFS

- Mortgage
- Medical Insurance
- Pension
- Rent Allowance

Mortgage

This is shown on the TFA as "home loan interest payable". It's based on the interest bill for both your mortgage and home-improvement loans in the coming tax year. The Revenue Commissioners use a complex formula to work it out. They give tax relief on a maximum interest ceiling of £2,500 (£5,000 for married couples) if you took out a mortgage before 6 April 1992. Then they take 80 per cent of your mortgage interest bill, less £200 for married people and £100 for a single person. In 1996/97, one quarter of your allowable mortgage interest bill gets tax relief at 48 per cent, and three quarters at 27 per cent.

Here's an example:

Jane Smith's interest bill on her mortgage was £2,625 in 1995/96. So the Revenue will give her relief on £1,900 in 1996/97 (which is 80 per cent of £2,500, less £100). A quarter of this sum — £475 — will get tax relief at 48 per cent, and three-quarters (£1,425) at 27 per cent.

So the sum looks like this:

48% of £475	=	£228.00
27% of £1,425	=	£384.75
Total Relief		£612.75

Jane is due a £612.75 cut in her income tax bill. To give her this sum, the Revenue gross *it back to £1,276.60, by dividing £612.75 by 48 and multiplying the result by 100. The £1,276.60 sum appears on Jane's TFA (see p. 199), and means that her non-taxable income has been increased by this sum. The mortgage interest relief formula will change yet again in the 1997/98 tax year, when all of Jane's qualifying mortgage interest will get relief at 27 per cent tax. To complicate matters further, if Jane had taken out her first mortgage after 6 April 1992, 100 per cent of her interest repayments (£2,500 maximum) would qualify for tax relief, not 80 per cent. See TFA certificate, p. 199.*

It's very confusing. How can you check whether the sums are wrong?

The TFA figure is a forward calculation. It shows what the Revenue Commissioners *think* you'll pay in mortgage interest in

1996/97. Most important, it is based on a predicted level interest rate. If you're locked into a higher rate — on a fixed-rate mortgage, for example — and your interest bill is below the top threshold (£2,500 for single people), ask the Revenue to change the TFA.

Get your bank or building society to confirm, in writing, what your mortgage interest bill will be in 1996/97. Send this letter to the Revenue Commissioners with the completed tax allowance claim form. If you're not on a fixed-rate mortgage, you'll have to wait until the end of the 1996/97 tax year to check whether the mortgage relief was accurate. Check the figure on your bank or building society's interest repayment certificate against the 1996/97 TFA figure. You can claim a refund if the Revenue underestimated your bill.

Medical Insurance Relief

This figure is based on the premiums you paid last year (1995/96). From 1996/97, all premiums will attract relief at the standard rate (27 per cent).

Jane Smith's VHI bill cost £250 last year. So she gets tax relief of £67.50 (£250 @ 27 per cent). This is "grossed" back up to £141 (£67.50 ÷ 48 x 100) on her TFA certificate (see p. 199).

Pension

This does not appear on your TFA, unless you have a personal pension plan. That's because people in company pension schemes get their tax relief when they pay their premiums through a "net pay" scheme of direct deduction — i.e., by paying lower premiums.

Rent Allowance

The 1995 Budget introduced a new "Rent Allowance" relief for tax-paying tenants. It is £500 for a single person, £750 for a widowed person and £1,000 for a married couple. But relief is only given at the standard rate.

The TFA is a marker for the next tax year. Having checked that all your existing allowances and reliefs are accurate, it's a good time to claim extra reliefs by making tax-efficient investments before 5 April.

ARE YOU CLAIMING THESE ALLOWANCES?

	1995/96	1996/97
Single Person	£2,500	£2,650
Married Couple	£5,000	£5,300
Widow/Widower	£3,000	£3,150‡‡
One-Parent Family Allowance:		
(a) Widowed Person	£2,000	£2,150
(b) Other Person	£2,500	£2,650
PAYE Allowance	£800	£800
PRSI Allowance	£140	scrapped
Incapacitated Child	£600	£700
Care of Incapacitated Person	£5,000	£7,500
Age 65+ (single)	£200	£200
Age 65+ (married)	£400	£400
Dependent Relative	£110	£110
Blind Single	£600	£700
Blind Married	£1,400	£1,600
Rent Allowance*:		
Single Person (under 55)	£500	£500
Widowed Person (under 55)	£750	£750
Married Person (under 55)	£1,000	£1,000
Single Person (over 55)	£1,000	£1,000
Widowed Person (over 55)	£1,500	£1,500
Married Person (over 55)	£2,000	£2,000
Maximum Mortgage Relief:†		
Single (80% of "gross" interest minus £100)‡	£1,900	£1,900
Married (80% of "gross" interest minus £200)	£3,800	£3,800
Local Authority Service Charge**	£150 (max.)	£150 (max.)
Charitable Donations††	£200–£750	£200–£750

* Relief allowances at standard rate (i.e. 27 per cent).

† First-time buyers qualify for relief on 100 per cent in the first 5 years of their mortgage.

‡ "Gross" figure is £2,500 for single people, £5,000 for married people. See also p. 196 for calculations. This did not change in the 1996 Budget.

** Relief allowed for actual service charges (excluding arrears) paid, up to maximum.

†† The Revenue Commissioners "top up" your donation to the charity by adding 27 per cent. You don't get the relief, but the charity does.

‡‡ Rises to £5,300 in the year of bereavement.

INCOME TAX PAY AS YOU EARN

NOTICE OF DETERMINATION OF TAX-FREE ALLOWANCES

The date of this Notice is 24 FEB 96

FOR THE YEAR 1996/97 AND FOLLOWING YEARS
COMMENCING 6 APRIL 1996

Ms Jane Smith
7 Lincoln Drive
Dublin 7

RSI No.	9876543A	When calling or writing to the **Tax Office - always quote the** RSI Number, the Employer Number and Unit Number.
Employer Number	3597264B	**Dept. of Social Welfare** always quote the RSI Number
Unit No.	612	

THE FOLLOWING DETERMINATION HAS BEEN MADE BY REFERENCE TO THE MOST RECENT INFORMATION AND TO THE LAW AT PRESENT IN FORCE.

ALLOWANCES and RELIEFS		DEDUCTIONS from Allowances & Reliefs	
SINGLE ALLOWANCE	2650	BENEFIT IN KIND CAR	4500
PAYE ALLOWANCE	800		
MEDICAL INSURANCE RELIEF 250 = ALLOWANCE OF	141		
TAX TABLE ALLOWANCE	4113		
HOME LOAN INTEREST PAYABLE 2500 = ALLOWANCE OF	1276		
Total	8980	**Total**	4500

Less Deductions from Allowances and Reliefs	4500
Annual Tax-Free Allowances determined	4480
Allocated to other employments (including spouse's, if in employment)	0
Tax-Free Allowance notified to your employer	4480

This amount and the Tax Table have been advised to your employer

BLOGGS & CO. LTD

MONTHLY Allowance	373.33
Weekly Allowance	86.15
TAX TABLE	B
Initial Tax Rate	48%

Issued By:
D. FOLEY
INSPECTOR OF TAXES
DUBLIN PAYE 4 DIVISION 98
HAWKINS HOUSE
HAWKINS STREET
DUBLIN 2 PHONE (01) 6775811

NOTES

1. The Tax Table and the Tax Rate have been determined on the basis of your estimated income. If your income exceeds this estimate tax may then be deducted at a higher rate.
2. When communicating with the Tax Office regarding this Notice you should always quote the RSI Number, Employer Number and the Unit Number (if shown).
3. If you have changed employment your should inform the Tax Office at once.
4. This form should be retained by you for future reference.

ACTION CHECKLIST

- Capital Acquisitions Tax ❑
- Deed of Covenant ❑
- Medical Expenses ❑
- Pension ❑
- Tax-based Investments ❑

Capital Acquisitions Tax

You can claim a £500 exemption on gifts made during the calendar year to 31 December. This applies to both cash and assets. The exemption is given on a calendar basis, and can be used to reduce gift-tax or inheritance-tax liability.

Action

Think about inheritance-tax planning (see Chapter 15). Then talk to an accountant.

Deed of Covenant

The 1995 Budget sharply restricted the use of covenants to pay for educational costs, but you can still use them to cut your tax bill. A covenant is a legal pledge to pay a sum for a period that can last at least 6 years (or the duration of third-level education, in the case of college-going children). However, you can still use a covenant to pay maintenance payments (to a separated spouse) or to pay for the support of an elderly person or for an incapacitated child (of any age). See Chapter 9, Children, for details on how the tax relief works.

Action

Work out what you can afford to pay each year. Then talk to an accountant.

Medical Expenses

If you haven't got a VHI medical insurance plan, then get one. It saves tax — albeit dwindling — and will help to protect you and your family from hefty medical bills.

You can also claim a refund for the 1996/97 tax year on medical expenses incurred up to 5 April which were not covered by the VHI. These include some consultants' fees, non-routine dental expenses (excluding cosmetic work, such as crowns), visits to your GP, diagnostic procedures, physiotherapy, prescription drugs, nursing-home costs, etc. The list includes expenses incurred by your spouse, children and other dependants.

The Revenue Commissioners will usually grant a refund at the end of the tax year. If you have large, recurring expenses, such as a nursing-home bill, your TFA may be amended. You cannot claim for the first £250 of expenses (£400 for a family) from 1 January 1996.

Action

Keep all your receipts and claim as soon as possible after 5 April. Fill in a MED 1 form (general medical expenses) or have your dentist fill in a MED 2 (dental costs) and send these, plus copies of receipts, to the Revenue Commissioners.

Pension

You can claim tax relief on premiums paid to a company or personal pension plan. The maximum ceiling is still 15 per cent of your gross (pre-tax) income. So, if you pay £4,000 into a pension scheme, it will cost just £2,080 thanks to tax relief.

If you're in a company pension scheme, and are below the 15 per cent contributions threshold, you can top up your pension premiums before 5 April with Additional Voluntary Contributions (AVCs). PAYE workers and self-employed people with personal pensions can make Retirement Annuity Contributions, which are similar to AVCs. Paying these before April 1996, for example, will also cut your 1995/96 tax bill.

Some PAYE workers contribute to both a company pension and to a personal pension, although the latter can only be taken out if they have additional "freelance" earnings. In this scenario, they can claim tax relief on 15 per cent of each income (separately) for pension purposes.

Action

Decide whether you can afford to pay a lump sum into your pension by 5 April. If you haven't got a pension, talk to an independent financial advisor.

Tax-based Investments

These include BES schemes, Section 23 film investments and property which qualifies for "Urban Renewal Allowances" (see Chapter 3 for details).

You can still invest £25,000 each year in a qualifying BES scheme and a further £25,000 in a Section 23 film project, and claim tax relief at the marginal rate. However, you can only claim tax relief on 80 per cent of your film-related investment. BES investors can claim relief at 48 per cent on their entire £2,500, but this may be clawed back if the scheme fails to meet tighter regulations. The investment thresholds are double for married couples if you both have an income in your own right. A £25,000 investment will cost a 48 per cent taxpayer £13,000, after tax relief.

You must invest this cash gross of tax (and supply the necessary paperwork) by 5 April 1996 to get relief in the 1995/96 tax year. The Revenue Commissioners won't send you an amended TFA unless you get it in early enough. You must claim a tax refund on your annual return, which can be filed after 5 April. Property investment is complex, and should not be leapt into as a last-minute tax dodge.

Action

See example in Chapter 3, Investments. Get literature on BES and film-investment schemes, but only commit cash you can afford to lose. These investments are tax-efficient, but involve commercial risk. Talk to a good accountant. Consider property investment as a longer-term option.

LOW-INCOME EARNERS

If you earn a very small wage, you may be exempt from tax altogether. This applies to people who earn slightly more than the total of their combined personal allowances and who would, ordinarily, be taxed on the balance.

People with dependent children who are just inside the 48 per cent tax net may qualify for marginal relief. This means that if your income exceeds the exemption limits but is less than twice the relevant limit, you only pay 40 per cent of the tax bill that you would normally have paid on your taxable income.

Here's an example:

A married person with two dependent children has income of £10,500 in 1996/97. Her income is in excess of the exemption limit of £8,700 (£7,800 plus £450 for each child). The tax bill is calculated as follows:

Income	£10,500
Less Married Allowance	£5,300
PAYE Allowance	£800
Taxable Income	£4,400
Taxable:	
£4,400 @ 27%	= £1,188
Tax Bill Restricted to:	
40% x (£10,500 – £8,700 (income exemption) =	£720

INCOME EXEMPTION LIMITS FOR 1995/96 AND 1996/97

Marital Status	1995/96	1996/97
Single and Widowed	£3,700	£3,900
Married Couples	£7,400	£7,800
Single and Widowed (aged 65+)	£4,300	£4,500
Married (either spouse aged 65+)	£8,600	£9,000
Single and Widowed (aged 75+)	£4,900	£5,100
Married (either spouse aged 75+)	£9,800	£10,200

Note: The income limits are increased for each dependent child as follows: First and second child (£450), third and subsequent child (£650).

OTHER TAXES

PAYE workers are very aware of income tax because it is deducted from their salaries. We pay many additional taxes, as well. The ones that concern most people are:

- Capital Acquisitions Tax (CAT)
  - — Gift Tax
  - — Inheritance Tax
- Capital Gains Tax (CGT)
- Probate Tax
- Residential Property Tax (RPT).

What are they, and how can you reduce the cost?

Capital Acquisitions Tax (CAT)

Broadly speaking, you pay CAT either when you receive assets as a gift (when the donor is still alive), or if you inherit them when the donor has died. The latter usually happens if you are left assets in a will or an estate. The amount of tax you pay depends on several factors:

- Whether the assets were received as a gift or inherited
- Your legal relationship with the donor
- The amount you receive.

See also Chapter 15, Wills and Inheritance Planning, for details of this tax, and tax-cutting tips.

Capital Gains Tax (CGT)

If you buy an asset — such as shares — and make a profit when you sell it, you may have to pay Capital Gains Tax (CGT) on this gain. This tax is charged at 40 per cent, except in the case of ordinary shares in small (unquoted) companies (27 per cent). If part of the gain was a result of inflation, and not of any real increase in value, you can reduce the CGT charge accordingly.

If you make a gain by selling an asset in another country — for example by cashing in your BMW shares — you are liable for CGT because they are deemed to be part of your "worldwide" income. A person who is tax resident here but not "domiciled" —

for example, a French person working on contract — only has to pay tax on income remitted back to Ireland from investments made outside Ireland and the UK.

Each person has an annual CGT allowance of £1,000. Married couples have a combined annual CGT allowance of £2,000.

Yvonne, who is single sells shares in AIB Bank on 25 February and makes a £2,000 profit. There is no tax charge on the first £1,000. Her tax bill (before indexation relief) is 40 per cent of £1,000, or £400.

Certain profits are exempt from CGT. These include any gain on the sale of the family home (which must also be your main residence) or a house occupied by a dependent relative, government gilts, life-assurance policies and deferred annuities. Assets with a life span of under 50 years — such as a car — are also exempt from CGT, as are lottery winnings, bets and similar windfalls. If you sell the family farm or business to a relative when you retire, you pay no CGT on this gain.

Tax-Cutting Tips

- Keep the CGT bill to a minimum by trying to keep your realised gains (profits from the sale of assets) to under £1,000 per year (£2,000 for a married couple).
- You can minimise the CGT charge on the sale of business assets (for example, shares in that company or machinery) by claiming *roll-over relief*. You have to reinvest the profits in similar assets, however.
- If your spouse transfers an asset to you, you don't pay a CGT charge.
- You can deliberately sell an investment that has made a loss, to help reduce the tax burden on a gain made elsewhere.

Yvonne also bought shares in a mining company, but these made a loss of £1,800. If she sells these shares before 5 April, she can wipe out the tax bill on her bank shares. She must sell them in the same tax year, however. Here's what the tax equation looks like:

Gain on AIB Bank Shares	£2,000
Loss on Mining Shares	£1,800
Net Gain	£200
Minus CGT Allowance	£1,000
Taxable Sum	Nil

Of course, Yvonne may prefer to hold onto her mining shares in the hopes that they recover. She could decide to sell just enough mining shares to cancel out her AIB Bank share gain.

Probate Tax

This is another form of inheritance tax. However, it is levied as a flat 2 per cent charge on the estate itself. It is not paid by the beneficiaries of a will, although probate tax may eat into the money that they finally receive. Spouses are exempt from probate tax, as are certain types of property. These include the family home and an estate valued at under £10,650. The probate tax charge on agricultural land and buildings is based on a 30 per cent reduction in the value of these assets.

See also Chapter 15, Wills and Inheritance Planning, for more details and tax-cutting tips.

Residential Property Tax (RPT)

This tax was not revised in the 1996 Budget. You must still pay RPT if your house is valued at £94,000 and the combined income of everyone in the home (spouse, children, etc.) is over £29,500. The rate is now 1.5 per cent.

You can still claim the following reliefs:

- If your combined household income is under £39,500 you can claim *marginal relief* — in other words, pay less tax.
- A 10 per cent cut in the bill for each child living at home (aged under 16, or older if incapacitated or a full-time student).

- If you are aged 65, or are widowed or incapacitated, you can claim these reliefs

  — The income of any resident who is not an owner and who is aged 65 or over, or is permanently incapacitated, is ignored.

  — If the (joint) owner/occupier of the house is aged 65 or over, the income of any other people (apart from the owner(s)) living there is ignored.

  — If the owner/occupier is widowed with dependent children, earnings of a live-in help should not be counted as part of "household" income.

  — Similarly, if the owner/occupier is permanently incapacitated, the earnings of a live-in nurse or home help need not be included.

  — People aged 65 or over can claim marginal relief on incomes up to £44,500.

The Revenue Commissioners may postpone the RPT charge in hardship cases.

The valuation should be made in the April before the tax is paid. If you receive an RPT form in the post, you must complete it, even if you are exempt from paying the tax. These forms are posted in August, and the tax must be paid and/or the form sent back by 1 October of each year. You don't need to have your house professionally valued. An estimate based on local selling prices and your own valuation is enough.

SAMPLE CHARGES (BEFORE RELIEFS)

House Value	RPT Bill
£100,000	£90
£120,000	£390
£150,000	£840
£200,000	£1,590

For further details contact:

The Revenue Commissioners
Residential Property Tax Section
Stamping Building
Dublin Castle, Dublin 2
(Tel: (01) 679 2777, Ext. 4626)

RPT/Tax-Cutting Tips

- If you and your spouse jointly own two residential properties (for example, a family home and a holiday home), consider putting a house in each person's name.

- You don't have to pay RPT if you live in an approved building which has historic, architectural, scientific or aesthetic merit, and if you open your house to the public and appropriate Revenue approval has been obtained. To apply for listing, contact:

  The Secretary
  Office of Public Works
  51 St Stephen's Green
  Dublin 2

- You can avoid paying RPT charge on a holiday home by renting it out for over 6 months of the year. This period must include 5 April.

- If you make alterations to your house to cater for an incapacitated person, you can *deduct* these costs from the house's value for RPT purposes.

OUTSIDE THE PAYE NET

What happens if you earn money outside your PAYE job? Simply put, you should treat yourself as a self-employed person as far as that income is concerned.

That entails filling in an annual tax return (no later than 31 January for the tax year ending the previous 5 April). People who hold company "directorships" must also do this, and face a hefty penalty if they don't. You should list all extra income sources on this form, including deposits that pay interest gross of tax (such as the credit union) and foreign bank accounts, rents, other income (including trading income and investment income). These non-PAYE *profits* are liable to income tax at either the standard rate of tax (27 per cent) or the marginal rate (48 per cent). However, you can reduce the tax bill in the *other income* category by claiming reliefs, allowances and costs.

You can also funnel up to 15 per cent of your "other income" into a personal pension plan and claim tax relief at the marginal rate. People who already belong to a company pension scheme may find this a useful way of cutting their non-PAYE tax bill and putting more cash aside for their pension.

However, you can only use certain Schedule D income for this purpose. This includes profits from:

- A trade
- Professional earnings, such as fee income
- Foreign salary not subject to PAYE.

These revenues are distinct from Section E income, which chiefly consists of your salary (see also Chapter 12, Self-Employed).

BENEFIT IN KIND (BIK)

PAYE workers pay tax on their "Schedule E" earnings. These sources of income include:

- Salary
- Benefits-in-Kind, — for example, Company Car, Subsidised Loans, Other Perks
- Bonuses.

Salary is taxed at the 27 and 48 per cent rates, as described above. Benefits-in-Kind (or BIK) are treated in a different way.

Company Car

The 1996 Budget gave a special perk for sales representatives, provided that they clock up at least 5,000 work-related miles per year and spend at least 70 per cent of their time away from the business premises. The perk allows them to reduce their benefit-in-kind tax charge by 20 per cent. If your employer normally provides a car for your use and pays all the running costs, you are taxed on the equivalent of 30 per cent of the car's original market value each year. For example, if you are an executive with a £25,000 car, you pay 48 per cent tax on £7,500 — which is £3,600. The new Budget perk will allow a rep to cut their BIK bill by 20 per cent, to £2,880.

If you clock up over 15,000 miles per year, you can also opt for a BIK bill based on your mileage. The charge decreases as the mileage figure rises. However, the tax charge will gradually rise in the 1996/97 tax year, as illustrated in the table below. The table shows the percentage of the BIK charge that the car user has to pay.

BIK/COMPANY CARS: HOW MUCH WILL YOU PAY?

Business Mileage (Lower Limit)	**95/96** %	**96/97** %
15,000	100	100
16,000	97.5	97.5
17,000	95	95
18,000	90	90
19,000	85	85
20,000	75	80
21,000	70	75
22,000	65	70
23,000	55	65
24,000	50	50
25,000	45	55
26,000	40	50
27,000	35	45
28,000	30	40
29,000	28	35
30,000	25	30
Over 30,000	20	25

Low-mileage users can also cut their BIK charge. For example, your 30 per cent bill drops by the following amounts if you pay for certain running costs yourself.

In the example below, the executive with a £25,000 car who does under 5,000 miles per year (and does not qualify for a 20 per cent cut in his BIK charge) can pay 48 per cent tax on 18.5 per cent of the car's original value, instead of 30 per cent, by paying for the following himself. This cuts the tax bill from £3,600, to £2,220.

Costs	Reduction
Petrol	4.5%
Insurance	3.0%
Repairs and Maintenance	3.0%
Road Tax	1.0%
Total	11.5%

Other ways of cutting the BIK company car bill:

- You can claim a reduction in BIK for each day that the car was unavailable for use by you or another family member — for example, if it was locked up in an airport car park during a business trip.
- Ask for a classic second-hand car instead of a new model. Because the original cost price is usually low, your BIK will drop accordingly.
- Give back the company car and ask your boss to pay you a Revenue-approved mileage rate instead. This is based on the vehicle's cc and mileage recorded by the employer (see the Appendix). It is supposed to cover petrol, repairs, tax, insurance and depreciation costs.

Subsidised Loans

If your boss gives you a loan at a preferential (below-market) rate, you should pay tax on this benefit. You pay tax on the difference between the interest you paid on the loan (if any) and the *specified* cost of this money. The specified cost is the interest rate set by the

Revenue Commissioners for this form of loan. In 1996/97, the specified rates are:

Loans to purchase/repair/improve your home	7%
Other loans	11%

Here's an example:

Joan, who is married, works for a finance company. She has a £50,000 mortgage subsidised by her employer at a preferential rate of 5 per cent. She paid £2,500 in mortgage interest in 1995/96. Her interest bill would have been £3,500 if she had been charged 7 per cent — which is the Revenue Commissioners' "specified" rate. The cash difference between the two is £1,000, and Joan has to pay 48 per cent tax on this. Her bill comes to £480, but she can claim mortgage interest relief on the full £3,500 — so she gets an extra perk. Because Joan is married, she can claim tax relief on the full £3,500, even though she has not paid all of it in cash. If she were single, she would not be able to claim this full amount because of her lower tax-relief threshold.

TAX PERKS AT WORK

PAYE workers get some benefits that are totally tax-free. These include the following:

- A lunch allowance (which must be agreed by the Revenue Commissioners) if you are working outside the office, or luncheon vouchers worth up to 15p per day
- Subsidised canteen meals, provided these are available to all employees
- Rent-free or low-cost accommodation on the business premises if this is required by the job
- Removal expenses, if you are posted to another location
- Staff entertainment, etc.
- "Golden handshakes"

- Pooled transport to the workplace
- Your company's contribution to the pension scheme. The scheme must be approved by the Revenue Commissioners
- Share in a Revenue-approved profit-sharing scheme
- Sporting and club facilities. These must be available to all employees
- Working clothes, tools, etc.

This is just a sample of the tax-free perks that your employer can give you. Ask a tax advisor for a full list.

VEHICLE REGISTRATION TAX (VRT)

The 1995 Budget introduced a new £1,000 "scrappage" scheme. This allows a person who is trading in a car aged 10 years or more to get a £1,000 discount on the price of VRT which is paid on a brand new car. You must have owned, taxed and insured the old car for at least two years to avail of the scheme. It will run until December 1996. For other details on VRT, see Chapter 14, pp. 258–60.

CONCLUSION

Tax is a big issue in Ireland. The top rate of income tax has dropped from 65 to 48 per cent since 1984, but we are hardly better off. Tax rates have fallen, but the reliefs and allowances which protect part of our salary against tax have not risen in line with inflation. Result? A larger part of our income is being taxed, albeit at a lower rate.

Tax evasion is illegal, but you can cut your income-tax bill by claiming legitimate reliefs and making tax-efficient investments.

These reliefs and allowances appear on your Tax-Free Allowances (TFA) certificate, which you receive from the Revenue Commissioners each January or February. You should check that the allowances and reliefs on your TFA certificate are accurate, and claim any new ones to which you are entitled. The end of the tax year (before 5 April) is also a good time to plan tax-efficient investments — if you can afford them.

The key issue is that you have to take the initiative. Unlike self-employed people, who calculate their own tax bill, PAYE workers have their incomes docked at source. It's up to you to reduce the tax bite, or claim a refund for qualifying expenses, such as medical costs. If you don't keep the receipts and claim the refunds you won't get it — it's as simple as that.

Other taxes — Capital Gains Tax (CGT), Capital Acquisitions Tax (CAT) and probate tax — are also hard to avoid. But you can minimise the tax bite through careful planning.

12

SELF-EMPLOYED

"A business with an income at its heels
Furnishes always oils for its own wheels."

William Cowper (1731–1800), "Retirement"

Life can be tough if you're self-employed or a contract worker. You have to sort out your own tax affairs under the "self-assessment" system (see below), unlike PAYE workers. You also have to arrange a pension, life assurance and PHI cover. If you fall sick, you can't claim disability benefit if you have been outside PAYE employment for over 18 months. Self-employed people also pay PRSI (Pay Related Social Insurance), but these contributions are only used to fund their pension. They don't provide short-term benefits such as sickness/disability pay.

However, there's good news, too. You can cut your taxable income by up to 25 per cent simply by taking out a pension and key "protection" policies. That gives you peace of mind, and a smaller tax bill.

SELF-ASSESSMENT

How Does it Work?

Under the old system (pre-1988), the Inspector of Taxes issued each self-employed person with an estimated tax bill. This estimate was based on the person's occupation and previous earnings. Delays were frequent, because taxpayers challenged the estimates and submitted their own figure. Under the self-assessment régime, you work out the tax bill and do most of the paperwork.

The new system is complex. Think of key dates in the tax calendar — 5 April, 1 November and 31 January — and use the 1996/97 tax year as an example.

The Deadlines

The 1996/97 tax year runs from 6 April 1996 to 5 April 1997. You have to pay a large chunk of your tax bill for 1996/97 by 1 November 1996, half-way through the year. This is called "preliminary" tax. It's not the full tax bill, but is either 90 per cent of the estimated liability for 1996/97, or exactly what you paid in 1995/96 (i.e. 100 per cent). If you miss the November deadline, you face an interest penalty of 1.25 per cent each month or part of a month thereafter.

You don't have to pay the balance until the 31 January after the tax year ends or within one month of the Revenue Commissioners confirming what your tax bill is. So the final settlement for 1996/97 isn't due until 31 January 1998 at the earliest. You must file an annual return for the 1996/97 tax year by the same date. This will list details of your earnings and expenditure (such as mortgage interest payments and other costs that qualify for tax relief).

> **Note**: From 1996/97 onwards, self-employed taxpayers can also pay their preliminary tax on a staggered basis by direct debit, instead of in one lump sum by 1 November of each year. You can opt for the 90 per cent or 100 per cent "rules" or pay 105 per cent of your tax bill for the pre-preceding year — 1994/95 — provided that you did have a tax liability that year. Then, you divide the chosen sum by 12, and start paying by monthly instalments from January 1996 to December 1996. You must still file your tax return by 31 January 1998, but have until 30 April to settle the final bill. If you plan to pay your preliminary tax in this way, tell the Revenue Commissioners (in writing) by 1 March 1996. If in doubt, talk to your local tax inspector or a fully-qualified accountant.

Preliminary tax can still pose a problem. How can you pay tax on income that you haven't earned yet?

Firstly, by saving part of your income each month for tax — ideally in a Special Savings Account (SSA) or another account that you can't dip into easily, but be conscious of the notice period required for withdrawals. Secondly, you can use the 90/100 per cent rule to juggle with payments. For example, if you paid £5,000 in tax for 1995/96, but expect your bill to be higher in 1996/97, you can legitimately pay £5,000 (by opting for the 100 per cent rule) on 1 November 1996, instead of paying a larger sum. You have until January 1998 to pay the balance. You can also cut your tax bill by taking out a pension, life assurance, permanent health cover or by investing in certain Revenue-approved investment schemes. But timing is critical.

Your business "status" is also important. Sole traders and partnerships are not treated in the same manner for tax purposes as directors of limited companies. This has a direct impact on pension planning and other aspects of your personal finances, as shown below.

CONTRACT WORKERS

"Fixed-term" contract workers account for a growing percentage of employees in the 1990s job market. Indeed, contract work is the only option for many college leavers.

Unfortunately, contract work should carry a "wealth warning". Unless you plan your finances carefully, it can do them a lot of harm.

If you are employed on a "Contract for Services", you are treated by the employer as an independent contractor. Essentially, you are a self-employed person and must pay your own income tax, PRSI (on a voluntary basis, if you wish) and pension contributions. You may also be denied benefits that permanent co-workers take for granted, such as sick pay, maternity leave, paid holiday leave (or any holidays at all), the protection of the Unfair Dismissals Act and the right to a lump-sum payment in the event of redundancy.

However, if you are hired on a "Contract of Service", you become a company employee (either full- or part-time) for the agreed period of time. Tax and PRSI will be deducted from your wages, and you are entitled to all the benefits above, plus paid holiday leave of at least three weeks a year (if you are a full-time worker). You will probably not be able to join the company pension scheme, however.

A "Contract of Service" gives you more protection as an employee. If you are hired on a "Contract for Services", you are really a self-employed person; read the following section to see how this affects your financial planning. It can be illegal for a company to hire workers on a series of rolling, short-term contracts to deny them rights under employment law. If this happens to you, talk to your union, a solicitor and/or the Department of Enterprise and Employment.

SOLE TRADERS/PARTNERSHIPS

Below is a shopping list of "needs" that you can satisfy while cutting your tax bill at the same time. At this stage we'll assume that you are a contract worker, sole trader or in a business partnership. If you're a director of a limited company, see pp. 223–6.

7-POINT CHECKLIST

(1)	Pension	❑	p. 218
(2)	Life Assurance	❑	p. 220
(3)	Mortgage	❑	p. 220
(4)	Car, or Other Vehicle	❑	p. 221
(5)	PHI	❑	p. 221
(6)	Critical Illness Cover	❑	p. 222
(7)	VHI, or Alternative Cover	❑	p. 222

(1) Pension

Self-employed people who can't join a company pension scheme may take out a personal pension plan. Chapter 10 explained how to buy a personal pension, so this chapter will deal only with the tax issues.

Suppose that you haven't got a pension plan already. If you sign a legally binding contract with a life-assurance company to take out a personal pension on or before 31 January 1997, you can claim full relief on your 1995/96 tax bill. This is the tax year that ends on 5 April 1996. You don't have to pay the pension premium (also called a Retirement Annuity Contribution) *until* 31 January 1997 (the deadline for filing the 1995/96 annual return). You can choose when filing your 1995/96 return to have relief set against your 1995/96 tax liability. But if you break the commitment, you will face a tax penalty.

Like PAYE workers, self-employed people can only claim relief on pension premiums equivalent to a ceiling of 15 per cent of their income. In their case, their net relevant earnings — income after costs and PRSI charges are deducted — is used as the benchmark, instead of salary. Here's an example:

Jack is a carpenter. He wants to start a personal pension. His net relevant earnings were £15,000 in 1995/96, so he pays up to £2,250 into a personal pension plan and claims full tax relief on that sum. He must pay the full pension premium of £2,250 on or before 31 January 1997, but can claim tax relief at 48 per cent. In effect, his premium will "cost" just £1,170. When he settles his final tax bill, he can deduct £2,250 from his taxable income. If he has already paid his full tax bill, he should qualify for a tax refund.

When Jack gets a copy of his personal pension contract from the life company, he must send a copy to his Inspector of Taxes in support of the claim made when he submitted his tax return.

Jack will probably invest a once-off lump sum into a pension plan. This is called a single premium investment. Alternatively, he may prefer to start a regular premium plan, which commits him to paying a fixed sum every month or year. He can claim tax relief on both sorts of pension contributions.

Self-employed people who have fluctuating incomes often prefer to save through a series of once-off lump-sum payments. This is called a recurrent single-premium investment. Each pension contract is separate from the other, unlike a regular premium plan, which grows as you pay in money each month/year, and the upfront charges are lower (see Chapter 10, Your Pension). If you can afford it, it's better to save a fixed monthly or annual sum into a regular premium plan and put any spare cash in a single premium plan at the end of the year. This disciplines you into regular saving, and allows you to "top up" the pension as required. It also spreads the risk, because you can take out separate policies with different life-assurance companies.

(2) Life Assurance

Tax relief on life-assurance premiums has been abolished. However, self-employed people who take out personal pensions can allocate up to 5 per cent of the 15 per cent tax relief ceiling for life-assurance cover.

To qualify for tax relief, the life assurance must be part of the pension contract. You can add it on to an existing pension policy, but you can't take out life cover with a separate assurance company. You must meet the same deadlines to qualify for tax relief, namely, 31 January (for payment of premiums).

Susan's net relevant earnings are £20,000, so her 15 per cent tax relief ceiling is £3,000. She can put all of this into a pension plan, with up to £1,000 for life-assurance cover. That would provide far more life cover than she needs, so she decides to allocate just £360 (£30 per month) for her life-assurance cover.

> **Warning!**
> "Bundling" life assurance into your pension contract will earn tax relief, but less of your cash will go towards your pension nest egg. Before taking out the plan, insist on two separate "illustrations" that show how fast the fund might grow with, and without, life assurance included. Shopping around for separate life cover may even prove cheaper.

(3) Mortgage

You can claim tax relief on mortgage interest repayments on your own home. If the house is also being used for business purposes — office space, for example — the situation is more complex. The Revenue Commissioners allow you to split the property for tax purposes. This means that you can claim tax relief on mortgage interest repayments for the part that is used as the family home. Costs relating to the business part — such as mortgage interest repayments, electricity, phone, etc. — can be deducted from your business profits.

Here's an example:

Harry is married and an architect. He paid mortgage interest relief of £5,000 in 1995/96. He uses a quarter of the family home as an office, so he can write off 25 per cent of the mortgage interest repayments — £1,250 — as a trading expense. This will be deducted from his consultancy income.

All of the remaining £3,750 qualifies for mortgage interest relief. See Chapter 11 for how this is calculated.

If you have two properties — a family home and a business premises — they will be treated separately for tax purposes. You can claim mortgage interest relief on the main property and write off expenses on the business property against your trading profits.

See also section on "Owner/Occupier" reliefs, p. 229.

Warning!

Using part of the house as a business premises may result in you paying a commercial, rather than a residential, mortgage rate. This may increase your monthly repayments. You might even have to pay some business rates. Using part of the house for business may also result in a Capital Gains Tax (CGT) liability on that part when the house is finally sold.

(4) Car, or Another Vehicle

If you use the car for business, you can claim expenses for it, including a proportion of running costs — insurance, maintenance, road tax, fuel, etc. — on your profit and loss account. But if the car is also used for domestic purposes, the claim may not be fully allowed. Keep all your invoices for the current tax year and include this information when you file the annual return. You can also claim capital allowances if you are buying a vehicle. This effectively writes off the cost of the car over seven years, subject to a maximum of £14,000. It's quite complicated, so talk to an accountant.

You can reclaim VAT if you buy a van and you are registered for VAT. You can reclaim VAT on diesel purchases, both for vans and cars. Keep all your receipts.

(5) Permanent Health Insurance (PHI)

PHI cover is useful if you are self-employed, as self-employed people can't get disability benefit from Social Welfare.

Unlike pension premiums, which can be used to reduce your tax bill in the previous tax year, PHI premiums must be written off against earnings in the current tax year. The maximum tax relief you can claim is equivalent to 10 per cent of your net relevant earnings in that year.

Michael is a computer programmer who earns a regular contract-based income of about £30,000 per year. He is anxious to protect his earnings, so he takes out PHI cover, which will replace up to two-thirds of his income, minus state Disability Benefit if he is unable to work because of disability.

Michael takes out a PHI policy on 5 July 1996 which commits him to paying £100 per month. He knows that his premium bill will be £900 in the tax year ending 5 April 1997, so he can factor this into his preliminary tax bill for 1996/97. If he is following the 90 per cent rule, and paying 90 per cent of his estimated 1996/97 tax liability on 1 November 1996, Michael can base his tax bill on a £29,100 income instead of £30,000.

(6) Critical Illness Cover

This is a policy issued by a life-assurance company which pays an agreed lump sum if the policyholder gets a serious illness covered by the insurer. Some policies also pay a daily cash sum if the person is hospitalised for any reason. You cannot claim tax relief on premiums paid into a critical illness policy, but the proceeds are paid tax-free.

(7) VHI, or Alternative

This reimburses you for specific medical expenses, such as a hospital stay, surgery, etc. These premiums used to be fully tax deductible at 48 per cent, but in 1996/97 they will qualify for tax relief at the 27 per cent rate. To complicate matters, your tax relief in any year is based on the premiums paid in the previous year. Here's an example:

Martina is a tour operator. She wants to settle her 1996/97 tax bill. Martina's VHI premium in 1995/96 was £233.56, but this only qualifies for relief at 27 per cent. Because the Revenue Commissioners give her tax relief of £63.06, Martina's VHI premium really costs just £170.50.

Starting Out as a Sole Trader

When people start their own business, they often find it hard to separate their personal finances from those of their business. This can be useful, because as a sole trader you can offset losses in the business against your personal income — thereby reducing the tax bill. On the other hand, swamping your current account with sales revenue is not a good idea. It's better to allocate yourself a small income, and open separate accounts for the business. You will need to keep clear financial records to see whether you are making a profit or a loss.

Get advice early, and try to keep your books and tax affairs in order. The Revenue Commissioners will already know from your P45 that you have left PAYE employment. Contact them to find out what your new reporting obligations are for PAYE (if you are employing another person), PRSI, VAT and income tax. If in doubt, contact a good accountant. If you're afraid of being distracted by tax and book-keeping worries, why not hire professional help to get the job done properly?

DIRECTORS OF LIMITED COMPANIES

Incorporating your business as a limited company has several advantages. As a company director, your personal assets are protected against creditors if the business fails. However, the Companies Act prohibits you from trading "recklessly". You can raise finance by issuing "share capital" in the company. Becoming a director in a limited company also gives you more scope for personal financial planning. This may suit older business people, who are anxious about their pensions (see also below).

Here's the checklist that we used for the sole trader. How does being a director in a limited company affect your tax situation?

CHECKLIST

(1) Pension	❑	p. 224
(2) Life Assurance	❑	p. 225
(3) Mortgage	❑	p. 225
(4) Car	❑	p. 226
(5) PHI	❑	p. 226
(6) Critical Illness Cover	❑	p. 226
(7) VHI, or Alternative Cover	❑	p. 226

(1) Pension

Sole traders are limited by the "15 per cent rule" when they pay into a pension scheme. Company directors aren't. The company can pay a percentage of the director's annual salary into a pension scheme and claim relief against corporation tax (10 or 38 per cent, depending on the nature of the business). The percentage is not fixed, and rises sharply as you — the director — approach retirement age. It is also determined by gender.

The table below shows the maximum that your company can pay into a pension scheme on your behalf (expressed as a percentage of salary, assuming no other benefits in force).

HOW MUCH CAN YOUR COMPANY PAY ON YOUR BEHALF?

	Female		Male	
Age Next Birthday	To Age 60 % of Salary	To Age 65 % of Salary	To Age 60 % of Salary	To Age 65 % of Salary
25	37.99	24.91	36.85	24.18
30	47.18	30.73	45.56	29.61
35	56.69	38.36	57.33	36.77
40	76.74	48.94	73.32	46.51
45	102.99	63.57	97.89	59.81
50	152.94	86.07	144.61	80.27
55	296.89	128.96	279.74	119.18
59	1,426.58	211.38	1,342.33	194.28
60	—	251.98	—	231.38
61	—	312.55	—	286.78
62	—	413.84	—	379.20
63	—	613.88	—	562.51
64	—	1,213.31	—	1,111.79

Note: Women can have a higher multiple of their salary paid into a pension scheme because they need to build a bigger nest egg to fund the same pension as a man (see Chapter 8). The Revenue permits two different scales to be used, depending on whether you plan to retire at the age of 60 or 65.

The maximum pension the company can fund is limited to two-thirds of your final salary. This can include a spouse's pension, and other benefits. If you have another pension plan, the company won't be able to pay as much into the scheme for you.

This arrangement has many advantages. In effect, the pension scheme is a tax shelter, because you can put a large chunk of your profits into a tax-free pension fund. Assets in the pension fund cannot be touched if the business fails. Last but not least, you can start drawing your pension as early as 50 years of age.

Pension schemes can be funded for more than one director — resources permitting.

> **Note**: Company directors who are close to retirement, and want to pay large chunks of money into their pension fund, have another option. They can set up a Self-Administered Scheme (SAS) with the approval of the Revenue Commissioners. See also p. 184 in Chapter 10, Your Pension.

(2) Life Assurance

This is also tax deductible, in certain circumstances. It has to be part of the pension package, and can pay a maximum death-in-service benefit of four times your salary. To qualify for the relief, this cover must normally lapse when you retire, but it may still pay out in the event of early retirement (before 65). Ask the insurance company before taking out the policy. Premium costs can be deducted from the company's profits for corporation-tax purposes.

(3) Mortgage

There are many possibilities here. If the company owns the business premises property, it can deduct mortgage interest payments — and other costs associated with the building — from its annual profits. Thus, if the interest bill is £5,000 and the annual profits £50,000 in 1996/97, the declarable profits will drop to £45,000. If the company owns the house you live in, you may be liable to pay Benefit-in-Kind (BIK) on the free rent.

If you own the business premises and lease them to the company, you can deduct mortgage interest payments from rental "profits" earned on the building. There is no ceiling on the interest repayments, which can be written off against tax. Limited companies do not qualify for "owner-occupier" reliefs. See p. 229.

(4) Car

You are liable for Benefit-in-Kind (BIK) on 30 per cent of the car's original value, regardless of whether you are an employee or company director. You can cut the bill in certain circumstances, however (see pp. 209–11 in Chapter 11, Tackling Tax).

(5) PHI

If you draw a salary from the company, and pay your own PHI premiums, you can claim full tax relief on them. If the company pays, it can write the cost off against its corporation tax bill.

(6) Critical Illness Cover

Neither you nor the company can claim relief on these premiums. Payouts on the policy are tax-free, however.

(7) VHI, or Alternative

If you pay your own premiums, you get the same tax relief as a sole trader (see p. 222). If the company pays the premium, you can still claim this relief from the Revenue Commissioners. But there is a snag. The relief that you get in 1996/97, for example, will be based on premiums paid in the previous tax year (1995/96), but you will be liable for BIK tax on the benefit received in the current year (1996/97). If the premiums go up in the second year, you face a shortfall. Note that relief is being restricted.

SOLE TRADER *v.* LIMITED COMPANY?

Opting for limited-company status is a big decision, and should not be seen as a "quick-fix" solution for financial problems, such as an under-funded pension.

Limited companies must be registered at the Companies Registration Office, Dublin Castle. There is an initial fee of £165, plus 1 per cent of the issued share capital (minimum one £1 share). The company must have at least two directors, one shareholder and a registered address.

Directors' Duties

Directors have clearly defined obligations. You must ensure that the company keeps proper financial records and files annual accounts at the Companies Registrations Office. The first set of annual accounts must be filed within 60 days of the company's first AGM (annual general meeting), which should be held within 15 months of incorporation. There is a £10 annual fee when filing accounts. This rises to £150 if the accounts are submitted over 77 days after the due date. Directors who fail to file annual accounts may be brought to court and their company struck off the register. You must update their file at the Companies Office if the company changes its directors or its registered address.

Directors also have to comply with key provisions in the Companies Acts. These include the responsibility to stop trading if the company becomes insolvent.

If you are a sole trader, you do not have to file information at the Companies Office, or publish annual accounts. Nor are you bound by regulations in the Companies Acts. However, you must comply with employment regulations, health and safety law and tax obligations.

A partnership is similar to sole-trader status, but duties and financial commitments are shared equally by all partners. If the business fails, your personal assets and those of your partner — including your family homes — may be at risk. However, your respective spouses may also have a stake in the home, thus protecting it from creditors.

WHICH ONE TO CHOOSE?

Business Status	Pros	Cons
Limited Company	Owner protected *v.* Business losses. May qualify for 10% tax. More flexibility with pension planning etc.	Must file annual accounts at Companies Office, plus other detailed information. Directors have strict legal obligations.
Sole Trader/ Partnership	Does not have to file annual accounts at Companies Office, etc. Simpler reporting duties and legal obligations.	Taxed at 48%/27%. Personal assets (including family home) exposed to creditors. Less flexibility with pension planning, etc.

Tax

Limited companies and sole traders/partnerships are taxed differently. In simple terms, company directors pay income tax on their salary, and corporation tax (10 or 38 per cent) on any company profits. Thanks to the 1996 Budget, all companies can pay corporation tax at 30 per cent on their first £50,000 of annual taxable income.

THE SELF-EMPLOYED TAXPAYER'S CALENDAR

Date	What it Signifies	Action
5 April 1996	End of 1995/96 Tax Year	
6 April 1996	Start of 1996/97 Tax Year	Start collecting mortgage interest statements, P60 form,* etc. for 1995/96.
1 Nov. 1996	Deadline for Preliminary Tax 1996/97	Avail of tax reliefs (e.g. pension contributions) before paying tax. Pay 90% of estimated 1996/97 liability, or 100% of 1995/96 bill.
31 Jan. 1997	Deadline for Settling 1995/96 Tax Bill	Pay outstanding tax if an assessment has been raised (i.e. tax sought) and file return, using information from mortgage interest statements, P60 form,* etc.
5 April 1997	End of 1996/97 Tax Year	Start collecting statements, etc. For 1996/97.
6 April 1997	Start of 1997/98 Tax Year	
1 Nov. 1997	Deadline for Preliminary Tax 1996/97	Follow 90% or 100% rule.
31 Jan. 1998	Deadline for filing 1996/97 Tax Return	File annual return, using gathered information.
30 April 1998	New deadline for settling 1996/97 tax bill	Start paying your preliminary tax by direct debit, but inform the Revenue in writing by 1 March 1996.

* If you are paying PAYE.

If you are a company director and a PAYE worker, you must file an annual tax return, even if you earn no income from your directorship. If you miss the 31 January deadline, you face a 10 per cent interest surcharge on your entire tax bill. That includes tax already paid under the PAYE system.

If you're a sole trader or partner, you pay income tax (27 or 48 per cent) on your annual revenues. You must submit your business/personal information on the annual return, not later than 31 January of each year. You face a surcharge of 1.25 per cent per month, or part of a month, thereafter if you file the return late.

"OWNER/OCCUPIER" RELIEFS

Thanks to the "designated areas" scheme, business people who buy a refurbished property to work/live in — such as a shop with an overhead flat — can qualify for tax relief on their income. The scheme was introduced on 1 August 1994 and expires on 31 July 1997.

You can reduce your income-tax bill by 10 per cent of the "qualifying cost" of the premises each year, for 10 consecutive years. If you buy new, as opposed to refurbished, premises, the tax allowance is halved to 5 per cent over the same 10-year period. To get the tax back, you must use the property as your sole or main residence.

If you sell the property within 10 years, the tax reliefs granted up to that time will not be "clawed back". You cannot transfer these reliefs to the new purchaser. This relief is available both in the "designated areas" and "designated streets". It can be claimed in addition to mortgage interest relief.

You can still claim Section 23-type reliefs on rented residential accommodation. In short, this means that you can write off rental profits against the cost of buying the new premises (see Chapter 3 for details). Here's an example:

Michael buys a refurbished unit for £60,000. He can claim relief on a qualifying tax cost of £50,000, because £10,000 is deducted for the site cost. He opens a shop in the unit and lives in a flat on the same premises. We'll assume Michael is a sole trader who pays tax at the 48 per cent rate.

Contract Price	*£60,000*
Qualifying Tax Cost	*£50,000*
<u>Cash Value of Relief</u>	
Annual Allowance, £50,000 @ 10%	*£5,000*
Tax Relief at 48%	*£2,400*
Cash Value over 10 Tax Years	*£24,000*

OTHER BUSINESS/PERSONAL TAXES

It is often said that the Revenue Commissioners can reach out beyond the grave! This means that your estate may be liable for tax when you die, and the beneficiaries — including close relatives — may also have an inheritance-tax bill (see also Chapter 11, Tax, and Chapter 15, Wills and Inheritance Planning).

CONCLUSION

Company directors, self-employed people and contract workers must take their personal financial planning seriously. They have few safety nets. They don't qualify for short-term Social Welfare benefits, like sickness/disability cover, because their PRSI contributions are used to fund their state pension, and they must provide for their own privately funded pension.

On the plus side, being your own boss is rewarding. With a bit of thought and planning, you can meet key needs — such as buying a car, home, business premises and taking out a pension — and reduce your tax bill in the process. The key thing is to understand how "self-assessment" works, and work with it. If in doubt, get advice but don't make hasty decisions based on tax needs alone, especially when buying a pension. All pension plans offer the same tax relief, but some are more suitable than others. Get a product that matches your needs. That means one that is flexible, has shown a good historical rate of return, and has a low cost.

13

BUDGETING

"A poor man's debt makes a great noise."

English Proverb

You don't have to be in financial trouble to need a budget. In fact, having one is a good way of avoiding problems in the first place.

Even high-income earners can find it hard to meet all the outgoings each month — the mortgage, tax, family car, their children's special educational needs, insurance and investment plans. It all adds up. The situation is more precarious for people living on a small wage, social welfare payments, or a pension/redundancy payout. Christmas, or a death in the family, or marital breakdown can put a huge strain on their home finances. That's where budgeting can help.

This chapter looks at ways of managing your money from month to month. In the past, people used to budget by stashing coins in a jar or putting away money in envelopes for the gas or electricity bill. This still works for some, but you can use quite sophisticated financial products and services, too. You can also get advice and help from different sources. Knowing where to turn if you fall behind with your mortgage repayments or get into debt is crucial.

DRAWING UP A BUDGET

TABLE A: YOUR MONTHLY OUTGOINGS

Home Bills		
	Electricity	£
	Gas	£
	Other Heating	£
	Telephone	£
	House Insurance	£
	Water/Refuse/Rates/Service Charges	£
Other Costs		
	VHI (or other medical insurance)	£
	TV (licence, rental, repayments)	£
	Holiday Expenses	£
	Entertainment Expenses	£
	Sports/Hobbies/Clubs	£
	Food, Household Items	£
	Fares to Work	£
	Clothing	£
Car(s) etc.		
	Road Tax	£
	Insurance	£
	Petrol	£
	Repairs etc.	£
Miscellaneous, e.g.		
	Savings/Investment Plans etc.	£
	Life Assurance etc.	£
	Other	£
Credit Commitments		
	Mortgage	£
	Car Loan	£
	Washing Machine etc.	£
	Credit Card	£
	Store Cards	£
Total Monthly Costs		**£**

TABLE B: YOUR MONTHLY INCOME

Salary (after tax and other deductions)	£
Guaranteed Overtime/Bonus (after tax etc.)	£
Payments/Commission	£
Income from Savings	£
Partner's Salary (after tax etc.)	£
Partner's Guaranteed Overtime/Bonus (after tax etc.)	£
Partner's Payments/Commission	£
Partner's Income from Savings	£
Social Welfare Payments, e.g. Child Benefit	£
Total Monthly Income	**£**
Total Monthly Costs	**£**
Balance	**£**

You have to know what you're spending before you can budget. The "Budget Planner" which appeared in Chapter 5 is divided above into two tables, A and B. Table A is for your expenses only. There's a new section at the bottom called "Credit Commitments" for other outgoings, such as the mortgage, car loan, hire purchase plans, credit card etc. Table B is for your sources of income. It has a new section for social welfare payments.

Work out what you spend each month. Does it match your income? Is there any spare cash left?

There are two solutions if you're spending more than you earn: spend less, or generate more income. Looking at the budget planner may help to cut or eliminate some costs. You can also restructure your debts, by remortgaging or paying off your credit-card borrowings, for example. We'll deal with those issues later in "Mortgage Arrears". Let's assume that you aren't in serious debt and just want to manage your money better, perhaps because you have separated from your spouse or partner. Here are six tips to help you to achieve this. Each tip is elaborated on below.

- Start Saving
- Open a Credit Union Account
- Borrow More Cheaply
- Sort Out Your Tax
- Claim What You're Entitled to
- Avoid Bank Charges.

Start Saving

Putting away just £20 a month can grow a healthy nest egg. If you pick the right investment, you'll be able to get cash in an emergency — if your car is written off, for example — but you won't be able to dip into it *too* easily.

Don't use a unit-linked savings plan or an ordinary deposit account, for precisely these reasons. Try a Special Savings Account (if you haven't got one already) or an An Post product, such as National Instalment Savings or Savings Certificates/Bonds (see also Chapter 2, Savings).

Open a Credit Union Account

This can give you access to funds, for example, in an emergency or at Christmas (see Chapter 4, Borrowing).

Borrow More Cheaply

Borrow as cheaply as possible. Don't pile up debts on a credit card. The interest rates are punitive. Restructure borrowings if necessary by taking out a credit union or personal loan.

Sort Out Your Tax

Don't pay surcharges for late payment. Claim all the reliefs and allowances that you can.

Claim What You're Entitled to

Find out whether you're entitled to claim more Social Welfare benefits.

Avoid Bank Charges

Choose a current account that doesn't have charges if you stay in credit. Better still, pick one that also pays interest on credit balances.

You can use financial products to help you to budget more efficiently. These include:

- Budget Accounts
- Savings Accounts
- Household Budget Scheme.

Budget Accounts

The main banks offer accounts that help to spread costs throughout the year and enable you to pay big bills, such as your car or household insurance. They all work on the same principle. You add up your annual bills (by using the Budget Planner on pp. 232–3, for example), add a percentage increase for inflation, and then divide by 12. You then arrange for this sum to be transferred into your budget account each month (usually from your current account).

This account is for paying bills. You can make payments with a cheque book, standing order or a direct debit facility. The account may go into the red if you make a large payment, but you'll have a credit balance at other times.

Banks usually charge a small quarterly fee for these accounts, plus an interest penalty during the months when you have to "borrow" money, and they may not pay interest on credit balances.

Savings Accounts

A savings account topped up by a direct debit each month can serve a similar purpose. Say your domestic bills average roughly £100 per month, but often fall together. You might also have a problem setting cash aside to pay them. Why not build a cash reserve by transferring £100 into a separate account each month? You can then dip into this account when payments coincide.

Household Budget Scheme

This facility is operated for the Department of Social Welfare by An Post. If you are getting unemployment benefit or assistance, you can arrange to pay certain bills by having money deducted from your welfare payments. The scheme covers the following:

- Local authority rents and mortgages
- ESB bills
- Gas bills
- Telephone bills.

You can only use the scheme if you're getting an unemployment payment and are being paid via the Postdraft method (at An Post). Only 25 per cent of your payment can be earmarked for direct payments. If the sum paid each week does not cover your bills, you're still liable to pay the balance.

Contact An Post's freephone number (1-800-707172) for details.

MORTGAGE ARREARS

People fall behind on their mortgage payments for all sorts of reasons, including sickness, redundancy, unemployment and marital breakdown. This problem affects people from all walks of life, including those who overstretch themselves to pay a large mortgage, although people on low incomes and those with families to support are most vulnerable. The outcome can also vary, depending on whether your luck improves and how your bank or building society reacts in the short term.

Common to the problem, however, is a sense of paralysing panic that most people experience when threatened by the loss of their home.

Fortunately, there are organisations that can help in this time of crisis. They can suggest coping strategies, put you in a stronger negotiating position and — ideally — save your home. Threshold, the housing advice agency, gives free counselling and budgetary advice for people who are in mortgage arrears. It can also help you to negotiate with the bank or building society. Threshold can be contacted at (01) 872 6311, or (021) 271250 or (091) 63080.

HOW THE PROBLEMS OF MORTGAGE ARREARS CAN ESCALATE

You miss one mortgage payment. The bank or building society sends you a warning letter, which you ignore. You then fail to pay for the second or third month, or make insufficient payments. Arrears are now mounting.

At this stage, the lender will probably write again and phone, or send a representative to the house to check out the problem. If it fails to make contact, the lender may send a solicitor's letter, warning that court proceedings will be initiated if the payment isn't made.

There is still time to negotiate, both at this and later stages, but you should do it as early as you can.

Legal Proceedings

If you fail to meet the lender's deadline, you'll probably get a Civil Bill stating that proceedings are about to start in the Circuit Court. Typically, you'll have 14 days to respond to the Civil Bill. There is no need to put in an appearance if you don't intend to contest the case at a full trial. If you miss this deadline, the civil bill is entered in the Cause Book for the court. You will be given a case number, for example No. 2,500 of 1996.

The lender will probably try to contact you again. If this attempt is unsuccessful or if the problem cannot be resolved to the lender's satisfaction, the lender's solicitor will issue a "Notice of Motion". This is effectively a summons. It will state the date, time and court number for the scheduled court case. If you wish to contest the case — for example, because you claim that the payments were in fact made or that the amount billed was incorrect (for whatever reason) — you can opt for a full trial. This is rare, however, and can be very costly.

Court Appearance

If and when the case appears in court, the lender will seek an order for possession but what they really want is for the arrears, plus any charges (interest and fees) to be paid off. You will have an opportunity to speak in court, or have your legal advisor

How the Problems of Mortgage Arrears Can Escalate

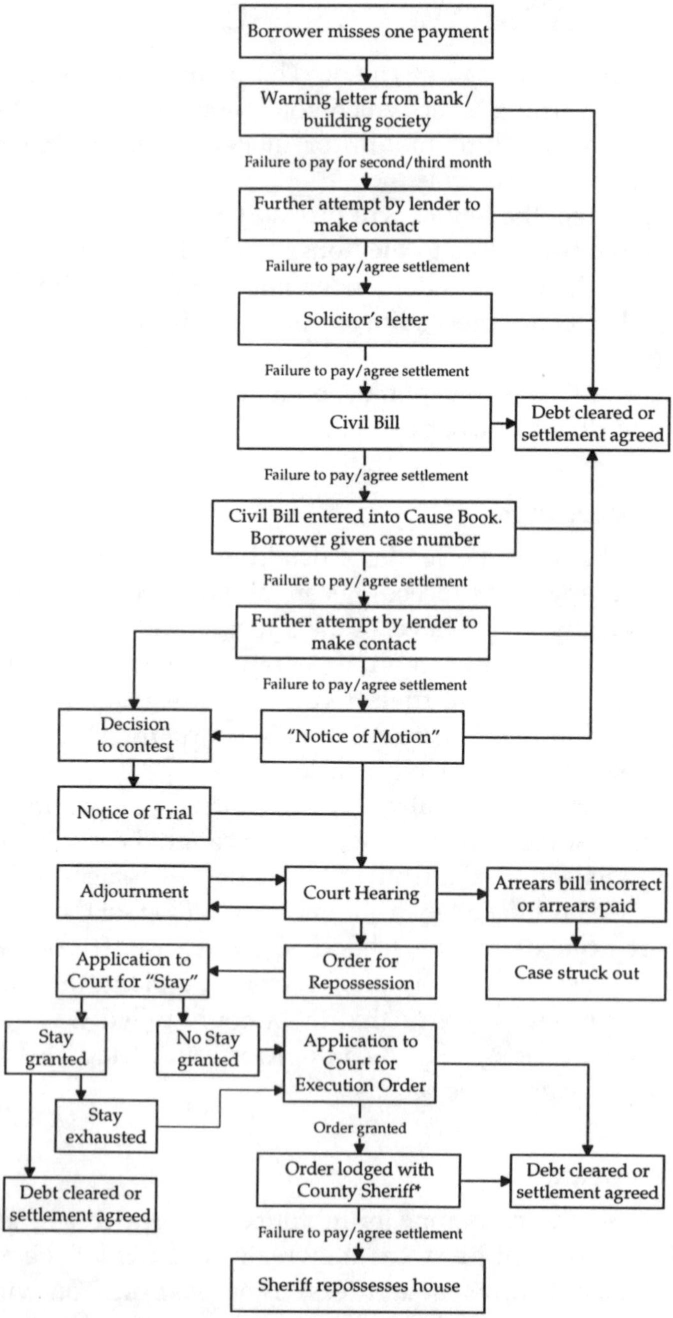

* Dublin and Cork have city and county sheriffs. The rest of the country has registrars who perform the same function.

(usually a solicitor) address the judge for you. Typically, the case may be adjourned on several occasions. This gives you more opportunity to find the missing cash, but each postponement can cost you up to several hundred pounds. These costs will probably be added to the lender's legal bill. If the lender wins the case and finally repossesses the house, these fees, along with arrears and mortgage interest, will be deducted from the sale price achieved on the house. Moreover, the lender can even charge interest on the "overdue" fees and mortgage repayments, thus hiking up your bill.

On each court appearance, you have an opportunity to plead your case by requesting more time or offering a financial settlement to the lender. You can also do this outside the court system, in letters sent direct to the bank or building society.

The lender may reject these offers, accept them or negotiate.

The judge has three options on each court appearance:

- Adjourn the case.
- Strike out the case (if the arrears bill is incorrect, for example, or the arrears have been repaid).
- Make an Order for Repossession.

Even if the judge takes the last course of action — for example, after ordering several adjournments — you can still prevent your home from being repossessed. You can ask the judge for a "Stay", which can buy time if you hope to be able to clear the debt or resume repayments (and negotiate a settlement) within a certain time. When the Stay has been exhausted, or if no Stay has been granted, the lender's solicitor can apply to the court office for an Execution Order. When the court office has issued the Order, it can be lodged with the Sheriff or County Registrar.

You can still try to reach a settlement at this late stage. If you fail, the Sheriff can then repossess the house.

Getting Help

The entire process is a long one which can take up to two years or more. Ideally, you should seek help at a very early stage. This can stop arrears from mounting, and make it easier to negotiate with the lender. You can also find other ways of generating income to pay the mortgage (see below). Banks and building societies will usually insist that the money be paid, and can be quite inflexible. However, your lender may agree to do one of the following:

- Reschedule the mortgage. Your monthly repayments will fall if the debt is spread over a longer term. The lender is more likely to agree to this if you suggest it at an early stage and have a mortgage that only has a few years left to run.
- Allow you to pay interest only. This is very rare. Your lender may agree to it for a limited period if you can promise to resume full payments in the near future. Or, your lender may agree to accept interest-only payments from your local Health Board (see below).
- Get help from another party, such as a friend or householder, to pay the mortgage. This might create legal complications, however.

If you face the problem early enough, it is easier to raise alternative sources of income to help meet all or a sufficient part of the repayments. Your lender is more likely to seek a repossession order if you have built up a large debt.

Ways of Boosting Your Income or Bridging the Gap

- Take in a lodger (but tell the mortgage lender, Revenue Commissioners and insurance company).
- Ask the local Health Board or community welfare officer for a mortgage supplement. The Health Board may agree to this, especially if you have children and can prove genuine hardship. This payment is means-tested (tel: Freephone 1-800-520520).
- Claim other social welfare benefits, for example FIS (see pp. 241–2).
- Claim extra tax reliefs and allowances.
- Seek emergency support from a voluntary agency, such as the Society of St Vincent de Paul (tel: (01) 838 4164). See also the Appendix, p. 296.

OTHER SOURCES OF ADVICE

FISC

The Leinster Society of Chartered Accountants runs a free and very useful information service for members of the public who need help with tax, budgeting, debt and other financial issues. It is called FISC (Financial Information Services Centre). FISC clinics are held at venues across Ireland. Contact FISC at (01) 668 2044 for details.

Money Advice Centres

The Department of Social Welfare is now funding over 25 money-advice and budgeting service centres across the country. These are chiefly designed to help low-income families to deal with the problems of moneylending and financial management. However, they also help middle-income clients who are having difficulty with debt. Like Threshold, they can try to negotiate with your creditors and raise other sources of income, such as social welfare payments. Contact your local Social Welfare office.

FAMILY INCOME SUPPLEMENT (FIS)

This can boost your take-home pay significantly, without affecting your entitlement to a medical card. Lone parents in full-time employment can qualify for FIS too. To qualify, you must:

- Be working at least 20 hours a week full-time employment
- Be maintaining a child aged under 18, or aged between 18 and 21 in full-time education
- Have gross weekly earnings below a certain threshold.

FIS is paid once a week by means of a book of payable orders which can be cashed at your post office. The size of the payment depends on the number of children you have and your income. From June, if you have four children, and earn £160 per week (before tax), for example, your FIS payment will be 60 per cent of the difference between £255 (your FIS income threshold) and £160. That means £57 per week (£2,964 per year).

The FIS thresholds were raised in the 1996 Budget as follows:

Family Size	Increase*	New Income Limit
1 child	£10	£195
2 children	£10	£215
3 children	£10	£235
4 children	£10	£255
5 children	£10	£280
6 children	£10	£300
7 children	£10	£317
8 children	£10	£334

* From June 1996.

If your spouse is working, that income will be added to your own to calculate your FIS payment.

CONCLUSION

Budgeting can help to avert problems as well as to solve them. For some families, even in the so-called middle classes, it's a way of scraping by.

Drawing up a budget can help prioritise spending. It can also highlight possible savings — for example, by restructuring debt — and pinpoint other sources of income. Opening a budget account at a bank or setting up a simple savings account for paying bills may also help you to manage your finances better.

If you get into financial trouble, such as mortgage arrears, it's best to get professional help. The earlier you do it, the better chance you have of resolving the problem. There is no shame about being in debt. The Society of St Vincent de Paul estimates that one third of the Irish population lives on or near the poverty line. That's about one million people. Many others, who might ordinarily view themselves as "comfortable" or "well off", can be pitched into debt by sickness, redundancy, marital breakdown and a host of other problems.

The one consolation is that you can get help, both by seeking it from voluntary and state-backed organisations and by drawing on your own personal resources.

14

HOLIDAYS AND WORKING ABROAD

"Travel light and you can sing in the robber's face."

Juvenal (AD60–*c*.136), Roman satirist

You've chosen the destination, saved for the holiday, bought the travellers' cheques and are ready to go. Right? Wrong!

Holidays and trips abroad are like any other part of life. They usually go more smoothly when you plan ahead. If you hit a problem when you're away, an insurance policy, telephone "help-line" or even a simple form can quickly defuse a crisis. Having extra plastic cards in your wallet or purse can also be very useful — for example, for charging telephone calls to a special account or withdrawing cash from an ATM machine as you do at home.

Very often, it's simply a question of organising things before you leave home.

Preparation is even more important if you plan to work abroad. Just a short working trip can interrupt your tax status and pension/PRSI contribution records. It also raises the problem of what to do with the family home. Rent? Sell? Leave it empty? You can avoid or minimise these problems by thinking ahead. You can even cut your tax bill!

This chapter gives tips on travel planning. It starts with

general topics, like picking the right mix of money when you travel, and how to insure you, your family and possessions. The second part covers the more tricky issues faced by people who plan to work abroad.

HOW TO CARRY MONEY

You have four basic options:

- Cash
- Travellers' Cheques
- Credit Card
- Eurocheques.

Cash

This is the simplest form of spending power. It's probably all you need on a very short trip, apart from a credit card in case of emergency. Cash is also handy for covering small expenses, such as a taxi fare, hotel tip etc., when you arrive on a longer trip. If you're travelling to a destination where the currency is shaky, dollars may be a better bet. Otherwise, bring local currency, or you could end up paying high bank charges for foreign exchange. Check with your bank or travel agent.

Don't bring large wads of cash. You could be in dire straits if your money is lost or stolen.

Travellers' Cheques

These are far safer than cash and almost as widely accepted. It's best to buy them in local currency of the country you plan to travel to, or in dollars or sterling. The latter are useful for destinations with less well-known currencies, such as Greece or Malta, especially if after the trip you have cheques left over, which you need to change back into Irish pounds.

You usually have to pay commission — typically 1 per cent — when buying travellers' cheques. Commission rates vary from one place to another, and some institutions don't charge at all. Shop around and look out for a good exchange rate too (see p. 247). Also, be careful when you cash them abroad. Banks tend to give better exchange rates than hotels and may charge a lower commission. Verify the rate, and find out what the commission is before signing the cheque. Some institutions charge a fixed fee, regardless of the cheque size, so you can save money by cashing several cheques at a time. Sometimes they may even be accepted as "cash".

When you buy travellers' cheques, you get a piece of paper for recording transactions. Keep it safe, separate from your cheques, and update it each time you cash one. This paper could be vital if your cheques disappear.

Credit Cards

These have many uses. They are widely accepted in hotels and restaurants, and business travellers can pay for virtually an entire trip with them. Costs are itemised on the monthly credit-card statement, which provides a record of business-related expenses. That makes it easy to separate your personal and business costs.

For tourists, a credit card is a safe, convenient payment method and a friend in need. Want to pay for a slap-up meal on your last night? Or book a plane ticket? A credit card is probably the answer, but remember that you'll have to settle the bill when you get back. Also, don't expect a local restaurant on a tiny Greek island to accept your Visa or Access unless they have the sign up.

You can use your credit card for purchases and cash withdrawals. If you have a Personal Identification Number (PIN) you may be able to take cash straight out of an ATM machine. Your Irish credit-card issuer can give you a new PIN, before you leave, if you've forgotten it. Alternatively, you can withdraw cash over the bank counter — but you'll need identification.

You'll have to pay the credit-card issuer a handling charge for each cash transaction. This is typically 1.5 per cent of the cash you withdraw. If you don't settle the credit-card bill in full after you get the statement, you'll also be billed for interest on the borrowed cash. You can avoid these charges by lodging cash to your credit-card account before you leave Ireland. You may earn interest on your balance, depending on the credit-card company.

Charge cards — Diners or American Express — can be used in much the same way as credit cards, and are very useful when travelling abroad. American Express card holders can withdraw cash at over 100,000 ATMs worldwide, and use a "poste restante" (mail-holding service) at around 1,900 Amex travel-service offices. Diners Card clients will be able to access roughly 53,000 ATMs in 27 countries and can order up to $1,000 per week at a bank or Diners Club office.

Warning!

Beware of fraudsters. Make sure that a trader doesn't make two "imprints" of your card when finalising the bill. If they make a mistake, keep the first receipt or destroy it. Notify your card issuer immediately if the card is lost or stolen. You should not be liable for any fraudulent transactions on the card, but some issuers will charge you £50 if you don't report a lost or stolen card immediately. Write down your card number and card issuer's telephone number, and keep them in a safe place, separately from your card, when you travel. The major banks offer a card-registration service which keeps a record of your card numbers.

Eurocheques

These allow you to write cheques on your current account when you're abroad. They are useful, but require a bit of pre-planning. You have to apply to your bank for a special chequebook and a guarantee card. The card, which costs about £5, guarantees each cheque written in local currency up to the value of IR£140. It can take up to two weeks to get the chequebook and card, so don't leave it to the last moment.

You can write cheques in the currency of the country/countries that you are visiting, and the money is later debited from your bank account in Ireland. There's a commission charge of about 1.6 per cent on each cheque you write (on sums between £57 and £240). On lower sums, you pay the Irish bank that sold you the cheques a flat 90p charge per encashment. Bank of Ireland, which co-ordinates Eurocheque payments, charges an extra 25p "handling fee". The foreign bank where you cash them also charges about 0.25 per cent of the cheque's value. Here's an example:

You write a Eurocheque for the equivalent of £100 in a Paris restaurant. This will cost you £1.60 (commission), plus 25p for Bank of Ireland's handling charge. Total cost: £1.85.

The bank card will only guarantee cheques up to the equivalent of £140, but hotels and retailers should let you write up to three cheques, up to a maximum value of £140 each, for the same transaction. However, you can write other cheques the same day for different transactions. Avoid writing too many small cheques, as the charges can mount up.

You can also withdraw cash across Europe from about 40,000 ATMs bearing the Eurocheque sign.

Buying Cash or Travellers' Cheques

Shopping for holiday money can be confusing, especially when most "bureau de change" display tables look like this one:

DATE 15/1/96

Currency	Buy Note	Sell Note	Buy Cheque	Sell Cheque
GBP	1.0579	1.0071	1.0560	1.0097
USD	1.6466	1.5654	1.6385	1.5651
FFR	8.1496	7.6409	8.1410	7.7485
GDM	2.3906	2.2339	2.3740	2.2616

Key: GBP = UK sterling; USD = US dollars; FFR= French francs; GDM= German marks.

Source: An associated bank.

Let's say you want to buy sterling notes. You can simply ask how much it will cost to buy stg£500. Ask whether this includes a commission charge. Or, you can do the sum yourself.

Divide stg£500 by the "sell note" rate, which is 1.0071. This is the rate at which the foreign exchange desk "sells" notes to you. The figure works out at £496.50. If the commission is 1 per cent, add an extra £4.96, which makes £501.46. To find out the rate for travellers' cheques, divide by the "sell cheque" rate, which is 1.0097. The cost in Irish pounds is £495.20, plus commission. Buying cash is usually more expensive, so you'll get less foreign currency for your Irish pounds.

To convert sterling back into Irish pounds, divide the amount you want to sell by the "buy note" or "buy cheque" rate for sterling. Then add on the commission (if there is one).

The procedure for converting a sum in Irish pounds — for example £100 — into another currency is slightly different: multiply £100 by the appropriate "sell note" or "sell cheque" rate.

Puzzled? The golden rule when comparing the price of buying your stg£500 is that the higher the "sell rate", the less it will cost you in Irish pounds. And when you're switching back into Irish pounds, the lowest "buy rate" will give you the best return. The latter rule also applies if you're changing sterling or dollar travellers' cheques into Greek drachmas when you start your holiday. Note that bureaux de changes often have tiered rates for larger transactions and commission rates can vary. Shop around, especially if you're buying a large volume of cheques or cash.

INSURING YOUR CAR

Firstly, check whether your own insurance policy covers travel outside Ireland. Ask your broker or insurance company and pay the supplement, if necessary. Don't leave it to the last minute, as you may need to get extra documentation.

Insurance that covers you in the event of accident and/or breakdown is also an excellent idea. This can repatriate you, your family and car if a crisis strikes, and it costs very little. Some policies also provide medical and other logistical support — such as free car hire and/or emergency accommodation. They operate in a similar way. You are given a freephone or contact number to ring in an emergency. If your car breaks down, for example, the English-speaking operator will tell you where you can get a towing service and/or a garage, or will order help for you.

You may have to part with some cash for these services. Or you may get vouchers, free service (up to a certain threshold) or a cash facility. It depends on the policy.

Where Can You Get this Cover?

Celtic International Insurance

This Galway-based company, now part of the Eureko group, provides a free "assistance" service to all its customers free of charge. Ireland Assist, which handles the service, gives free motor breakdown rescue and car hire within Ireland. Customers are also entitled to medical, accommodation and travel expenses when travelling in Europe.

The PMPA Insurance Company

PMPA clients can buy supplementary cover as an optional extra — the service is also provided by Ireland Assist.

The Automobile Association

The "Five Star Vehicle Service" can be purchased by both AA and non-AA members, but the latter pay a surcharge. You also pay an extra premium if your car is aged over 15 years and if you are travelling to Continental Europe, and not the UK.

A full Irish driving licence is accepted throughout the EU and in the US, but you may be asked for an international licence if you are hiring a car. "Visitors" can use their Irish licence for up to one year. You can get an international driving licence from the AA at a cost of £4. Bring a passport-size black and white or colour photograph, along with your Irish licence.

HOLIDAY INSURANCE

This is often a mandatory part of the "sun-holiday" package tour, but an optional extra for others. It should not be forgotten.

Travel policies cover you for various holiday disasters. These include:

- Cancellation
- Delays (through strike or bad weather)
- Lost baggage
- Theft
- Medical expenses
- Repatriation.

If insurance is included in your travel package, read the policy. Is there adequate cover for your personal belongings, medical costs, and so on? You may need to take out a supplementary package. People with a medical history — such as heart disease — may not be covered by the policy for that illness. Check the policy and talk to your GP before you go. Also, people aged 65 or over may not be covered at all. If you're buying an air ticket only, talk to your broker about "stand-alone" cover, especially if you're travelling to the US, where medical costs are high.

> **Note:** A travel agency cannot insist that you buy insurance from them, but they can insist on proof that you have taken out alternative cover. Travel policies are available from most insurance companies.

Other Medical Cover

Extra cover is available from other sources, and it doesn't cost a penny. Irish citizens are entitled to free, reciprocal health care in any EU state. The level of cover will vary from one country to another. Basically, if you fall sick in Germany, you'll be entitled to the same free/charge-based services that a German national would get there. You can either get basic care (free of charge) or pay abroad and claim a refund from the health board on your return. You need an up-to-date E111 form to be sure of receiving attention. Ask your local health board for one, and get it stamped before leaving Ireland.

VHI members can claim large transportation expenses — if they fall sick in a faraway land — plus logistical support through the VHI Assist scheme at no extra cost. You will also be covered for medical service appropriate to your VHI "class" when abroad. You will need a VHI Assist identity card, so contact the VHI before you leave. This cover is useful, but will not repay high medical costs. It is not a substitute for medical cover in a holiday insurance plan.

TRAVELLERS' CHECKLIST

- **Credit Card**
  - — Renew PIN number, if necessary. ☐
  - — Lodge cash to credit-card account, if possible. ☐
  - — Check whether your destination has many authorised outlets/ATMs. ☐
- **Other Holiday Money**
  - — Book Eurocheques two weeks in advance. ☐
  - — Shop for a good rate on foreign currency/travellers' cheques. ☐
- **Travel Insurance**
  - — If booking a package holiday, check the policy ☐
  - — Otherwise, ask your insurance broker for good "stand-alone" cover. ☐
- **Health Insurance**
  - — Get an E111 form at the Health Board. Have it stamped and bring it with you. ☐
  - — Ring the VHI about VHI Assist (if you're a VHI member). ☐
  - — If you've got special medical needs, talk to your GP ☐
  - — Get any necessary vaccinations. ☐
- **Telephone**
  - — Ask Telecom Éireann about its "chargecard" service. Find out how much the charges are. ☐
  - — AIB Bank Visa card holders can use a similar service. Ask the bank for an application form. ☐
  - — Contact AT&T or MCI if you want a special telephone chargecard — especially if you're travelling to the US. Calls from hotels and motels tend to be very expensive. ☐

TRAVELLERS' CHECKLIST (CONTINUED)

- **Car**
  - — Ring your broker. Arrange supplementary cover, if necessary. ☐
  - — Contact the AA about "Five Star" cover. ☐
  - — Get an international driving licence. ☐
  - — If you rent a car abroad, read the contract fully and have it explained to you. Where should you drop off the car? What surcharges are there? Be wary of signing blank credit-card vouchers. ☐
  - — Study the "Rules of the Road" of the country you visit. Ignorance is not an excuse in the eyes of the law. Observe speed limits and know what to do after an accident. ☐

DUTY-PAID AND TAX-PAID GOODS

Holidays are a good time for building up stocks of wine, spirits and cigarettes. You can bring a large amount with you when you return home, provided that you have already paid duty/VAT. Here are the EU guidance levels for these goods:

Cigarettes	800
Cigarillos	400
Cigars	200
Smoking Tobacco	1 kg
Spirits	10 litres
Port, Sherry etc.	20 litres
Wine*	45 litres
Beer	55 litres

* Only 30 litres can be sparkling

If you bring in more than these quantities, you must be able to prove that the foods are for personal use. Otherwise they may be seized.

DUTY-FREE AND TAX-FREE SHOPPING

The limits on duty-free goods (which are usually bought in the airport or on the ferry) are much lower, and are listed below.

These limits only apply to goods bought in other EU countries. Different rates apply for other places, including the Canary Islands, the Channel Islands and the US.

Cigarettes	200 *or*
Cigarillos	100 *or*
Cigars	50 *or*
Tobacco	250g
Spirits	1 litre
Wine**	2 litres
Still Wine	2 litres
Perfume	50g (60 ml)
Toilet Water	0.25 litres (250 ml)

** Sparkling and fortified

Note: The limits to the above tables may change. If in doubt, contact the Revenue Commissioners

WORKING ABROAD

Planning a longer trip abroad, for work or study, is more complicated. That's especially the case for people who are already working and in the PAYE/PRSI net, and who plan to spend more than a few months away. These points are mainly drawn from a Coopers and Lybrand guide on working abroad.

CHECKLIST

- Irish tax(es) ❑
- Your PRSI/pension contributions ❑
- The tax and social-welfare system in your new host country ❑
- Your house ❑
- Investments/other financial arrangements ❑

Irish Tax

Depending on your departure date, you may be able to claim a rebate on Irish tax if you cease to be resident. This is because your personal tax allowances are granted for a whole year, even if you stop work after six months. So, if you leave Ireland in October, for example, your tax-free allowances will be reallocated over six months instead of twelve, resulting in a tax rebate. You should apply for this rebate on a P50 form, which should be submitted with your P45 (the form you get when you leave a job).

The same situation can arise if you leave your host country midway through a tax year. Working abroad can affect your residency for tax purposes (see below), creating a potentially complex situation for you, so it's a good idea to get professional advice.

Talk to a trusted accountant or the Revenue Commissioners. The latter have a walk-in centre on Dublin's Cathedral Street, called the Central Revenue Information Office (CRIO).

PRSI/Pension Contributions

Working abroad can interrupt your Irish PRSI contribution record. In theory, this means that you may lose entitlement (or reduce your entitlement) to some benefits — such as maternity pay or pension rights. There are compensations, however.

Firstly, social insurance contributions paid in another EU state and some other countries (most notably, the US) can be added to your Irish record for pension purposes, which means that if you spend three years working in Britain, you can transfer benefits paid into the state-run (National Insurance) system back to Ireland when your lifetime contribution record is finally being assessed. If you work abroad for a long time, and then return to Ireland, you may qualify for a separate pension from the foreign country. This will be paid in addition to, or in lieu of, your Irish pension.

Secondly, people who are transferred abroad by their employers may be able to continue paying into their Irish company pension scheme for three years, or more by extension. For example, someone who is posted to Britain for a short period may continue to pay into their Irish-based company pension scheme but will get tax relief on their British salary. Also, a person who is posted to the US or any EU country can continue paying Irish

PRSI contributions for up to five years. Reciprocal agreements exist with other countries — Canada and Australia, for example. Contact the Department of Social Welfare before you leave.

People who leave their Irish employer and look for new work abroad can't deduct PRSI payments from their foreign salary. However, they can keep up their PRSI payments separately if they wish, by making voluntary contributions. Contact the Department of Social Welfare at (01) 874 8444 for details.

Tax and Social Welfare System in Your Host Country

A bit of homework may pay off here. For example, a contract worker who has the choice of being paid locally or through their Irish bank account should compare the pros and cons of each. That person will also have to find out if they will be regarded as ordinarily "resident" in Ireland for tax purposes or not. If they are, income earned on overseas investments — such as high-yielding bank accounts — may be liable for Irish tax.

It's complex, as the section "Are You at Home?" (p. 260) shows. Contract workers should ask their employers to explain the full tax implications of either choice. They should also seek independent advice from an accountant who specialises in this area, preferably at one of the larger firms. The Revenue Commissioners will be able to help too.

If the public health services are quite basic in the country where you plan to work, check out the cost of private health cover there. It can be prohibitive. You may want private medical cover to be included in your remuneration package.

Your House

Leaving a family home for a year or more poses quite a serious question. You must decide whether you want to:

- Sell
- Let
- Leave your house unoccupied
- Lend your house to a friend or relative.

Profits earned on the sale of a primary residence are usually exempt from Capital Gains Tax (CGT). However, working abroad can complicate matters, especially if you buy another house in another country when you leave Ireland. CGT is charged at 40 per cent, and you may have to pay some tax on this profit. Generally speaking, you can avoid CGT if you live in the house after returning from abroad. A lot depends on your personal circumstances, so it's a good idea to consult a qualified professional.

If you decide to let the house, you'll be liable for Irish income tax on any rental income. You can deduct many expenses from this "profit", thereby cutting or totally wiping out the tax bill. Tax-deductible costs include:

- Interest (no upper limit) on borrowings for the purchase, improvement or repair of the building
- Insurance of the property and its contents
- Utilities such as gas, electricity, telephone rental
- Repairs and maintenance
- Agent's fees and commissions (incurred in letting the property)
- Yearly wear and tear allowance of 15 per cent of the cost of furniture and fittings. This is not automatic, and must be granted by the Revenue Commissioners.

These costs must relate to the period when the property was actually let. This can be very relevant for large outlays — for example, for repair and renovation. Losses incurred in one rental year, arising from these costs, can be offset against profits in a future year. You can also write off losses against rental income from another property.

The tax is usually collected in one of two ways if you are not resident in Ireland:

- By your agent who can withhold the portion of tenants' rent which should be paid in tax, and pay this to the Revenue Commissioners.

- If no agent has been appointed, your tenants should, in theory, deduct income tax at the standard rate (27 per cent) and pay the rent net of tax. You must submit your tax return (by 31 January for the tax year ending the previous 5 April). Any overpaid tax can be reclaimed at the end of the tax year, although you may face a cash-flow problem in the meantime. An agent may help to eliminate the problem by making allowances for costs etc. when calculating the amount earmarked for tax.

You can also leave the house unoccupied. In that case, you cannot offset the running costs against your Irish income-tax bill. Living outside Ireland may not exempt you from Residential Property Tax.

Investments and Other Financial Arrangements

If you are not resident in Ireland for tax purposes, you may be exempt from CGT here. However, you have to spend three years outside the country to qualify because CGT liability is determined by your so-called "ordinary residence". See the section below.

CGT is quite punitive, so it may be a good opportunity to arrange the sale of certain assets — such as shares apart from your main residence — if your absence is prolonged. However, you may have to pay this in the country in which you are living.

This advice only applies to assets that you sell at a profit. It's not a good idea to sell loss-making investments, however, because you may not be able to offset these losses against any gains made in the future. In other words, you may not be able to use them to cut a CGT bill which might arise when you sell profit-making assets.

If in doubt, talk to an accountant!

RETURNING HOME

As has been discussed briefly already, you can claim a tax refund and legally skirt payment of certain taxes by timing your return to Ireland.

Also, bear the following in mind:

- Family Home
- Tax
- Relocation Expenses
- Car.

Family Home

Because the family home is deemed to be your main residence, if you work abroad on a temporary assignment, you can protect it from any potential CGT liability by living in it when you return home. If you sell the house as soon as you return, you may have to pay some CGT on the proceeds. Ask an accountant to clarify this for you.

Tax

You can claim a full year's tax allowances even if you come home halfway through the tax year. It's a good idea to file a tax return as soon as you return to get a tax-free allowance certificate, which will mean that your tax reliefs and allowances will be spread through the rest of the tax year (up until 5 April). It should also prevent you from being put on emergency tax. Talk to an accountant too, especially if your stay will be brief or intermittent. Liability to Irish tax is triggered by a complex web of factors.

Relocation Expenses

If you are being posted back home, you are entitled to certain tax-free relocation costs, provided that your employer claims them in advance. Get advice.

Car

When you return to Ireland, if you import a car from any EU state, you must pay both VAT (21 per cent of the car's invoice value — including freight and insurance) *and* Vehicle Registration Tax. This must be done by the end of the next working day after the car is imported unless you can claim relief (see below). If the car is less than six months old or has travelled less than 6,000km, you must pay VAT at a rate of 21 per cent of the car's invoice value. The VAT is payable irrespective of whether you have already paid VAT in another EU state.

You must go to the nearest Vehicle Registration Office (VRO) in the county where you live. A VRO officer will examine the vehicle, estimate the tax and process the paperwork. You must pay any VRT or VAT due immediately.

In return, you will get a receipt stating the vehicle's new registration number.

The VRT payable is based on several factors, including the car's age, condition, mileage and enhancements. VRT is calculated on either a percentage or flat basis, depending on the type of vehicle.

The following are the rates for VRT:

Cars:	Up to and including 2,500 cc, charged at 23.2 per cent of the vehicle's open market selling price (OMSP). Over 2,500 cc, charged at 29.25 per cent of the OMSP.
Small Vans:	Car-derived vans, chargeable at 13.3 per cent of the OMSP.
Motorcycles:	Charge based on engine capacity and age of machine.
Other Vehicles:	Tractors, large vans etc. attract a flat charge of £40.

Vehicles that have been modified may incur an extra VRT charge.

Relief from VRT

If you have established your normal residence outside Ireland and were the sole user and possessor of the car outside Ireland for at least six months prior to returning, you may be totally exempt from VRT. You must fulfil several conditions, however. For example, your presence abroad must not have been on a contract of one year or less. Also, you must have paid all the local and national taxes on the car/vehicle before bringing it back to Ireland. You will be expected to prove this by providing documents like the car's foreign registration book and insurance certificate.

ARE YOU AT HOME?

Determining whether you are resident in Ireland for tax purposes is tricky, especially if you go abroad for short working trips (on contract work, for example). You may find — as is often the case — that two sets of tax authorities have a claim on your earnings! If so, you shouldn't have to pay tax twice if the second country has a double taxation agreement with Ireland (see Appendix, p. 297). The agreement will decide which of the two countries has the right to tax certain sources of income, or capital gains.

The tests to determine residency are:

- If your visits to Ireland total 183 nights in that tax year.
- If your visits to Ireland in that tax year and the previous one total 280 nights or more, you are deemed to be resident in the second tax year. If you have spent fewer than 31 nights here during either year, this rule does not apply.

The 1994 Finance Act defined the elusive concept of "ordinary residence". This is acquired after you have been resident for tax purposes for over three years. Conversely, you do not lose "ordinary residence" until you have been a non-tax resident for three years.

Some Irish people who work abroad for short periods will remain both resident in Ireland for tax purposes and ordinarily resident — which means that they are liable for Irish income tax on their worldwide income, but they can claim a tax deduction on employment income for the time spent working abroad.

Employees who work outside Ireland and the UK, but remain "resident" because of the length of time spent in Ireland, can claim a "working abroad" deduction for days spent abroad. You can qualify for this if you spend at least 90 days working outside Ireland and the UK, either during the tax year in question or during 12 calendar months. Also, you can only claim a deduction for periods of 14 days or more spent abroad. If you meet these conditions, there's a complex formula to work out the tax deduction.

A person who goes to work abroad for a short period but is still "ordinarily resident" in Ireland does not have to pay Irish tax on foreign investment income — for example, on money in a Jersey bank account — up to £3,000 per annum.

> **Note:** Leaving Ireland mid-way through a tax year can trigger special tax rules or "split year" assessment. Like anything else to do with tax, it's a minefield. Check it out.

WORKING ABROAD: STUDENTS

Roughly 30,000 students work abroad each year. For most, the main issue is getting to another country, finding work and getting any spare cash back home again. USIT, the youth and student travel service, and your own student union can give quite detailed information on this. However, it's worth bearing a few things in mind:

- Bureaucracy
- Spending Money
- Social Welfare Rights
- Tax.

Bureaucracy

Opening a bank account outside Ireland can be difficult. Bring plenty of identification with you, including a birth certificate, passport, letter from your new landlord/employer in the host country. This is especially relevant in Britain, where EU money laundering legislation is interpreted very strictly.

Social Welfare Rights

If you go to live in another EU country, you'll be entitled to the same social-security rights as nationals of that country. But you'll have to meet local criteria to qualify, which means that you may need to have an employment record in that country.

Britain is a bit more flexible — and generous — than other EU countries, because of its historical relationship with Ireland. Irish people were exempted from stricter controls on payment of non-contributory state payments which were imposed in 1994. Wherever you go, don't expect to be embraced by the welfare state. Check out your rights before you leave Ireland and bring plenty of documentation with you, including your birth certificate, passport, letter from your Irish employer/college, Department of Social Welfare, new landlord etc.

Spending Money

Bring enough cash to tide you through. If you're looking for a flat, you may need a month's rent plus the deposit in advance. You may also have to wait several weeks for your first pay cheque.

Tax

You can claim a refund of tax paid during short working spells abroad. This refund applies to many countries, including EU Member States, the US, Canada, Australia and New Zealand. Before your work spell comes to an end, ask the local tax authority how to claim a refund. Better still, check with the Revenue Commissioners and USIT before leaving Ireland. You can use the services of an accountant to get your money back, but you can manage it yourself, with a bit of paperwork and patience.

Students who work in the US on a J1 visa are exempt from US federal tax and, in some destinations, state taxes.

RETIRING ABROAD

Each winter, thousands of British and Irish pensioners fly to Spain and other parts of Southern Europe in search of sun and easy living. They are known as "snowbirds".

Some people like the idea of retiring abroad, and staying warm all year round. It's a lovely notion, but there's a bit more to it than meets the eye.

You can transfer a contributory state pension (but not a means-tested one) to any other EU country, but this will be paid in Irish pounds, and payments will fluctuate with exchange rates. The same applies to income from another (private or company-based) pension plan. Also, an index-linked pension may not keep pace with inflation in the country where you have chosen to live. Your monthly income may plunge as a result.

If you're still at work, but plan to retire abroad, try to sort out your pension entitlements as early as possible. People who have worked in other EU countries (or even places like the US and Australia) may need to amalgamate these credits when claiming their Irish pension. Also, contact the office that will pay your pension and give them details of your new address, etc. If you have contributed to a company pension scheme, contact a trustee for the scheme. You may have to set up a special bank account — in Ireland and abroad — to arrange for the transfer of these pensions. Check whether Ireland has a double tax treaty with that country and work out in which country — if any — you will be taxed.

As an EU citizen, you are entitled to claim health and social-welfare benefits abroad. But these may be means-tested, and will certainly be paid in accordance with the rules in that country.

Read up on your entitlements before leaving Ireland. The appropriate Embassy and the Department of Social Welfare EU Records or EU/International sections (tel: (01) 874 8444) should be able to help. It would also be wise to talk to an accountant. Last but not least, take language classes and do some research on the culture and traditions of the country in which you plan to live.

When you finally leave, be sure to pack an E107 form. You can post this back to the Irish Department of Social Welfare if you are finding it difficult to prove entitlement to certain benefits.

CONCLUSION

Travel broadens the mind, but it also empties the pockets. Like many other aspects of life, you can't predict how it will work out or cost, but a bit of planning helps.

It's only when a crisis strikes — anything from a car breakdown to a sudden illness — that you appreciate the value of a motor travel or another insurance policy. This, and a few key phone numbers — such as an emergency line for reporting a lost credit card — can prevent an emergency from ruining your holiday or business trip.

Travel involves other complications, too. Students who work abroad during the summer, pensioners who settle in Spain for short- or long-term stays and people who leave Ireland to further their careers all need to prepare for both departure and return.

Few people in their twenties or thirties will lose much time worrying about tax residency and pension planning. But for people in their forties and fifties, and those on large salaries, working spells abroad can have a serious impact on their tax status, PRSI record and pension contributions.

You could lose valuable benefits — and pay more tax than you need to — by missing out on a few simple preparations.

15

WILLS AND INHERITANCE PLANNING

"Tomorrow is often the busiest day of the year."

Spanish Proverb

Most of us avoid thinking about death, if we possibly can. That's understandable, but not very wise when it comes to personal financial planning. Some people never make a will, or take out life assurance, even when they have young children or other people to support. The key issue — who will look after their family if they die — is often too painful to contemplate. Others just never get around to it. When you are in your thirties or forties, the prospect of death can seem very remote.

Here are some good reasons *not* to procrastinate about long-term financial planning.

- For Your Family's Sake
- To Save Tax
- To Provide "Fair" Settlements
- To Protect Your Business
- For Your Peace of Mind.

For Your Family's Sake

If you have dependants — a spouse, children or elderly parents — they could suffer financially if you die. They may not have enough income to live on. It may also affect their future plans, like school or a college education. If you die without leaving a will, your estate will be carved up according to rules laid down in the 1965 Succession Act (see p. 268). This may not suit you, or your family. Bitter family rows could ensue. Also, you may wish to provide for a disabled child or other dependant. This can be done by creating a "trust" and/or taking out life-assurance cover (see also pp. 167–8 in Chapter 9, Children.

To Save Tax

The Revenue Commissioners' arm reaches far beyond the grave. Inheritance planning can help to reduce or pay any necessary taxes. It can also avoid a situation where a relative or friend has to a pay a huge tax bill on their inheritance.

In some cases, a farm may have to be sold to pay the probate tax bill, which is a flat 2 per cent charge on the estate. This can also happen if someone who isn't a relative — and is thus a "stranger in law" — inherits an asset. They can only receive £12,170 before they start paying Capital Acquisitions Tax (CAT). See pp. 270–74.

To Provide "Fair" Settlements

Separated people, especially those in second relationships, need to think about inheritance planning. If they die, their first partner (wife or husband) may receive the lion's share of the estate, regardless of whether that would seem appropriate or not. The second partner (with whom they may have had a long-standing relationship and possibly children, but no legal bond) could be cut out or face a big tax bill on any inherited assets.

You can provide for both partners and, indeed, two sets of children through inheritance planning.

To Protect Your Business

Inheritance planning is vital in a family-owned business. It can ease the transition of power and wealth from one generation to another. If you fail to address this problem, the business may not survive you.

For Your Peace of Mind

This sort of planning can be positive and reassuring — once you start. As an article in *Consumer Choice* magazine pointed out, you can view your will as a "posthumous presents list", not just as a safety net for your dependants. Making a will itself won't kill you!

HOW TO MAKE A WILL

Making a straightforward will costs roughly £50. Home-made wills can cause a lot of problems, so it's worth spending a few pounds to get it done professionally. At the very least, get it checked by a solicitor. Here's how to go about making a will.

Seven Steps

(1) Make a list of your possessions and get an idea of their value.

(2) Decide to whom you want to give them.

(3) Talk to a trusted solicitor about potential inheritance tax costs. It may be better to pass on some possessions as a "gift" when you are still alive.

(4) Choose one or more executors whom you can trust to sort out your affairs.

(5) Draw up your will with a solicitor.

(6) If you opt for a home-made will — which is not advisable — keep it simple. Make sure it is also dated, signed and witnessed by two people.

(7) Keep your will in a safe place, preferably a bank or solicitor's office. Review it regularly.

Witnesses do not have to read the will, but neither can they or their spouses be beneficiaries. If they are, the will is not invalid, but the witness or spouse cannot receive any assets. You should pick the executor carefully. This person must try to ensure that your wishes are carried out when you die. Some people pick their bank to do this job, but the fees can be very expensive and will be docked from your estate. It's best to appoint two people, so a trusted friend and a family member may be a better choice, but choose people who are younger than you and in good health! If you are elderly or have no close family, you could appoint your solicitor.

When you die, the executor must take out a "grant of probate" to see that your possessions are properly divided. Executors must also pay any debts owed (from the estate) and see that assets are duly allocated. They can take out probate by hiring a solicitor or applying directly to the Probate Office. You can contact the latter through the local circuit court offices.

Your will remains valid until you marry or make a new one. You can, however, make a will in anticipation of marriage. Remember to check it periodically as your family and personal circumstances change.

If You Die Without a Will

This is called dying "intestate".

Firstly, your next of kin (perhaps your spouse, brother/sister or parent) will have to apply for a Letter of Administration to divide your estate. This could be distressing for that person, given their recent bereavement. In effect, your next of kin will be the administrator of your estate and must do the job that is normally carried out by the executor. However, instead of following the wishes laid down in your will, the administrator must divide up your belongings in accordance with the 1965 Succession Act (see "If There is No Will" table, p. 269).

This carve-up may not suit your wishes. You might want to leave the family home to a particular child, perhaps the youngest or a handicapped member of the family. By making a will you can make sure that these plans will be carried out. Furthermore, if you die without a will, an administration bond is required. This is usually obtained from an insurance company and acts as a guarantee that the administrator will carry out their duties according to the law.

IF THERE IS NO WILL

Heir	Entitlement
Surviving Relative	Share of estate
Spouse Only	Whole of estate
Spouse and Children	Two-thirds to spouse, one-third to children in equal shares. The share of a deceased child passes to the children of the deceased child
Children, No Spouse	Whole of estate to children in equal shares. The share of a deceased child passes to the children of the deceased child
Parents, Brothers/Sisters	Whole estate to surviving parent(s). None to brothers and sisters
One Parent, Brothers/Sisters	Whole estate to surviving parent. None to brothers and sisters
Brothers and Sisters	Divided into equal shares. The share of any deceased brother/sister passes to his/her children
Nephews and Nieces	All get equal shares

Your Spouse's Rights

No matter what your will states, you cannot cut your spouse out of your estate, except in certain circumstances. Spouses are legally entitled to half of their partners' assets if they have no children, or one third if they do. Your spouse's rights do not extend to any property that you have held in joint names with another person, provided that the title is held in true *joint tenancy*. That property will pass automatically to the other person, but that person may face a CAT bill. However, if the joint tenancy was created to deprive a spouse of their legal right, or a child of their succession rights, the other person's claim on the property could be contested. If you hold a property jointly as *tenants in common,* your half will automatically pass into your estate when you die. The other joint tenant will not benefit.

You don't have to include your children in the will, but there is a strong moral obligation to do so. They could also make a legal claim on your estate under the 1965 Succession Act, if they feel that they have not been properly provided for.

Both a husband and wife should make a will to include provisions covering for a situation where both die simultaneously or the survivor does not, or cannot, make a new will. This can avoid problems in a situation where the man leaves all of his property to his wife in a will, but both die together in a tragic accident.

TAX

Tax is a key part of inheritance planning. Taxes are hard to avoid, but you can ease the burden. Here are the taxes you have to look out for:

Tax	Who Pays It?	How Much Do They Pay?	When is It Due?
1) Capital Acquisitions Tax (CAT)			
Inheritance Tax	The beneficiary	Depends on their blood/legal relationship with you. A spouse pays no CAT, a "stranger in law" pays CAT on assets worth £12,170+.	When they receive the asset after your death.
Gift Tax	The beneficiary	Ditto, but the tax penalty is 75% of the total CAT charge (see below).	When they receive the asset more than two years before your death.
2) Probate Tax	Your estate	2%	Within nine months.

CAT

As shown in the table above, CAT must be paid on both large gifts and inheritances.

CAT RATES

Amount	Tax Payable
Up to exemption threshold (see below)	No Tax
The next £10,000	20%
The next £30,000	30%
The balance	40%

However, if the assets are passed on as gifts at least two years before the donor dies, the bill is 75 per cent of the regular CAT charge. So, it makes sense to start inheritance planning before you die, and "gift" some of your assets. The size of the tax bill also depends on:

- The beneficiary's blood/legal relationship with the donor
- The amount the person receives.

HOW MUCH CAN YOU INHERIT BEFORE PAYING CAT?

Blood/Legal Relationship of Beneficiary	Tax Threshold*
Husband/Wife	No CAT payable
Child	£182,550
Grandchild under 18 (parent deceased)	£182,550
Father/Mother (absolute inheritance only)	£182,550
Father/Mother (other benefits, including gifts)	£24,340
Grandfather/Grandmother/Grandchild	£24,340
Brother/Sister	£24,340
Niece/Nephew	£24,340
Other†	£12,170

* These thresholds were introduced on 1 January 1996, and are raised each year in line with inflation. The 1995 thresholds were £178,200, £23,760 and £11,880, respectively.
† Includes unmarried partner, live-in or otherwise.

Here's an example:

Aoife receives a £65,000 inheritance from an elderly benefactor. Aoife's tax bill would have dropped to £12,099 if she had received the money as a "gift" when her friend was still alive. However, she would have had to have paid the full inheritance tax bill if he had died within two years of giving her the money. Her tax bill works out like this:

AOIFE'S INHERITANCE TAX BILL

Amount	Tax Rate	Amount Payable
£12,170	Exempt	No Tax
The next £10,000	@ 20%	£2,000
The next £30,000	@ 30%	£9,000
Remaining £12,830	@ 40%	£5,132
Total Tax Bill		£16,132
Net Inheritance		£48,868

Note that many types of asset can qualify as a "gift". They include cash, jewellery, a car, the transfer of house or lands, the use of a house etc.

If Aoife receives an inheritance or gift from another person, she must add this sum to the inheritance she has already received:

Her grandmother leaves her a £20,000 inheritance the same year. Aoife now has an aggregate inheritance of £85,000, and must pay some tax on the money she has just received — even though the CAT threshold for a granddaughter is £24,340. The fact that she received a taxable sum from a stranger has eroded this threshold. Her new CAT threshold is taken to be the value of the second gift, which is £20,000, instead of the £24,340 threshold which might appear logical.

If she had inherited money from her grandmother several years later, the "allowance" given for tax already paid would be eroded in value. She might end up paying more tax. This is because the tax-free threshold of the current year is used when calculating her "credit" for tax already paid on past gifts and inheritances.

Aoife's new bill looks like this:

AOIFE'S NEW INHERITANCE TAX BILL

Taxable Value		£85,000 (aggregate)
CAT Threshold		£20,000
Taxable		£65,000
Amount	**Tax Rate**	**Amount Payable**
£10,000	@ 20%	£2,000
£30,000	@ 30%	£9,000
£25,000	@ 40%	£10,000
Total Tax Bill		**£21,000**
Credit for Tax Paid in Same Year		(£16,132)
Tax Now Payable		**£4,868**

CAT is complex! If in doubt, talk to a fully qualified tax advisor and/or solicitor.

Special Reliefs and Concessions

Business and Agricultural Relief

The 1996 Budget increased the percentage of qualifying business assets which are exempt from CAT from 50 per cent to 75 per cent. It also extended this relief to agricultural property. Both measures are intended to smooth the passing on of a family enterprise, but the full 75 per cent reliefs only apply if the assets are held by the beneficiary for at least 10 years. Otherwise they will be clawed back.

Thus, if an entrepreneur bequeaths her business to a nephew, for example, and these business assets are worth £500,000, the value of these assets will by cut by 75 per cent (or £375,000) for tax purposes. Her nephew will be taxed on £125,000, minus his inheritance allowance of £24,340.

If the gift or inheritance involves agricultural land, the beneficiary has the option of having their CAT bill based on a special set of reliefs introduced in the 1995 Budget if this would reduce the tax bill. Also, the person can cut their tax bill further if they are classed as a "farmer" for tax purposes (because most of their assets are agri-based). This is a very complex area. Talk to an accountant who specialises in the topic.

Tips for Cutting CAT

- Your beneficiaries pay less tax if they receive the asset as a gift, rather than an inheritance.
- You can take out a Section 60 life-assurance policy and earmark it to pay taxes and charges arising on your death or that of your spouse from your estate or your spouse's estate (see section below).
- You can reduce the inheritance or gift-tax bill by staying close to the tax threshold for each relative and spreading the bequests as wide as possible.
- Gifts for public and charitable purposes are exempt from tax.
- Payments for the support, maintenance and education of the deceased's children or other dependent relatives are also exempt.
- A beneficiary of a will can decide to disclaim — not accept — the inheritance. In a case where shares are passed to a niece and nephew, for example, one person may inherit the whole estate and will be liable for the tax as if they had inherited the entire asset from the deceased uncle or aunt.

Probate Tax

This is another form of inheritance tax. It was introduced in the 1993 Budget, and softened slightly the following year. It applies to the estate of any person who dies after 17 June 1993. All assets in the estate, minus debts, are liable to the charge. There are some exceptions, however (see below).

Unlike CAT, probate tax is levied as a flat 2 per cent charge on the estate itself. All assets (with the exception of those listed below) are subject to this tax. Probate tax is not directly paid by the beneficiaries of a will, but it may eat into the value of the dead person's assets. In some cases, it could force a beneficiary of the will to sell an asset — such as a large house — in order to be able pay the tax debt. Here's an example:

Mary and June are sisters. They have inherited their aunt's family home, which is valued at £75,000. Neither sister was living in the house before their aunt died. There are no other assets in the will, or other beneficiaries, so the sisters have to pay the probate tax themselves.

The sisters face an effective total tax bill of £6,946. Probate — which makes up £1,500 of this sum — must be paid within nine months. They get a 1.25 per cent discount for each month by which they beat the deadline. If they miss it, however, they face a 1.25 per cent penalty each month. It may be necessary for the sisters to sell the house to pay these taxes as they cannot be paid by the "estate". Or, one sister may decide to keep the house and buy the other out by taking out a mortgage.

Mary's tax bill is identical to June's. It breaks down like this:

MARY'S TAX BILL (BASED ON £37,500 SHARE OF INHERITANCE)
(less £750 share of probate tax = £36,750)

Amount	Tax Rate	Amount Payable
Probate		£750
CAT:		
Niece's CAT exemption:		
£24,340	Nil	No Tax
The next £10,000	@ 20%	£2,000
Remaining £2,410	@ 30%	£723
Total CAT Bill		£2,723
Final Tax Bill		**£3,473**

Note: Value of Mary's Share: £37,500
Probate Bill (2% of £75,000): £1,500
Mary's Share of Probate Bill: £750 (deductible from inheritance).

Exemptions from Probate Tax

Spouses are exempt from probate tax, as are certain types of property. These include the family home, if the deceased's spouse has already died, in which case any share inherited by surviving dependent children (i.e. aged under 18 or in full-time education).

Estates valued at under £10,650 are also exempt, but if the value exceeds this sum, the entire estate is taxable. The tax charge on agricultural land and buildings is based on 30 per cent of the value of these assets.

Probate is not charged on any property transfers carried out before the donor dies. Assets which are held in joint names (such as a home owned by an unmarried couple in a true joint tenancy) are also exempt.

Tips for Cutting Probate Tax

- Take out a life assurance policy to cover charges arising on the estate when you die (see Section 60 policy below).
- Pass on the asset as a gift before you die.

Section 60 Policies

Remembering someone in your will is a generous thing to do. However, as the examples of Joe, Aoife and Mary have shown, it can cause a financial headache for the lucky beneficiary. All three face a large tax bill. In the case of a separated person in a "second" relationship, tax can create huge problems.

Here's an example:

Seán and Deirdre are living together, and have a small baby. They have taken out a mortgage in joint names on their £65,000 house. Seán dies unexpectedly, without a will. His share of the house passes automatically to Deirdre, thanks to the life-assurance protection policy which is part of the mortgage contract. Also, she is exempt from probate tax because the house was in joint names. However, Deirdre was a "stranger in law" to Seán, so she must pay a large CAT bill.

Her bill looks like this:

TAX BILL*

Amount	Tax Rate	Amount Payable
£12,170	Exempt	No Tax
The next £10,000	@ 20%	£2,000
Remaining £10,330	@ 30%	£3,099
Total CAT Bill		£5,099
Plus Probate Bill		none
Final Tax Bill		£5,099

* Value of Deirdre's Inheritance: £32,500.

Note: If either of them puts up the entire deposit and makes most of the repayments, the other partner is deemed to have taken a gift of their half if the home is recognised in joint names. This would give rise to a double tax burden when the person who owns the asset dies. This situation can create a tax nightmare. It's vital to get specialist advice.

By taking out a special life-assurance policy, you can earmark the proceeds for any taxes arising on the estate when you die. This is called a Section 60 policy. To return to the above example:

Seán could take out life cover. He could do this for a few pounds a month on a "term basis", but this will only pay out if he dies within a specified period. Alternatively, he can get a "whole of life" contract, which is more expensive but will pay whenever he dies.

He gets cover for £20,000 to cover an increase in the value of his house or additional taxes. Alternatively, he can take out an index-linked policy which will increase his life cover in line with inflation. Any surplus from the policy will pass into the estate, and can be used to pay off other debts. It will not go to waste.

You can avoid the problem of an inherited tax bill in another way. When bequeathing a cash sum, you can stipulate that this be given net of tax. For example, your will might state:

> "I leave £15,000 free of tax to my friend John."

In theory, John should inherit the full amount without paying inheritance tax. The CAT charge should be borne by the estate, but there could be a problem if there are insufficient assets within the estate to foot this bill.

PASSING ON THE FAMILY BUSINESS

This topic can only be touched on briefly here, as it merits a whole book in itself. Planning your succession could be vital if you want the business to survive your death. Only 24 per cent of businesses survive the first generation, and only 14 per cent make it beyond the third, according to Irish research commissioned by BDO

Simpson Xavier. Sometimes the firm will be wound up in an orderly way, but it may also collapse because you — the founder — fail to manage the complex and highly emotional issue of succession.

Passing on the family business is not just about tax. It touches on many delicate areas, including family politics, power, your own financial and personal needs. It's vital to get good advice.

Here are some useful tips:

- Take a systematic and structured approach to succession planning. If you do nothing, you may be overwhelmed by events!
- Start planning early.
- Decide, at an early date, whom you want to inherit the business. Pick a retirement date and stick to it.
- Think hard about who you want to run the business. To ensure that it ends up in the right hands, you may need to favour one heir — your successor.
- Talk to your future successor and explain what you are trying to achieve through estate planning.
- Talk to the rest of the family so that they won't feel left out — and cause problems for your successor after you retire or die.
- Minimise estate taxes through the use of lifetime gifts and trust settlements. You can use Section 60 policies to foot any remaining tax bill.

Source: Philip Smyth, a family business counsellor with BDO Simpson Xavier.

FUNERAL COSTS

A burial can be very expensive. It's important to be aware of the potential costs, and make provision for them — either for you, or for others. A no-frills funeral usually costs around £2,000. The costs break down like this:

Plot*	£650
Offering or Honorarium†	£50
Flowers	£50
Death Notice	£100
Undertakers' Fees:	
Removal	
Hearse and Limousine	
Coffin	
Use of Funeral Home	
Embalming etc.	£1,200
Total	£2,050

* Cost of plot in Glasnevin Cemetery, Dublin. Includes opening of grave.
† This is the fee paid to the priest or Church of Ireland minister.
Source: Patrick Massey Ltd., 1995.

A funeral can cost as much as £3,500, if you pick a very expensive plot. Or, you can get a very basic undertaking service (excluding limousine) for £850, plus about £250 for a cremation service. Taking a shared plot with your spouse or other family members will probably also cut the cost.

Some people arrange to pay this by scaling down their own life-policy cover as they get older. It may no longer be necessary to have £100,000 cover for you or your spouse, if your children are grown up and the mortgage has been repaid. Scaling down an existing life policy may make sense if you have "whole-of-life cover", which pays out whenever you die, and you have no other plans for this payment. You can also adjust the policy conditions if you have "convertible" life assurance (see Chapter 6). Alternatively, you can take out a special, low-cost life policy to pay the funeral costs. A 65-year-old couple (both smokers) who want to provide for a £2,250 funeral each, would pay a premium of £27.16 for the two at one leading life company. The same policy can also be taken out by that person's relatives.

WIDOWHOOD

Losing your partner through death is a traumatic experience, no matter what age he or she is. It is best to avoid major financial decisions just after your spouse's death, such as whether to sell the family home or another major asset. Other "housekeeping" matters, like getting access to bank accounts, paying for the burial and claiming on life assurance policies cannot be postponed as long.

Tidy paperwork can spare a lot of anguish. It's best to keep your insurance policies, bank books and other bits and pieces together and in a place where they can easily be found. Let your spouse know where these documents are. If you are worried about security, leave them with the family solicitor or in a bank safe. Ideally, a will should be kept in a fire-proof container — if possible. If you change your will, you should tell your partner, and vice versa. If your spouse dies, and there is no sign of any papers, contact your spouse's bank or solicitor. Failing that, family members or trusted friends may be able to tell you where the documents are. See also Personal Portfolio Planner at the back of this book (pp. 313–20).

You can only cut your spouse out of a will, or be disinherited yourself, in certain circumstances. For example, if you or your partner was guilty of a criminal offence or had deserted the other spouse for at least two years previously. Succession rights can be waived (voluntarily, by either spouse) or "extinguished" by a court if the couple have ended their relationship with a Judicial Separation. Unpleasant shocks — and huge tax bills — can be avoided if both partners know the contents of the will. Knowing where the will is also helps.

Life-Assurance Policy/ies

If you think that your spouse had taken out a life-assurance policy, contact your insurance broker or the life company that you think may have sold it. Basic details, such as the date of birth and address may be enough to trace the missing policy. You should still be able to claim the payout, even if the policy document is missing, but you must provide sufficient personal evidence. Your spouse's solicitor, bank manager or accountant may be able to help here.

Bank Accounts

If you have a joint bank account and either of you can sign cheques, you can access this money immediately. It is yours, and will not go into your spouse's estate.

If there is joint signing authority on the account, which is unusual for married couples, withdrawing cash may be more complicated. This is because you need to have two signatures to cash a cheque or withdraw money. If the account is held in your partner's sole name and you need money urgently, ask your solicitor to contact the bank. The bank should be able to arrange an "executor's" overdraft, or an "administrator's" overdraft. This is essentially a loan on the money in the estate. If there is a substantial sum in the account — over £5,000, for example — the bank manager may ask for a "grant of probate" or "letters of administration" to obtain authorisation to release the funds. Remember that this happens when the estate is already being carved up.

The Family Home

A house that is held in joint names should pass to the surviving spouse when the first partner dies. If there is a life-assurance protection policy on the home, the outstanding mortgage will be paid off automatically. Life-assurance cover has not always been obligatory, so it's worth checking while both partners are still alive if such a policy exists on your mortgage. Ask the bank or building society which gave you the mortgage. Also, check that it is payable on "first" as opposed to "second" death. Otherwise, it will not clear the mortgage until *both* you and your spouse die.

As we have seen, inheritance can be tricky and further complicated by tax matters. If there is no will, the surviving partner automatically inherits two-thirds of their spouse's estate. The rest is divided equally among the children. So, if your wife dies intestate, and the house was in her sole name, you will not inherit the full amount if you have children, unless there are other assets in the estate that can pay their third. You may also be liable for CAT if your children "gift" the remaining third of the house to you.

If there is no mortgage, make sure that the deeds of the house are kept in a safe place. This is the record of title to the property.

Don't rush into selling your family home. It is best to wait — perhaps a couple of years — before making such a major financial decision.

Pension

If your spouse was a member of a company or public-sector pension scheme, you will probably be entitled to a pension. This may even apply to people in long-standing "live-in" relationships, be they heterosexual or homosexual. If your spouse was a public-sector worker, you should be entitled to a "death-in-service" payment — usually a lump sum which is a multiple of their salary. You should also be able to draw a "survivor's" pension from the Department of Social Welfare immediately, whatever your age, but it may be small. Sadly, many women never claim their husbands' pensions, even though they are entitled to do so if their husband was a private/public-sector worker who had paid PRSI contributions.

Company pension schemes vary enormously. You may be entitled to a death-in-service benefit, if this exists in the scheme. You may not be entitled to draw a pension until the age of 65, however. Contact the pension scheme.

The scheme's rules will determine how much cash you get, and when you are paid. In general, the sum will be between one-third and a half of your deceased spouse's entitlement. If you have children, they may also be entitled to a payment. The situation may change if your spouse had already retired before dying. Most annuities guarantee the pension for the first five years after the scheme member dies. If your husband or wife is unfortunate enough to die six months after retiring, you will get the full pension for the guaranteed period. Thereafter, your pension will drop sharply to the spouses' rate.

Tax and Social Welfare Benefits

The surviving spouse may qualify for extra tax reliefs and social welfare benefits. In the year of bereavement, you are entitled to a boosted widowed person's allowance of £5,300 (1996/97). This is the same as the married person's allowance and twice the single person's rate. In the following year, your tax-free entitlement shrinks to £3,150, which is only marginally more than the single rate of £2,650. You may be entitled to an additional allowance if you have dependent children.

These allowances should cut your tax bill — if some of your income is taxable — because they raise your tax-free income threshold. Last but not least, you may qualify for either the widows' non-contributory pension, which will be £64.50 per week from June 1996, or the "survivors'" pension which was introduced in October 1994. The rate is higher for people aged over 80. The maximum pension, based on PRSI contributions, is £68.10 a week (from June 1996). You will only get the former if your income is below a certain level. You can only claim the latter if you, or your deceased spouse, made a sufficient number of PRSI payments. Check at your local Social Welfare office.

Shared Roles

Ideally, pension, tax and inheritance planning should be decided in consultation with your spouse, not unilaterally. Trying to shield your husband or wife from important financial decisions does them no favour. It may result in a widow or widower not knowing about the existence of a life-assurance policy or will.

Also, if one spouse controls the budget and bank accounts, the partner can be doubly traumatised when widowhood forces them to make independent financial decisions for the first time in many years. Sharing responsibilities and pre-emptive planning can spare both parties a lot of difficulty.

More Help

You can get advice and valuable support from several organisations. These include the National Association of Widows in Ireland, 12 Upper Ormond Quay, Dublin 7 (tel: (01) 677 0977), the Retirement Planning Council, 27 Pembroke Street Lr., Dublin 2, (tel: (01) 661 3139) or the Bereavement Counselling Service Office, Dublin Street, Baldoyle, Co. Dublin (tel: (01) 839 1766). The latter only gives counselling on dealing with grief, not financial affairs.

CONCLUSION

Death is a stark word, which most of us avoid thinking about at all costs. We put off writing a will, getting life assurance — in short, doing anything which reminds us of our mortality. That's only natural. But good financial planning is a matter of life *and* death.

Many people leave inheritance planning until they are approaching their late fifties. This is often too late. Couples who procrastinate about writing a will can create unwanted distress for their family if they die unexpectedly. Shrewd inheritance planning can also take tax considerations into account and smooth out any potential problems. It's important to talk to an accountant as well as a solicitor before parcelling your assets into neat little bundles. Otherwise, your well-meaning bequest could create a major financial worry for the person who inherits it.

16

HELP!

"A consumer is a shopper who is sore about something."

Harold Coffin

The year 1995 was a good one for Irish consumers, and a bad one for the "sharks" that prey on them. It brought two major pieces of legislation: the Consumer Credit Act and the Investment Intermediaries Act. Pension and savings products came under a media spotlight, and some life companies reacted by changing products to give their customers better value.

There was also lively debate over fee- versus commission-based advice, early encashment values on life-assurance savings plans and investment yields. People woke up to the fact that life companies *charge* for managing their money and that, crucially, these fees can eat up all of the first two years' premiums on a regular premium policy, for example. More people became consumers, with a strong sense of their rights — not just shoppers with money to spend.

However, people still fall victim to "bad" advice. In other words, they make financial decisions, like taking out a mortgage or pension, on advice that is faulty (because they are not clear what they want or the person giving it is unqualified) or biased (because the salesperson is motivated by the commission they will earn on the sale, rather than the customer's own best interests). Some even lose their money to fraudsters.

The old saying "buyer beware" is as true as ever. An alert, confident consumer can do a lot to avoid the fraudster's clutches. Being aware of *your* needs also makes you less likely to accept a salesperson's patter. If you have problems, there are several places to go for help. This chapter gives tips on avoiding fraud, suggests how to get high-quality financial advice and where to get assistance if you need it.

THE REGULATORY FRAMEWORK

Irish legislation is more piecemeal than Britain's all-embracing Financial Service Act, 1986 (which came into force on 29 April 1988).

The UK Act created a single watchdog body, SIB, which monitors self-regulatory bodies and professional groups, representing lawyers, accountants, etc. In Ireland, there is no all-powerful watchdog, and much of the industry is still "self-regulated". Banks, building societies and insurance companies all have their own representative bodies. These act as a police force, of sorts, ensuring that their members comply with the law. They also draw up "Codes of Conduct" to regulate certain activities, but do not fine or publicly reprimand their members — as SIB does in Britain — for breaches of these standards.

Here, supervisory duties are split between the Central Bank, the Director of Consumer Affairs and several government departments, among others. Each body "polices" a number of laws — well over 100 in the case of the Director of Consumer Affairs.

The sale of "consumer" financial services is covered by a legal patchwork, the most recent elements being the Consumer Credit Act (1995) and the Investment Intermediaries Act (1995). Earlier legislation includes the Building Societies Act (1989), the Insurance Act (1989) and the Pensions Act (1990).

The Consumer Credit Act (see pp. 65–6) and Investment Intermediaries Act will police the sale of loan products and investment advice, respectively. The latter is especially welcome, as it finally regulates people who sell non-insurance investment products, such as unit trusts and deposit-based products.

From 1 November 1995, a person or company who advises on

or sells these products must be authorised by the Central Bank and/or the Department of Enterprise and Employment. They must also have a written letter of approval from the financial institution that they represent, and may have to be "bonded" (see p. 289 later in this chapter) at a future date. Separate plans are also underway for compensation schemes covering insurance and non-insurance based investments (see pp. 293–4).

Sadly, none of these initiatives is a solution to the problem of fraud or "bad advice". The Consumer Credit Act, for example, will force salespeople and financial institutions to give you — the consumer — more warnings and information about the products you buy, but you must absorb and understand it. The Investment Intermediaries Act will force salespeople to go through a registration process. But, before you do business with them, *you* should check with the Central Bank and/or Department of Enterprise and Employment whether they have done so.

Finally, to get compensation or redress of any sort, you must keep clear records. In other words, receipts for monies invested, copies of letters and investment reports, and so on.

WHO GIVES FINANCIAL ADVICE?

You can get financial advice from many sources. This has complicated life for many consumers.

Most people first get financial advice from a staff person in their bank or building-society branch. This may happen when they open a savings account, or look for a mortgage. Those who have insurance brokers probably use them to shop around for cheap household or car cover. A broker who sells "life" as well as "general" insurance may also provide investment advice.

Under the Insurance Act (1989), a broker should have agencies with at least five different insurance companies. Insurance brokers should give independent and "best" advice. In other words, they should offer a product that is competitively priced and suits your needs. They get a commission by selling these products. Good brokers should also suggest products that don't provide them with a cash return, such as An Post's savings plans, but they may ask for a fee instead of a commission. An insurance agent can represent up to four companies. This gives them a more limited range of products to sell. Finally, a tied agent has an agency with just one company. They are really employees of that company. Their main aim is to sell products sold by one company. It may be good advice, but cannot be best advice.

Solicitors, accountants and auctioneers also give financial advice. In some cases they have an agreement with a life or general insurance company to sell their products. This may make them a broker, agent or tied agent as well. Some may also act as an agent for a building society, which licenses them to take deposits. Consultants who give advice on non-insurance products — such as cash deposits or unit trusts — are now policed by the Investment Intermediaries Act.

However, people can still set themselves up as financial consultants, even when they have no professional qualifications or a commercial relationship with an insurance company or building society. They may not even be trained. Sometimes they get business just on the strength of being a family friend or acquaintance.

WHERE TO GET "BEST ADVICE"

Choosing the right advisor is crucial. It can mean the difference between a good pension and a lousy one. It can save you from fraud, or plain old bad management. So where can you find it? The best way is to shop around, or ask a few tough questions when a salesperson tries to sell you a financial product, such as those listed below.

These questions are most appropriate for people who sell insurance products, but some apply to all financial advisors.

(1) Do you give independent advice?

(2) Are you bonded?

(3) Do you have professional indemnity (PI) cover?

(4) Are you qualified?

(5) Do you offer fee-based advice?

1. Do You Give Independent Advice?

Step number one is to find out whether the person is a tied agent, an agent or an insurance broker.

If they're a broker, ask whether they belong to the Irish Brokers' Association. All IBA members should be able to answer "yes" to questions 2 and 3.

If you want to check who your advisor represents, contact the Insurance Intermediaries Compliance Bureau (IICB) (tel: (01) 478 2205). This is part of the Irish Insurance Federation (tel: (01) 478 2499). Any person or company who sells insurance products must register with the IICB each autumn, and supply basic documentation. This information is available to the public.

2. Are You Bonded?

A bond is a form of insurance that should protect you in the event of fraud. Note that an advisor may only be bonded for a specific business, such as insurance. You may not be covered if the consultant gives you investment advice — on deposits, shares, etc.

Tied agents do not need a bond. Their insurance company is responsible for any potential losses.

3. Do You Have Professional Indemnity (PI) Cover?

This is another form of insurance. It pays out if the holder loses your money through negligence or mismanagement. Again, the PI cover may be restricted to a certain area of business and is not required by tied agents.

4. Are You Qualified?

Would you pay an amateur to fix your plumbing? Or allow a person who wasn't a surgeon or doctor to operate on you? People who manage your money should also be qualified.

Beware of people who claim to be "experts" in all fields. An accountant who understands taxes may not be the best person to advise you on investment decisions. Large accountancy firms offer a range of specialisations — including tax, pension and inheritance planning and investments — under the one roof. Unfortunately, this advice can be expensive. An alternative is to create your own panel of advisors. Don't entrust all your business affairs to one person.

5. Do You Offer Fee-based Advice?

Most insurance brokers earn commissions. These eat into your premium payments, and affect the return on your investment in the early years. You may be better off paying an up-front fee, instead of choosing commission-based advice, although you may miss out on tax relief on this sum.

It's a good idea to talk to several different advisors before opting for one. That allows you to compare the quality of this advice. Good advisors should ask pertinent questions. For example, if you plan to invest a large lump sum, they should ask questions such as:

- What's your attitude to risk?
- Do you want to keep your capital sum safe?
- Do you need an income?
- Should you use some of this cash to reduce your costs? Should you, for example, pay back a personal loan or cut back a mortgage?

Beware of salespeople who don't listen or who push a particular product. They may be more interested in the commission.

Insurance brokers, accountants and solicitors are all listed in the Golden Pages. That's probably not the best place to find one, however. Nor is it wise to accept referrals blindly from friends, relatives and others. Professional bodies, such as the Incorporated Law Society (tel: (01) 671 0711) or the Institute of Chartered Accountants in Ireland (tel: (01) 668 0400) may be able to help.

AVOIDING RIP-OFFS

You can do a lot to protect yourself. Apart from choosing the right advisor, that means doing your homework, working out what you want — for example, security, an income, a risky but potentially lucrative investment — and stating your needs clearly and firmly.

You can also take a few simple precautions. These will partly depend on the person you are dealing with and the nature of the advice. Say you want to buy a life assurance-based investment:

- Prepare questions before you meet the advisor or talk business with them on the phone.
- Take notes of your conversation and the advice that you get. Record it if necessary.
- Ask the advisor to confirm what product they want to sell and what the terms and conditions are. This may prove vital later on if you want to claim that the product was sold under false pretences.
- Read the policy document. Even after signing it you've got a 15-day "cooling off period" to cancel the agreement. Check the policy for any hidden surprises.
- Make out the cheque to the insurance company, and then cross it. Or make it payable to your own name. Get a receipt.

You can modify this approach when shopping for a loan, or another product. Just remember a few key rules. Ask for confirmation in writing. Confirm the terms, conditions and cost of your investment. Ask whether you can change your mind at a future date.

GETTING HELP

It's important to know where to find help when things go wrong. Chapter 13, Budgeting, listed the organisations that give advice and support to people in debt. Other bodies — notably the Ombudsman schemes (pp. 291–3) — can help to resolve disputes between the consumer and financial institutions.

In the consumer finance world, there is a key demarcation line between insurance and non-insurance investment products. Not surprisingly then, you must go to a different Ombudsman for each type of product.

The Insurance Ombudsman of Ireland

The Insurance Ombudsman of Ireland tackles disagreements between policyholders and insurance companies. You must receive written confirmation from the insurer that the dispute has not been settled, and take your case to the Ombudsman within six months. Your case will not be heard if you have issued legal proceedings, or if it involves a sum exceeding £100,000 (£10,000 for "protection policies"). Also, the Insurance Ombudsman of Ireland cannot intervene if the dispute involves:

- The value (surrender or investment) of a life-assurance policy
- An insurance broker (only tied agents are covered by the scheme)
- Issues that would be more appropriate for a court of law, etc.

The Insurance Ombudsman does not charge a fee for this service. For further details, contact:

Insurance Ombudsman of Ireland
77 Merrion Square, Dublin 2
Tel: (01) 662 0899, Fax: (01) 662 0890.

The Ombudsman for the Credit Institutions

The Ombudsman for the Credit Institutions handles disputes between consumers, small businesses and their banks. Like the Insurance Ombudsman, this Ombudsman can only take up cases that have not been resolved through the financial institution's internal channels. However, the Ombudsman for the Credit Institutions can encourage dialogue by referring you — the consumer — to a designated person within the bank or building society. If that fails, the Ombudsman can then take up the case.

The service is provided free of charge. The Ombudsman cannot take on some cases. These includes complaints relating to:

- A loan refusal, for example, and other "commercial" decisions by the bank or building society
- General interest rates
- Issues that would be more appropriate for a court of law, etc.

For further details contact:

The Ombudsman for the Credit Institutions
8 Adelaide Court, Dublin 2
Tel: (01) 478 3755, Fax: (01) 478 0157.

The Small Claims Court

Outside the financial-services arena, the Small Claims Court can handle disputes between consumers and retailers and/or people who have provided a service. The procedure is very simple, and administered by the District Courts. It costs just £5, but you can only bring a case if the amount involved is very small. The limit went up to £600 on 22 January 1996.

For further details, contact your district court or:

The Department of Justice
72 St Stephen's Green, Dublin 2
Tel: (01) 678 9711.

The Consumers' Association of Ireland

The Consumers' Association of Ireland provides a range of services. Some are available only to members of CAI, but others are open to the public. CAI can be contacted at:

45 Upper Mount Street, Dublin 2
Tel: (01) 661 2466.

The Office of the Director of Consumer Affairs

This office polices a huge body of legislation, and also offers a consumer helpline. It can be contacted at:

Shelbourne House,
Shelbourne Road, Dublin 4
Tel: (01) 661 3399.

Compensation Schemes

The IBA already runs a compensation scheme for customers of IBA members who lose their money through fraud. This only covers insurance-based investments, however. Plans for a broader investor compensation scheme (like those operating in the UK) are underway, but may not materialise this year.

Thanks to a draft EU Directive, Irish government officials are preparing an Investor Compensation Bill. This may reimburse clients for losses up to ECU20,000 (£16,000 approx.) or 90 per cent, whichever is the greater, in the event of fraud. It is expected to cover losses arising from non-insurance products (such as deposit accounts). The Irish Insurance Federation may create a second scheme for insurance-based investments sold by all industry representatives, be they agents, brokers or non-IBA members. Or, these two compensation schemes may be blended into one.

The Irish Insurance Federation is still planning other reforms, including mandatory bonding for all insurance representatives and a personal identity number for all people who act as insurance representatives. This should prevent "rogue" salespeople from moving from one insurance company to another. In the meantime, if you have a problem with an agent or tied agent, contact the insurance company that issued the product. If it involves an independent broker, contact the IBA (tel: (01) 661 3061).

CONCLUSION

Like most challenges, taking your personal finances in hand can be rewarding. You can plan your savings and investments more appropriately, save tax, get value-for-money protection for you and your loved ones, and budget more efficiently.

You don't have to tackle everything at once. Even small steps, like starting that savings/investment plan, or dealing with long-neglected tax issues, can save money and give you a greater feeling of independence and control. That said, it's good to keep the big picture in view. What are your needs? Plans? Fears? How can you cater for them?

Some people will have to face big challenges in 1996: marriage breakdown, redundancy, the loss of a partner. In these crisis situations, getting timely advice can help you to cope.

This book tries to put *you* more in control. Banks, building societies and insurance companies are very powerful. They provide a valuable service, but they are also driven by the desire to make a profit. You, the consumer, need to make sure that their financial products meet *your* needs — not just theirs.

APPENDIX

A. USEFUL ADDRESSES

Bank Statement Checking Services

Irish Small & Medium
Enterprises Association
(ISME)
32 Kildare Street,
Dublin 2
Tel: (01) 662 2755

Taylor Investment Group
Investment and Financial
Brokers
Clyde House
15 Clyde Road,
Dublin 4
Tel: (01) 668 1499

Divorce/Advice Groups

Accord
(formerly Catholic Marriage
Advisory Council)
39 Harcourt Street,
Dublin 2
Tel: (01) 478 0866

AIM
(Family law information, mediation and counselling centre)
6 D'Olier Street,
Dublin 2
Tel: (01) 670 8363

AIM (Help Centre)
32 Upper Fitzwilliam Street
Dublin 2
Tel: (01) 661 1473

Family Mediation Service
(State-run)
5th floor, Irish Life Centre
Lower Abbey Street
Dublin 1
Tel: (01) 872 8277

Gingerbread
(Voluntary advice and support group for one-parent families)
29 Dame Street
Dublin 2
Tel: (01) 671 0291

Industry/Representative Bodies

Irish Brokers' Association
87 Merrion Square
Dublin 2
Tel: (01) 661 3061

Irish Insurance Federation
Russell House, Russell Court
Stephen's Green, Dublin 2
Tel: (01) 478 2499

Legal

Free Legal Advice Centres (FLAC)
(Voluntary)
49 South William Street
Dublin 2
Tel: (01) 679 4239

Legal Aid Board
(State-run)
St Stephen's Green House
Dublin 2
Tel: (01) 661 5811

Voluntary/Advice Agencies

Threshold (mortgage/rent problems)
Head Office
Church Street, Dublin 7
Tel: (01) 872 6311
or
8 Fr Matthew Quay, Cork
Tel: (021) 271250
or
Ozanan House
St Augustine Street, Galway
Tel: (091) 63080

FISC (Financial Information Service Centres)
87–89 Pembroke Road
Dublin 4
Tel: (01) 668 2044

Society of St Vincent de Paul
Head Office
8 New Cabra Road
Dublin 7
Tel: (01) 838 4164

Stockbrokers (for smaller clients)

Bloxham Stockbrokers.
11 Fleet Street
Dublin 2
Tel: (01) 677 6653

Butler & Briscoe
3 College Green
Dublin 2
Tel: (01) 677 7348

Miscellaneous

Director of the Office of Consumer Affairs
Shelbourne House
Shelbourne Road, Dublin 4
Tel: (01) 660 6011

Irish Policy Exchange Company
13 Ely Place
Dublin 2
Tel: (01) 661 1800

National Deposit Brokers
88 St Stephen's Green
Dublin 2
Tel: (01) 478 2564

Society of Chartered Surveyors (in the Republic of Ireland)
5 Wilton Place
Dublin 2
Tel: (01) 676 5500

B. DOUBLE TAXATION AGREEMENTS

If you are resident in two countries for tax purposes, a double taxation agreement between those countries will decide which of them may tax your income or gains. This is done by giving one of the countries an exclusive right to tax the income or gains or, where both countries continue to have taxing rights, by ensuring that a credit is given in one country for the tax already paid in another country.

Ireland currently has double taxation agreements in force with the following 29 countries:

Australia	Hungary	Poland
Austria	Italy	Portugal
Belgium	Israel	Russia
Canada	Japan	Spain
Cyprus	Korea	Sweden
Czech Republic	Luxembourg	Switzerland
Denmark	Netherlands	United Kingdom
Finland	New Zealand	United States
France	Norway	Zambia
Germany	Pakistan	

Ireland is in negotiation with Mexico and Greece for new treaties. It is renegotiating treaties with other countries.

C. MOTOR MILEAGE RATES (APPROVED BY THE REVENUE COMMISSIONERS)

These rates are used to reimburse employees who use their cars in the course of work.

Inclusive Rate per Mile	**Engine Capacity**		
Official Mileage in a Year	**Under 1138 cc**	**1138 cc–1387 cc**	**1388 cc +**
	p	p	p
Up to 2,000	49.87	57.70	66.50
2,001–4,000	54.98	62.98	72.50
4,001–6,000	29.44	33.38	38.04
6,001–8,000	27.74	31.35	35.69
8,001–12,000	24.33	27.30	30.98
12,001 +	20.92	23.25	26.27

Source: Revenue Commissioners.

D. WOMEN'S GROUPS

The Department of Social Welfare gives grant support for groups involved in voluntary and community work. These include those run for, or on behalf of, women, such as:

- The community development programme
- Voluntary organisations
- Locally-based women's groups
- Projects which tackle the problems of moneylending and indebtedness
- The respite care fund
- Groups assisting lone parents who are returning to the workforce, or are taking up "second-chance" education
- Special once-off grants are also provided.

Contact the Department of Social Welfare's Voluntary and Community Services Section, Floor Five, Áras Mhic Dhiarmada, Store Street, Dublin 1. Tel: (01) 874 8444, extension 3827 or 3864. Or, ring your local Social Welfare office or the Department's information service, at (01) 874 8444.

E. YOUR RIGHTS UNDER THE PENSIONS ACT (1990)

The Pensions Act is a key piece of legislation. It gives you — the pension scheme member — important rights. These include:

- The Right of Information
- The Right to Funding Data
- The Right to Elect Member Trustees
- The Right to a "Portable Pension".

The Right to Information

You are entitled to information about the way in which the scheme is structured, the benefits it provides and how your investment is performing. However, you have to request most of this information, as you will not get it automatically.

For example, you are entitled to see the documents which set up the pension scheme, including the trust deeds, the scheme rules and any changes to them. You can also get a yearly benefits statement which confirms your retirement age, the size of your premium contributions, value of your fund to date and additional benefits (life-assurance cover and disability cover) in the pension scheme. You may have to request these documents.

Your trade union automatically gets audited annual accounts and an annual report for the scheme. You can ask for a copy of both.

The Right to Funding Data

Trustees of defined benefit funded schemes must submit actuarial funding certificates to the Pensions Board every three and a half years. These confirm that there are sufficient assets in the fund to meet its current liabilities. They also reveal if the pension scheme has "self-invested", in other words, lent money to the parent company. The percentage of funds that can be self-invested is restricted by law.

As a pension scheme member, you are entitled to get this information, but you have to ask for it. Your trade union automatically gets this information in the annual report for the scheme.

The Right to Elect Member Trustees

The trustees of a pension scheme have an important job, because they police the running of the scheme. They also have access to key information and are responsible for paying out benefits from the scheme.

Employees who belong to schemes with over 50 members have the right to elect at least two member trustees. But this right must be sought by a trade union representing at least 50 per cent of active members of the pension scheme, or at least 15 per cent of the scheme's qualifying members (pensioners and non-pensioners) or by the employer.

The Right to a "Portable" Pension

Thanks to the 1990 legislation, pensions are far more mobile and you don't have to lose benefits when you change jobs. See section "When You Leave your Job" below for more details.

For further information about your rights, contact the Pensions Board, Holbrook House, Holles Street, Dublin 2; Tel: (01) 676 2622.

F. HOW BIG A LUMP SUM CAN YOU TAKE?

Years of Service to Retirement	Max. Lump Sum as a Fraction of Final Pensionable Salary
1–8	3/80ths for each year
9	30/80ths for each year
10	36/80ths for each year
11	42/80ths for each year
12	48/80ths for each year
13	54/80ths for each year
14	63/80ths for each year
15	72/80ths for each year
16	81/80ths for each year
17	90/80ths for each year
18	99/80ths for each year
19	108/80ths for each year
20	120/80ths for each year

G. WHEN YOU LEAVE YOUR JOB

In the past, people who left their jobs also had to leave valuable pension rights behind them. Now, thanks to the Pensions Act, your pension is far more "portable".

Under Five Years

If you have been with a company for less than five years, you have full access to your own pension contributions. The typical options available to you are as follows:

- Take a cash refund of your contributions, including AVCs. Tax will be deducted at 25 per cent, however.

or

- Leave the value of your contributions in the scheme. These will be paid to you as a pension at your normal retirement date. This is called a "deferred pension". The drawback is that this sum will be frozen in money terms at the date you leave your job, and not revalued between then and your retirement date.

or

- Transfer the gross amount of your contributions into a new company pension plan with your new employer or, alternatively, into a personal retirement bond with an insurance company.

You can never take a refund of the contributions made by your employer to the scheme on leaving service. However, some schemes give "vested rights" after a minimum period of service, usually five or ten years. This means that you are entitled to a deferred pension based on both your own and your employer's contributions.

Over Five Years

After five years you are entitled to "preserved benefits" under the Pensions Act. This means that if you leave a scheme before retirement date, having five years' service (at least two of which were after 1 January 1991), you have the following choices:

- Preserve the benefits you have built up after 1 January 1991 in the scheme you are leaving. The way in which your preserved benefit is calculated depends on whether you are a member of a defined benefit or a defined contribution scheme. If it is a defined benefit scheme, the formula is as follows:

  Your preserved benefit is calculated as the "long-service benefit". That is, a pension expectation at normal retirement age multiplied by the reckonable service (i.e. the period of your scheme membership, which is not necessarily the whole period of employment, and excluding any time when covered for death benefits only), after 1 January 1991. This is divided by the number of years of reckonable service to normal pension age, including service before 1 January 1991. Preserved benefits granted under a defined benefit scheme will be revalued every year, starting from 1 January 1996, until the benefits become payable on retirement.

  The situation is much simpler for a defined contribution scheme. The preserved benefit is the accumulated value of contributions paid by you, and on your behalf, after 1 January 1991, or the date you started work, if later.

or

- Transfer your preserved benefits to your new employer's scheme.

or

- Transfer these benefits to an approved insurance policy or contract.

If you qualify for preserved benefits, you cannot get a refund of any contributions paid after 1 January 1991. This also applies to AVCs. However, you can get a cash refund (minus 25 per cent tax) of contributions paid before that date.

Moving jobs can be stressful enough, without the added worry of sorting out your pension benefits. Contact the Pensions Board (tel: (01) 676 2622) or the pension scheme's broker if you need advice. You can also get a copy of the Pension Board's leaflet, "What Happens to My Pension If I Leave?"

Note: Information for this section was provided by the Pensions Board.

H. *1996 BUDGET*: HOW WILL IT AFFECT YOU?

CHANGES IN TAKE-HOME PAY: SINGLE PERSON

Gross Annual Income	Private Sector			Public Sector		
	Take-Home Pay		(£)	Take-Home Pay		(£)
£	**95/96**	**96/97**	**Change**	**95/96**	**96/97**	**Change**
10,000	7,597	7,685	**88**	7,881	7,926	**45**
12,500	9,194	9,317	**123**	9,564	9,672	**108**
15,000	10,301	10,496	**195**	10,785	10,967	**182**
17,500	11,407	11,603	**196**	12,006	12,188	**182**
20,000	12,513	12,709	**196**	13,228	13,409	**181**
25,000	14,898	15,045	**147**	15,701	15,875	**174**
30,000	17,365	17,499	**134**	18,188	18,361	**173**
40,000	22,315	22,431	**116**	23,162	23,335	**173**
50,000	27,274	27,381	**107**	28,137	28,308	**171**
60,000	32,239	32,339	**100**	33,111	33,283	**172**
75,000	39,691	39,784	**93**	40,573	40,745	**172**

CHANGES IN TAKE-HOME PAY: MARRIED (ONE SPOUSE WORKING)

Gross Annual Income	Private Sector			Public Sector		
	Take-Home Pay		(£)	Take-Home Pay		(£)
£	**95/96**	**96/97**	**Change**	**95/96**	**96/97**	**Change**
10,000	8,328	8,574	**246**	8,650	8,814	**164**
12,500	9,903	10,032	**129**	10,302	10,388	**86**
15,000	11,534	11,663	**129**	12,048	12,134	**86**
17,500	13,166	13,295	**129**	13,794	13,880	**86**
20,000	14,797	14,926	**129**	15,541	15,626	**85**
25,000	17,967	18,291	**324**	18,770	19,121	**351**
30,000	20,434	20,745	**311**	21,257	21,607	**350**
40,000	25,384	25,677	**293**	26,231	26,581	**350**
50,000	30,343	30,627	**284**	31,206	31,554	**348**
60,000	35,308	35,585	**277**	36,180	36,529	**349**
75,000	42,760	43,030	**270**	43,642	43,991	**349**

Source: Adapted from *The Irish Times*/Craig Gardner Price Waterhouse.

GLOSSARY

Additional Voluntary Contributions (AVCs): can be used to "top up" (increase) premium payments into a pension fund, to maximise tax relief. Can be paid as a lump sum, or in regular instalments.

Annual Percentage Rate (APR): total cost of credit including charges, expressed as an annual percentage of the amount of credit given.

annuity: annual payment which a life company agrees to pay you in return for a lump sum. Also called a pension.

Automated Teller Machine (ATM): popular term is the "hole in the wall" machine, or cash dispenser. This is a terminal, located in public places and inside banks, which allows you to make transactions on your bank/building society account, with a plastic ATM card.

bid price: price at which "units" are sold in a unit-linked fund. They are bought back by the company at the "offer" price. Typically, there is a 5 per cent difference in these prices. This is the "bid offer spread".

broker: person who acts as an agent or go-between when buying or selling financial products or services. Note: An "independent" broker should represent at least five insurance companies.

Business Expansion Scheme (BES): this allows 48 per cent taxpayers to claim full tax relief on approved BES investment projects. This facility was extended for three years in the 1996 Budget. Section 35 film investments qualify for similar relief.

charge card: like a credit card, can be used to buy goods and services on credit. However, it does not offer a "revolving" credit facility, and your bill must be settled in full when the statement arrives.

commission: sum of money paid to insurance intermediary — i.e. broker/agent/tied agent — in return for business sold by that person.

Compound Annual Return (CAR): reflects the true return (before tax) on a savings/deposit account, allowing for the rolling up of interest.

credit: use of someone else's funds — e.g. bank or department store — in exchange for promise to repay, usually with interest, at a later date.

credit card: allows you to buy goods/services on credit, subject to limits and rules set by the company (usually a bank) that issued the card.

death-in-service benefit: payment made if you die in employment, usually by a pension scheme to your dependants.

debit card: this is a plastic card that works like an electronic "cheque". It allows money to be deducted directly from your bank account to pay for goods or services.

direct debit: instruction from a customer to their bank to debit their account with a sum of money (fixed or variable) to pay another party. It is often used to pay bills.

Dublin Inter-Bank Offer Rate (DIBOR): a "wholesale" rate quoted on the "interbank" market where banks lend surplus cash to each other. Commercial loans sometimes expressed as DIBOR plus *x*%.

hire purchase: literally, a combination of hiring and purchasing. You have the use of goods — but do not own them — while paying for them. Ownership automatically transfers with the last payment.

leasing: a method of obtaining the use of a large asset — usually a car or office machinery — in return for regular payments. In car leasing, you can often arrange to purchase the vehicle at the end of the lease agreement. You may have to pay an extra cash sum, however.

life assured: the person whose life is covered by an assurance policy.

maturity: the life expectancy of a loan from the date when it is taken out to the last repayment date.

mortgage: a loan provided for buying a home or any other property.

security: assets like a house, life-assurance policies and other items, which are pledged to support a loan.

self-administered scheme: a special pension arrangement for company directors, whereby they can invest in Revenue-approved assets (outside the life-assurance industry) and still qualify for zero tax on any pension-fund profits.

standing order: an instruction from a customer to their bank to make a regular payment (often monthly) from their account. It is often used to arrange mortgage repayments.

sum assured: the amount of cover that you have on a life policy.

term assurance: a life-insurance policy which is taken out for a specified period and guarantees to pay a lump sum if the policyholder dies within that time. "Convertible" term assurance permits you to extend or otherwise change the original policy.

unit-linked fund: a life-assurance investment. Premiums paid by thousands of investors are "pooled" and used by a "fund manager" to trade in assets, in the hopes of making a profit.

"whole of life" assurance: a life-assurance policy which gives policy-holders permanent cover on their lives. It does not have to be renewed, unlike term assurance, but is a lot more expensive.

"with profits" policy: a life-assurance investment which pays the policy-holder a return that is related to the profits earned by that life company. Profits are added through the annual bonus and a final — terminal — bonus. Once added, they cannot be taken away.

NOTE: This glossary is largely drawn from three sources:

Banking in Ireland, Irish Banks' Information Service.

"Fact File", the Irish Insurance Federation.

"The Way We Talk", Irish Life staff training document.

INDEX

PERSONAL PORTFOLIO PLANNER

This Personal Portfolio Planner, which is adapted from a longer document published by Cork Publishing, is designed to summarise and record relevant information about your personal affairs so that, in the event of your death, your executor, surviving spouse or relatives can locate key documents, make appropriate claims under life assurance and pension arrangements, and protect your property and other assets.

Complete this section carefully and properly, and then keep it in a safe place, as it contains a great deal of confidential information. Make sure that your family knows where to find it, should they have cause to need it.

PERSONAL FACTS

Name ________________________________

Address ________________________________

____

____

Telephone ________________________________

Date Portfolio completed ________________________

Date(s) reviewed ____________________________

PLEASE NOTIFY

In the event of your death or other emergency, a number of people will need to be told. Only you can draw up the list. First, your family: your parents, brothers and sisters, or children who no longer live at home. Next, your neighbours, who may be more able than your family to cope with the day-to-day responsibilities of house security, or pets. Your employer or business partner needs to know, if someone is expected to carry on in your absence. Finally, there are your professional advisers who need to be told so that they can continue with responsibilities you are no longer able to fulfil. Make sure that you give full information on how to reach each person you list.

Name ______________________
Relationship ________________
Address ____________________
____
____
Telephone __________________

Name ______________________
Relationship ________________
Address ____________________
____
____
Telephone __________________

Name ______________________
Relationship ________________
Address ____________________
____
____
Telephone __________________

Name ______________________
Relationship ________________
Address ____________________
____
____
Telephone __________________

Name ______________________
Relationship ________________
Address ____________________
____
____
Telephone __________________

Name ______________________
Relationship ________________
Address ____________________
____
____
Telephone __________________

Name ____________________
Relationship ______________
Address _________________
____
____
Telephone ________________

Name ____________________
Relationship **ACCOUNTANT**
Address _________________
____
____
Telephone ________________

Name ____________________
Relationship **EMPLOYER/ BUSINESS PARTNER**
Address _________________
____
Telephone ________________

Name ____________________
Relationship **SOLICITOR**
Address _________________
____
____
Telephone ________________

FUNERAL ARRANGEMENTS

The arrangements you have made already can be recorded here, along with any personal wishes you may have.

Funeral Director ___________
____
Address _________________
____
____
Telephone ________________

Cemetery ________________
____
Address _________________
____
____
Plot Number _____________

My personal wishes for my funeral are:

____

____

____

____

____

____

____

____

____

____

____

____

____

WILL

When you die, the most important document that your family will need is your will. It should be kept in a safe place and a copy lodged with your solicitor.

Date will made ______________________________

Drawn up by ______________________________

Kept ______________________________

____

____

Date last reviewed ______________________________

LOCATION OF OTHER DOCUMENTS

Birth Certificate ______________________________

Marriage Certificate ______________________________

Bank & Building Society Passbooks ______________________________

List of Investments ______________________________

Share Certificates ______________________________

Tax Records ______________________________

Property & Mortgage Deeds ______________________________

Life Assurance Policies ______________________________

Pension Scheme Documents ______________________________

Other ______________________________

____

LIFE ASSURANCE & OTHER PROTECTION

The information needed to complete this section should be available from the documents in your possession. If not, your financial adviser will be able to supply the missing information.

LIFE ASSURANCE

Assurance Company ______________________________

Policy Number/Type ______________________________

Amount Assured ______________________________

Other Information ______________________________

____

ANNUITIES

Source ______________________________

Amount ______________________________

Other Information ______________________________

____

PENSIONS

Source ______________________________

Amount ______________________________

Other Information ______________________________

____

Source ______________________________

Amount ______________________________

Other Information ______________________________

____

PERSONAL ACCIDENT

Insurance Company ______________________________

Amount ______________________________

Other Information ______________________________

OTHER

Source ______________________________

Amount ______________________________

Other Information ______________________________

ASSETS

This section is for property, bank and building society accounts and other assets. Most of what you own will be known to your family. The purpose of this section is to remind them of items that otherwise might be overlooked.

PROPERTY

	Property 1	**Property 2**
Address	____________ ____________ ____________	____________ ____________ ____________
In Names of	____________ ____________	____________ ____________
Mortgage Lender	____________ ____________ ____________	____________ ____________ ____________
Lender's Reference No.	____________	____________
Insurer — Buildings	____________ ____________	____________ ____________
Insured Value	£ ____________	£ ____________
Insurer — Contents	____________ ____________	____________ ____________
Insured Value	£ ____________	£ ____________

Bank/Building Society and Branch ____________________
Sort Code ____________________
Account Number ____________________
Type ____________________
In Name(s) of ____________________

Bank/Building Society and Branch ____________________
Sort Code ____________________
Account Number ____________________
Type ____________________
In Name(s) of ____________________

Bank/Building Society and Branch ____________________
Sort Code ____________________
Account Number ____________________
Type ____________________
In Name(s) of ____________________

OTHER MAJOR ASSETS

Asset ____________________
Value £ ____________________
Other Information ____________________

Asset ____________________
Value £ ____________________
Other Information ____________________